# Selected
# U.S. Government
# Series

# Selected
# U.S. Government
# Series
A Guide for Public
and Academic Libraries

## Nancy Patton Van Zant

American Library Association

Chicago 1978

**Library of Congress Cataloging in Publication Data**

Van Zant, Nancy P
   Selected U. S. Government Series.

   Bibliography:  p.
   Includes index.
   1.  United States--Government publications--Biblio-
graphy.  2.  American periodicals--Bibliography.
I.  Title.
Z1223.Z7V36 [J83]     015'.73       77-10337
ISBN 0-8389-0252-9

CONTENTS

iii

## ACKNOWLEDGMENTS

J. D. Livsey, Director, Library and Statutory Distribution Service, Government Printing Office, has been of valuable service to me in the preparation of this guide. He supplied <u>Daily Depository Shipping Lists</u> and item cards, as well as answered questions as they arose.

Numerous librarians around the country have offered encouragement and advice, all of which has been appreciated.

The following persons provided valuable comment and verification for my selection of series:

Prof. Craig Allin
Political Science Department
Cornell College
Mt. Vernon, Iowa

Mary Burton
Reference Librarian
Iowa City Public Library
Iowa City, Iowa

Mary Jane Duncan
Peoria Heights Public Library
Peoria Heights, Illinois

Dorothy Heisel
Reference and Adult Services
Pekin Public Library
Pekin, Illinois

Harold V. Hosel, formerly
Documents Librarian
Grinnell College
Grinnell, Iowa

JoAnne Johnson
Reference Librarian
Free Public Library
Council Bluffs, Iowa

Janet Lyons
Head, Documents Branch
Illinois State Library
Springfield, Illinois

Candace Morgan
Public Services Librarian
Oregon State Library
Salem, Oregon

Mildred K. Smock
Director
Free Public Library
Council Bluffs, Iowa

Carol Spaziani
Community Services Librarian
Iowa City Public Library
Iowa City, Iowa

Joan Tucker
Catalog Librarian
Iowa City Public Library
Iowa City, Iowa

Doris Wanek
Reference Librarian
Free Public Library
Council Bluffs, Iowa

The time, experience, and encouragement of these persons have been important to the completion of this guide. Any errors in judgment or content are my own.

This guide grew out of the need for an aid in the selection of federal documents series by public and academic librarians. Several good bibliographies of individual publications and guides to the administration of collections are available. However, little in the literature calls attention to major series or offers assistance in the selection of documents by series.

The guide is intended for the use of librarians in academic libraries with collections up to 300,000 volumes and in small- to medium-size public libraries serving a population up to about 50,000. The listings herein may be considered a basic collection for depositories and a guide to purchases of documents by nondepositories.

About six hundred items are annotated according to their usefulness to the libraries under consideration. The basic source is the List of Classes of United States Government Publications Available for Selection by Depository Libraries (Washington, D.C.: U.S. Government Printing Office, Superintendent of Documents, March 1977). New items and series are added frequently and old ones discontinued, but this guide recognizes a relatively stable core of depository publications.

The organization is by broad subject area with some subdivisions for specific topics. The General Publications listed for most agencies are sometimes more varied than their subject classification would indicate because of the miscellany of publications issued in these series. More specific subjects are added in the index.

Each annotation includes a brief statement of the work of the agency which issues the series if that information is not evident from the publications and subject matter noted. Most annotations include a statement of the range of topics covered both by subject and level of treatment, a few examples of titles issued in the last five years, and a statement of recommendation. Because the frequency of individual titles may be a factor in selection, an estimate of the number of titles a year is given, based on the average for the past few years. Other information pertinent to the acquisition of the series or individual publications is noted. Library of Congress catalog numbers are included as available.

All annotations are headed by the depository item number and the Superintendent of Documents classification (SuDoc) number for the series within that item. The format of the entry follows the current practice of the Library of Congress and/or the Monthly Catalog of United States Government Publications (Washington, D.C.: U.S. Government Printing Office, Superintendent of Documents, GP3.8, item 557) insofar as possible. Titles given as examples in the annotation are identified by their book number or by that number which follows the colon, and not by the complete SuDoc number;

that is, Current Policy: Persian Gulf/Arabian Peninsula, no. 85, rather than S1.86/2:85. Titles occasionally or regularly revised may have a year in their book number (St2/1970 or St2/1973) but the year is omitted here.

Item numbers do not usually change, but because of frequent reorganization within the structure of the federal government, the issuing agency and, therefore, the SuDoc number may change several times in the history of a series. The establishment of the Department of Energy in 1977, and the subsequent changes in the publications series of the Federal Energy Administration, the Energy Research and Development Administration, and the Federal Power Commission are examples of this situation. This guide does not reflect the classification changes which result from the above reorganization, because the changes are not evident at this writing. The subject organization of this guide should eliminate some of the confusion which results. The index to item numbers is another point of access.

The term series is used throughout the guide to denote all those publications issued under the same SuDoc number or classification. A1.1, Annual Report, A1.2, General Publications, and A1.38, Miscellaneous Publications, of the Department of Agriculture are each series and treated as series titles. For consistency in organization and format, periodicals follow the same pattern.

The term item is used only to refer to a number assigned by the Superintendent of Documents to one or more series or SuDoc classifications for the purposes of their selection and distribution. The Annual Report of the Department of Agriculture is item number 6, and most items have only one series assigned. However, the publications of the Office of Education are frequently grouped so that the item number contains two or more different series. Thus depository libraries selecting the item will re-

ceive all of the series. However, the nondepository library has the choice, in some cases, of establishing a standing order for only one of the series or of observing its issuances in the Monthly Catalog and selecting individual publications for purchase.

The term document, except as noted, always refers to publications of the United States government.

Each annotation bears some statement of recommendation, be it specific or implicit. This recommendation is intended to guide nondepository librarians in their selection of series or individual titles issued in the series. The list attempts to be basic to the needs of the libraries under consideration, but it does not exhaust all the possibilities for document series pertinent to possible, specialized needs of smaller academic and public libraries. The same selection criteria which govern the acquisition of commercially published materials should govern the selection of federal documents. But the selection criteria of depository libraries go beyond those exercised in the acquisition of commercial materials to include consideration of the social, economic, and cultural character of the community served. The statement of recommendation in the annotation, if it is exclusive, should be heeded only to the extent that the character of the entire community served by the depository is taken into consideration. When the series serves special information needs, particularly some which may not be universal, the annotation notes that fact.

Selections for inclusion were made after the examination of all depository series. The publications issued in each series over the past five years (and the past ten years for those with less frequent issuances) were examined and evaluated according to the appropriateness of subject matter and level of treatment of material. Likewise, the standard bibliographies of individual titles of federal publications were consulted in an attempt to identify other SuDoc classifications which frequently include titles of general interest. Many series were automatically omitted because of their in-house nature, their highly technical or scientific presentation, or the probability that their existence is due to their being required by law.

The conservation of space and the maintenance of a controllable collection in the available facility were considered in the compilation of this guide. Series whose importance and potential usefulness are outweighed by their consumption of shelf space are omitted. Examples include the Army Corps of Engineers, Port series, D103.8, which is well known and included in many bibliographies but which is impractical in small collections. Although the National Aeronautics and Space Administration, NASA SP series, NAS1.21, includes valuable resources, several shelves are filled by it in a few years. For each of these the Monthly Catalog may be checked for individual titles of local interest.

Furthermore, in most cases, series which have not issued any titles in the last five to ten years, or only one or two, are omitted because they are inactive and appear to have little to offer. Exceptions to this were made if the few issuances are of exceptional interest or if the nature of the agency is such that libraries should not miss what might be issued, the Government Printing Office or the Library of Congress, for example.

Another category of agency publications omitted is laws. Federal laws relating to the work of a bureau or agency are sometimes issued separately or compiled for issuance (Bureau of Reclamation, Laws, I27.27; Bureau of the Mines, Laws, I28.114; National Park Service, Laws, I29.46), but they are not included here because Statutes at Large, GS4.111, item 576, is. Other similar instances of obvious duplication of material are avoided. Libraries that do not receive Statutes at

Large but that support some of these specific interests may want to look into the acquisition of individual Laws series.

Depository librarians are served by this guide in their decisions to select items from the depository list. Nondepository librarians may use it in conjunction with the Monthly Catalog and other selection tools for current and retrospective acquisitions, and to establish standing orders with private dealers and jobbers, a service which is becoming increasingly available. Depository and nondepository librarians frequently make individual title selections from the Monthly Catalog, Selected United States Government Publications, and department and agency publications lists. Familiarity with the series and items noted in the guide will aid in more effective use of these catalogs. Too often a title selected from the Monthly Catalog arrives and is not found to be what was expected. The guide will not completely solve this problem, but it can help. Consulting the guide for the series title of the individual publication provides an added selection aid. The guide is useful for locating information about annual reports, research reports, periodicals, reference tools, and other types of publications. Nondepository librarians who work closely with depository collections both through interlibrary loan and referrals will find the guide a source of description of that collection.

Within many series are titles which are occasionally revised. An annotation may note this fact, but in its absence, librarians should look out for, and dispose of, superseded material.

The concern noted here for a pertinent, qualitative, and space-saving collection of documents goes beyond that of selection and includes the retention of long runs of series. Document collections should be weeded just as the general library collection is; most libraries are faced with problems of shelf and building space. Some annotations note desirable periods for the retention of series or make suggestions about summary issues which might be retained. In general, however, this policy must be established locally. Librarians too often operate under the desire to acquire and retain documents because they are free (to depositories) and boost the total number of holdings. In the new era of "no-growth" and "steady-state" institutions, libraries should not add document series injudiciously, but rather should establish reasonable selection and retention policies. Regional depositories now assist smaller depositories in the disposal of unwanted publications, in reference service, and in interlibrary loan. The guide serves a secondary purpose for some libraries by identifying titles to retain and others to weed.

The fact that documents are free to depositories, and frequently reasonably priced to nondepositories by comparison to commercially published materials, is a good reason for librarians to more fully explore the availability of documents as alternatives to expensive commercial titles. A balanced documents collection is best achieved by careful scrutiny based on the considerations of space, subject needs, and timeliness. This guide helps meet that goal.

References have been made here to the administration, selection, and disposal of federal publications. These statements should be interpreted in the context of the statute creating depository libraries. The following federal publications state the law, interpret its provisions, and amplify the system:

U.S. Congress. Joint Committee on Printing. Government Depository Libraries. Washington, D.C.: Government Printing Office, issued annually. Y4.P93/1:D44/year

U.S. Government Printing Office. An Explanation of the Superintendent of Documents Classification System. Washington, D.C.: GPO, 1973.

U.S. Government Printing Office. Instructions to Depository Libraries. Washington, D.C.: GPO, 1974.

"Regional Depository Libraries for U.S. Government Publications," Government Publications Review, vol. 2 (1975), pp. 91-102, by LeRoy C. Schwarzkopf, is an important analysis of the implementation of the provisions of the Depository Library Act of 1962. The article gives information about assistance in the disposal of unwanted depository publications, interlibrary loan, and reference service provided by regional depository libraries. These functions ease the burden on smaller depositories.

No attempt is made in the list below to provide a comprehensive bibliography of the administration and control of federal government publications. The following is a selected list of recent publications and services which enhance the effective organization and dissemination of the information. They have also been useful in the preparation of this work.

American Statistics Index. Washington, D.C.: Congressional Information Service, 1974- .

A master guide and index to all statistical publications of the U.S. government. Statistical data of the government are identified in its publications, cataloged, and described in the Abstract section. The Index section provides full subject access. ASI coverage dates from the 1960s by way of ASI retrospective edition, 1960-73. Monthly supplements cumulated quarterly, and annual cumulations.

Congressional Information Service. Index. Washington, D.C.: CIS, 1970- .

Abstracts and indexes congressional documents, except for the Congressional Record. Especially important for hearings, committee prints, House and Senate reports,

House and Senate documents, public laws, and elusive publications. Abstract section and Index section. Monthly supplements cumulated quarterly, and annual cumulations.

Cumulated Subject Index to the Monthly Catalog of the United States, 1900-1971. Washington, D.C.: Carrollton, 1973.
Combines forty-eight annual indexes, two decennials, and one half-year index into a single alphabetical subject index. Also included in this cumulation is the original indexing of thirty early Monthly Catalogs never before indexed by subject. 15 vols.

Documents to the People. Chicago: American Library Assn., Government Documents Round Table, 1972- .
Published six times a year. Information on federal, state, local, and international documents. Reports news from the Government Printing Office, conferences, advisory groups, workshops, etc.

Government Publications Review. New York: Pergamon, 1973-
Quarterly journal. Reports on current practice in the production, distribution, processing, and use of government publications around the world. International in scope, it reviews books on the subject, reports news, and abstracts significant literature. The documents of national governments throughout the world, of the United Nations, international agencies, and federal, state, and local documents of the United States are within the scope of the journal.

Government Reference Books 74/75; comp. by Alan Edward Schorr. Littleton, Colo.: Libraries Unlimited, 1976.
A biennial guide. Annotates individual titles published by GPO and government agencies, 1974 and 1975. Useful in selection of individual titles.

Index to U.S. Government Periodicals. Chicago: Infordata, Jan. 1974- .
An index to the contents of government periodicals. About ten percent of the total government periodicals are analyzed. Quarterly indexes and annual cumulation.

Leidy, W. Philip. A Popular Guide to Government Publications. New York: Columbia Univ. Pr., 1976. Fourth ed.
Annotated. Organized by subject. Includes individual publications issued between 1967 and 1975. Earlier editions cover publications prior to 1967. Useful in selection of individual titles.

Morehead, Joe. Introduction to United States Public Documents. Littleton, Colo.: Libraries Unlimited, 1975.
Provides background on the functions of the Government Printing Office, the Superintendent of Documents, and the Depository Library System. Discusses the administration of documents collections. The final chapters focus on the organization and publications of the presidency, departments, agencies, Congress, judiciary, advisory committees and commissions.

Item 830-C
NAS1.2:  NATIONAL AERONAUTICS AND
    SPACE ADMINISTRATION.  General
    publications.
    The activity of NASA today con-
sists of six major programs:  aeronautics and space technology, applications of space research, energy
programs, manned space flights,
space science, and tracking and data
acquisition.  This wide range of activities produces a similar range of
publications, both technical and
popular, in this series.  Space activities have been in the public eye
for two decades, and this is an important series to chronicle the
technology.  Many of the titles,
which accumulate at a rate of eight
to ten a year, are useful teaching
aids.  There is a wide variation in
length and format.  Recent titles
include:
    Viking mission to Mars, no. V69
    Washington, D. C. area as seen
      by NASA satellite, no. W27
    Applications of Skylab earth
      resources data, no. Sk9/16
    Mission-oriented R and D and
      the advancement of technol-
      ogy, no. I22/6
    Kennedy Space Center story, no.
      K38
    Research in aeronautics and
      space, no. L26.
The item is recommended for academic
and public libraries.

Item 830-G
NAS1.19:  NATIONAL AERONAUTICS AND
    SPACE ADMINISTRATION.  NASA EP
    series.

These titles are designed to
accelerate the process of intro-
ducing scientific knowledge into the
classroom, with the intention of ap-
prising the educational community of
the relevance of the information to
the secondary school curriculum.
The Skylab concept composes a portion of this literature.  One subseries is called Skylab experiments,
no. 110-115, the purpose being to
inform teachers; it also provides
curricular suggestions for physical
sciences, life sciences, astronomy,
physics, etc.  Other publications
are reprints of articles from other
sources and public relations materials of NASA.  All are attractively designed and relatively nontechnical in content.  Examples
include:
    Our prodigal sun, no. 118
    Skylab:  Outpost on the fron-
      tier of space, no. 124
    Exploration of the solar sys-
      tem, no. 122.
Two or three publications are
issued annually.  Useful to the educational community, these are
recommended for academic and public
libraries.

Item 830-H
NAS1.20:  NATIONAL AERONAUTICS AND
    SPACE ADMINISTRATION.  NASA
    facts.
    Described as educational pub-
lications of the agency, the titles
cover highly technical subjects but
are written in nontechnical style.
The format varies from a standard
booklet to a folded map or chart to

large folded diagrams of orbits.
The quality of the photography is
good and the "facts" appear to be a
valuable teaching aid.  Recent issuances include:
> Viking mission to Mars, no.
>   NF-76, a booklet of photo-
>   graphs, diagrams, and text
> Space shuttle, no. NF44/72-7,
>   a large, folded diagram
> The Jupiter pioneers, no.
>   NF-56, a booklet of photo-
>   graphs, diagrams, and text.

The series is recommended for curriculum collections of academic libraries and without qualification
for public libraries.  Three or
four titles a year are issued.

Item 830-H-1
NAS1.46:  NATIONAL AERONAUTICS AND
SPACE ADMINISTRATION.  NASA
activities.
Published monthly for the employees of NASA, this periodical is
a significant publication for the
layman.  Activities of the agency
are briefly noted.  Personnel notes
reveal a sampling of the success of
women and minorities in gaining en-
trance to a highly technological
agency.  Other articles note traveling exhibits, projected launches,
and research in progress.  Pictures
accompany a number of the articles.
Issues are 20 to 25 pages in
length.  While not an essential title, it is recommended for patrons
of popular science.

Item 830-H-4
NAS1.49:  NATIONAL AERONAUTICS AND
SPACE ADMINISTRATION.  NASA
report to educators.  v.1-
Feb. 1973-  LC 73-643910
Published four times a year,
this newsletter is aimed at the educational community.  Teachers in
elementary and secondary schools
will find it useful in planning
lessons.  It contains information
about new discovery, classroom vis-
its, NASA films, quiz ideas, and
notes on other services available
through the agency.  Recommended
for academic and public libraries.

Item 830-J
NAS1.9/2:  NATIONAL AERONAUTICS AND
SPACE ADMINISTRATION.  Bibliographies and lists of publications.
This series consists of two annual lists and other occasional
lists.  NASA educational publications, no. Ed8, reports titles
available for classroom use.  NASA
special publications:  A selective
catalog, no. Sp3, reports advances
in science, engineering, and technology in the course of space exploration.  Both catalogs include
basic bibliographic information, annotations, and ordering information.
Recommended as a reference tool for
academic and public libraries.

Item 856-D
NAS1.52:  NATIONAL AERONAUTICS AND
SPACE ADMINISTRATION.  Report
to Congress from President of
United States, United States
aeronautic and space activities.
An annual summary of all federal activity in the areas of aeronautics and space, the report includes articles from NASA and from
the many other agencies engaged in
the technology.  The departments of
Defense, Commerce, Transportation,
Interior, and State, the National
Science Foundation, the Smithsonian
Institution, the Environmental Protection Agency, and several others
contribute to space activity by
their use of satellites for monitoring the environment, support of
atmospheric research, control of air
traffic, and plans for international
cooperation.  This report has a
broader scope and therefore more
popular appeal than does the Semi-
Annual Report (NAS1.1, item 830-A),
which has been discontinued.  The
consolidation of reports of this
federal activity is a useful approach.  Recommended for academic
and public libraries.

Item 909-B
SI1.12/2:  SMITHSONIAN INSTITUTION.
Smithsonian contributions to

astrophysics.  No. 1-    1956-
LC 56-63728
Research conducted at the As-
trophysical Observatory in Cam-
bridge, Massachusetts, is published
in this irregular series of technical articles.  Subjects of investigation are primarily the sun, earth,
and solar system.  Before the
series began, Annals of the Astro-
physical Observatory (1900-54) recorded this research.  Recent titles
include Distribution and ages of
Magellanic Cepheids, no. 16, and
Period, color, and luminosity for
Cepheid variables, no. 17.  Papers
varying from a few pages to a few
hundred pages in length include bibliography, charts, and illustrations.  This series is recommended
for academic libraries which support these areas of research.
Three to five studies are issued
a year.

## AGRICULTURE AND HOME ECONOMICS

Item 1
A1.47:  DEPARTMENT OF AGRICULTURE.
    Agricultural statistics.  1936-
    LC Agr. 36-465
    The Yearbook of agriculture
formerly included the battery of
statistics now found in this annual
volume begun in 1936.  The time period of each volume is usually ten to
fifteen years except for occasional
volumes which expand the series to
provide a long-term reference.
These volumes have appeared in 1942,
1952, 1957, 1962, 1967, and 1972.
Their existence means that reference
to previous volumes is seldom necessary.  The 1967 annual includes historical tables beginning in 1866 and
1867 for some crops and livestock,
while by comparison, the 1972 annual's tables for the same data be-
gin with 1929 and 1930.  In addition, the 1967 volume contains
earlier data for some other tables.
Retention of the 1967 volume, the
most recent expanded series annual,
and supplementary annuals is adequate for most collections.  Statistics are presented from three
different types of data:  actual
counts, estimates made by the

Department of Agriculture from sam-
ple surveys, and data obtained from
censuses of agriculture.  The publication includes extensive crop and
livestock production data, economic
data, minimal social data, conservation data, and foreign trade summaries.  Most statistical subjects
have a table of breakdowns by
states.  An index is included.  Recommended for academic and public
library reference collections.

Item 3
A1.76:  DEPARTMENT OF AGRICULTURE.
    Agriculture handbook.  No. 1-
    1950-   LC Agr. 50-554
    Most titles are handbooks, man-
uals, or guides providing reference
and teaching aids in home economics
and agriculture.  Recurring subseries include Handbook of agriculture charts and Compilation of statutes relating to soil conservation.
Older titles with some established
reference value are
    Snow avalanches:  A handbook of
        forecasting and control
        measures, no. 194
    Index of plant diseases in the
        United States, no. 165

A manual of conservation of
soil and water, no. 61.
More recent examples are
Preparing statistical tables,
no. 433
Guidelines for the use of
insecticides, no. 452.
Other subjects include food
purchase, food processing, natural
resources, commerce, and wildlife.
Recommended for libraries serving
teachers and students of agriculture and home economics.

Item 4
A1.75:  DEPARTMENT OF AGRICULTURE.
Agriculture information bulletin.  No. 1-    1949-
LC Agr. 49-680
Summaries of major reports, in-
structional materials, popular
science, consumer guides, and general topics related to agricultural
enterprise are the components of the
series.  Bulletins vary from leaflets to monographs of 100 pages.
Eight to ten may be issued annually.
Representative materials include:
Wheat in the United States,
no. 386
Condensation problems in
your house:  Prevention and
solution, no. 373
Balance sheet of the farming
sector, no. 376
Insects and diseases of vege-
tables in the home garden,
no. 380
Nutrition labeling, no. 382.
These titles and others are aimed at
the general audience and are an important component of household, consumer, and maintenance literature.
Recommended for academic and public
libraries.

Item 6
A1.1:  DEPARTMENT OF AGRICULTURE.
Report of the Secretary of Agriculture.  1894-    LC Agr. 31-
1035
Libraries in rural areas and
schools serving farming communities
and programs will find this an essential reference as it chronicles
the year for farming and ranching.
In urban areas, patrons will be more
interested in the consumer-
oriented publications of the department.  This annual report is grad-
ually becoming briefer than
formerly, about 25 pages at present.  From 1963 through 1972, the
report was not distributed by GPO.
Commencing with the 1973 issue, it
is once again a depository item.

Item 9
A1.9:  DEPARTMENT OF AGRICULTURE.
Farmers' bulletins.  No. 1-
1889-    LC Agr. 16-325
The farmer's guide to crops,
animals, projects, and problems,
this series follows a standard format in a pamphlet of 10 to 40 pages.
Home gardeners, handymen and handy-
women also find these useful.  Using
concrete on the farm, strawberry insects, vegetable diseases, plumbing,
roofing, and beef cattle breeds are
recent topics.  Most bulletins are
instructive, though occasionally
some are only informative, and all
are well illustrated and easy to
understand.  New topics are added to
the series, but old ones reappear
periodically as revisions.  When
this is the case, the publication
advises the reader.  Five to ten
titles are issued a year.  Recommended for public libraries and for
academics serving farm and gardening
interests.

Item 10
A1.2:  DEPARTMENT OF AGRICULTURE.
General publications.
This series is of interest to
the citizen as consumer and to the
rural patron.  Most titles are pamphlets, 8 to 50 pages in length,
covering a spectrum of agricultural
subjects.  Publications of the past
few years have included such titles
as Food is more than just something
to eat, no. F73/38, creatively designed pamphlet about nutrients at
various stages of human life; What's
happening to food prices?, no. F73;
and You can poison yourself, your
family, and your livestock if you
don't use poison carefully, no. P75.
Animal and crop research, land use
planning, ethnic groups in

United States farming, and careers in agriculture are also current topics in this series. Occasionally a publication resembles a research report, but most titles are intended to transmit information to the non-specialist. Titles accumulate at a rate of three to eight a year. Recommended for public libraries and for academic libraries as the need exists.

Item 11
A1.77: DEPARTMENT OF AGRICULTURE.
   Home and garden bulletin.
   No. 1-   1950-   LC Agr. 50-589
   This collection of short pamphlets on homemaking and gardening is similar in style and level of treatment to the Leaflet series, A1.35, item 12. The titles are instructive and easy to understand. Representative examples are
      Interior painting in homes and
         around the farm, no. 184
      How to buy cheese, no. 193
      Soybeans in family meals, no.
         208.
Home and Garden Bulletins accumulate rapidly but they are usually brief. Revisions are issued and noted. Libraries which cannot afford to keep up with all of these subjects in commercial books will find the use of this series a reasonable alternative.

Item 12
A1.35: DEPARTMENT OF AGRICULTURE.
   Leaflet. No. 1-   1927-
   LC Agr. 27-387
   Of the same nature as Farmers' Bulletins, the Miscellaneous Publication series, and the General Publication series, these are 4- to 10-page briefs. Subjects appear to follow crops and animals closely, to the exclusion of consumer information, maintenance guides, and farm-improvement ideas found among the other series. Recent Leaflets cover the topics of irrigating grains, mulch tillage, rhubarb production, insect control in grain, raising guinea fowl, and growing black walnuts. Topics do occasionally vary from animals and crops: firewood

selection and use, energy-saving kitchens, and rural zoning. Revisions of older leaflets are made as needed and noted in the publication. Five to eight titles are published a year. Recommended for public libraries and for academics who serve rural patrons.

Item 13-A
A1.38: DEPARTMENT OF AGRICULTURE.
   Miscellaneous publications.
   No. 1-   1927-   LC Agr. 27-747
   Included here are formats and subjects found throughout the department's other series. Bibliographies, symposium proceedings, statistical summaries, research reports, and building plans known as Cooperative farm building plans are available in summaries for all types of farm buildings: milk houses, grain-feed handling centers, farm houses, hotbeds, etc. Recent miscellaneous titles are
      Atlas of United States trees,
         no. 1146
      Annotated list of generic names
         of scale insects, no. 1015
      Jobs with Forest Service, no.
         843
      Bibliography of tree nut pro-
         duction and marketing re-
         search, 1965-71, no. 1255
      Proceedings of National Nutri-
         tion Education Conference,
         1971, no. 1254.
Revisions are noted. Annual cumulation at present does not exceed the space of one linear foot. Recommended for academic and public libraries.

Item 15
A1.34: DEPARTMENT OF AGRICULTURE.
   Statistical bulletin. No. 1-
   1923-   LC Agr. 23-1185
   The subjects are the same as those of Agricultural statistics, A1.47, item 1. However, individual bulletins are devoted to one agricultural feature and expand it statistically. Among the annual reports of statistics in the series are Annual report on tobacco statistics, Poultry market statistics, and Commodity futures statistics.

Continuing series of estimate reports occur:
> Meat animals, revised esti-
> mates, 1965-69, no. 510
> Farms, revised estimates,
> 1959-70, no. 507
> Vegetables for processing, re-
> vised estimates, 1964-1970,
> no. 494.

Most reports are routine and
treatment of the data does not vary
from year to year or from one reporting period to another. Among
these basic statistics and their
summaries is an occasional social
report or a study indicating the
relationships between data of two
or more agricultural subjects:
> U.S. food consumption: Sources
> of data and trends, 1909-63,
> no. 364
> Fluctuations in crops and
> weather, 1866-1948, no. 101
> Poverty dimensions of rural-
> to-urban migration, no. 511.

Eight to ten titles are issued
annually. Recommended for libraries
serving rural communities or agricultural economics programs and re-
quiring the detail of this series.
The needs of many libraries are met
by item 1.

Item 16
A1.36:  DEPARTMENT OF AGRICULTURE.
> Technical bulletin.  No. 1-
> 1927-   LC Agr. 27-509

Original scientific and technical research is reported here.
Representative examples include:
> Econometric models of cash and
> and futures prices of shell
> eggs, no. 1502
> Factors associated with level-
> of-living in Washington
> County, Mississippi, no. 1501
> Structural design procedure for
> corrugated plastic drainage
> tubing, no. 1466.

Older but often cited titles in the
series are Major uses of land in the
U.S., no. 1082, and Productivity of
of agriculture, United States, 1870-
1958, no. 1238.  Recommended for libraries utilizing agricultural or
agricultural economics materials.
Eight to twelve titles are issued

annually.

Item 17
A1.10:  DEPARTMENT OF AGRICULTURE.
> Yearbook of agriculture.  1894-
> LC Agr. 7-1035

Since 1936 the annuals have focused on a subject of special interest to farmers and ranchers, as well
as to the general public.  Early in
the century this publication served
agriculture as more of an annual report.  The thematic approach has led
the Yearbook to become a popular series because it frequently advises
on consumer issues and serves the
household.  Scientific subjects also
occur, and the Yearbooks may provide
ideas for projects suitable for
science fairs if used creatively.
Recent editions have a tendency to
focus on agriculture and the quality
of life it supports:
> Contours of change, 1970
> A good life for more people,
> 1971
> Landscape for living, 1972.

Older editions have become classics
for their reference value:
> Climate and man, 1941
> Animal diseases, 1956
> Seeds, 1961.

After a hundred years, the 1962
Yearbook, is a history of the Department of Agriculture, and agricultural development in this country.  Each volume is indexed.  The
item is recommended for academic and
public libraries.

Item 19
A92.23:  Agricultural situation.
> 1920-   LC 26-1797

Subtitled the "crop reporter's
magazine," this monthly periodical
is about 15 pages in length and is
written in a popular style.  It is
issued by the Statistical Reporting
Service.  Each issue contains three
main features:  "Surveyscope," which
spotlights various surveys; "Brief-
ings," agricultural news from recent
U.S. Department of Agriculture reports; and "Statistical barometer,"
which features comparative data on
farm income and expenses.  Several
short articles in each issue have

broad appeal to farmers and to ranchers. Recommended for public libraries and for academics in rural areas.

Item 21-H
A93.16: National food situation.
    Issued by the Economic Research Service, the National food situation began during World War II to report on the state of the national food supply, demand, and prices. The publication continues to cover these subjects as well as food-related developments of interest to consumer affairs professionals. Agriculture outlook (A93.10/2, item 42-M), also published by the ERS, provides monthly information on food demand, prices, and supply, while National food situation reports a quarterly analysis. The reporting is comprehensive. The quarterly periodical requires some familiarity with economic analysis for maximum usefulness. Recommended for academic and larger public libraries.

Item 25-A
A77.12: Agricultural research.
    v.1-   Jan./Feb. 1953-
    LC Agr. 53-137
    This monthly is a 12- to 20-page publication with brief articles reporting technical research of the Agricultural Research Service. Articles about animal science, insects, plant science, crops, soil and water, marketing, utilization, and diseases are regular features. Some are directly translatable into farming activity, while others require additional information and guidance for application. The publication is useful to some work in natural sciences as well as to agricultural research. Recommended for academic and public libraries.

Item 42-F
A93.33: The farm index.  v.1-
    Oct. 1962-   LC Agr. 62-486
    Published by the Economic Research Service, this monthly journal is 25 pages in length and contains general farm articles of 4 to 6 pages in length. Regular

features include "Outlook," an editorial column, "Recent publications," and "Economic trends," a chart of comparative data. With the exception of the latter, the journal is not statistical. Recent articles have included such subjects as the success of the soybean, grain needs of the Soviet Union, houseplants, fuel prices, farming during the Depression, vegetable popularity, and rural development. The journal is illustrated and is one of the more attractively designed periodicals of the department. Recommended for public and academic libraries with the interested clientele.

Item 42-M
A93.10/2:  Agriculture outlook.
    v.1-   1976-
    Issued monthly except in December by the Economic Research Service, the periodical is a digest of articles on the variables of the agricultural economy. The reports note major interrelated developments in farming, its support industries, marketing, and the impact of these developments on U.S. agriculture and the consumer. Each issue analyzes the outlook in the following areas: food, marketing, commodities, inputs, transportation, world agriculture and trade, and policy developments. In addition, articles focus on farmers' capital expenditures and their effect on the U.S. economy, the cost of producing major crops, and energy requirements in the food system. Each issue contains statistical indicators and notices of reports issued. The publication has a greater audience than that of the agricultural community; it embraces the interests of economists and business people as well. Agriculture outlook appears to have been merged with or replaced some other periodicals of the Economic Research Service. Recommended for academic and public libraries.

Item 74-A-3
A98.11:  Food and nutrition.  v.1-
    June 1971-   LC 73-649337
    The Food and Nutrition Service

and its food assistance programs are the focus of this publication. The periodical is published six times a year and contains four to ten articles about these activities. Articles typically feature food stamp programs, school breakfast and lunch programs, nutrition for the elderly, and general concern about nutrition. They are brief and serve to publicize the programs of the Food and Nutrition Service. Recommended for public libraries.

Item 76
A67.7/2: Foreign agriculture. v.1-
    Jan. 7, 1963-   LC 66-6212
    This publication of 16 to 20 pages is not an essential to any collection, but yet it has the potential for broadening the interest and understanding of its readers. There is little available commercially which provides the interested reader or the farmer with a view of foreign agriculture. It is published by the Foreign Agriculture Service. Given the great concern about agricultural trade of the present decade, this weekly seems to have a mission. The articles are not always profound, and they may have the bias of the department. Nevertheless, they are quite readable. Recent subjects are France's grain crops, cotton in Central America, meat in East German, and Portugal's food imports. A regular feature is the section "Crops and markets." A small back file may be desirable. Recommended for libraries with a little extra space for a browsing item.

Item 80
A13.1: FOREST SERVICE. Report of
    the chief of the Forest Ser-
    vice. 1883-   LC Agr. 12-394
A13.66/1: PACIFIC NORTHWEST FOREST
    AND RANGE EXPERIMENT STATION,
    PORTLAND, OREGON. Research
    progress.
    Libraries serving patrons in recreation areas or students of forestry programs will find this report important as it chronicles forestry activity each year. It includes a

section on meeting public needs, protecting the environment, legislation highlights, major research publications, and statistical tables. Other Forest Service publications have a broader popular interest. The Report is less than 100 pages in length.
    Research Progress is brief annual reports of new ideas and findings for forestry in the Pacific Northwest. This title is not essential to the general collection, but it accompanies the Forest Service Report.
    The item is recommended for academic and public libraries.

Item 83-A
A13.55: FOREST SERVICE. Forest
    Service films available on
    loan for educational purposes.
    1962-   LC Agr. 52-366
    An annual listing of films available on loan for educational purposes to schools, civic groups, churches, and television, this booklet provides an annotation, viewing time, recommended age group, and ordering information for each film. Libraries serving an active film program or recreational interests related to forestry should maintain the current catalog.

Item 84
A13.2: FOREST SERVICE. General
    publications.
A13.82/2: NORTH CENTRAL FOREST EX-
    PERIMENT STATION, ST. PAUL,
    MINNESOTA. General publica-
    tions.
    Some titles in the Forest Service series are not of popular interest but those in the area of recreation and career information are worth noting:
    Ski the intermountain region,
        no. Sk5
    So you want to be a forester?,
        no. F76-75
    Forestry schools in the United
        States, no. Sch6
    A summer job with the Forest
        Service, no. Su6/2
    Mining and mineral claims in
        national forest wildernesses,

no. M66/2
Discover the national forests
of Washington, no. W27/2.
The publications are well designed
and some have beautiful pictures.
They run in length from 4 to 20
pages and are issued at a rate of
three to five a year.

Recently added to this item
number is the General Publications
series of the North Central Forest
Experiment Station. Identifying as-
pen diseases, controlling needlecast
and fungus, and general research are
subjects of the attractively designed brochures.

The item is recommended for libraries serving recreational interests.

Item 85-A
A13.11/2: FOREST SERVICE. Lists of
    publications.
A13.27/7: FOREST PRODUCTS LABORA-
    TORY, MADISON, WISCONSIN.
    Lists of publications.
A13.82/9: NORTH CENTRAL FOREST EX-
    PERIMENT STATION, ST. PAUL,
    MINNESOTA. Lists of publica-
    tions.

One title is issued regularly
by each of these series. Materials
to help teach forest conservation,
no. A13.11/2:T22, is revised once
every three or four years. It is
brief, lists titles and annotates
them, and includes a recommended
grade level, as well as a list of
nonprint materials. Ordering information is given. Dividends from
wood research, no. A13.27/7:W85/15,
is a bibliography of recent publications of the Forest Products
Laboratory, the Forest Service.
Issued semiannually, it includes a
brief description of each publication cited and ordering information. An annual publications list
is issued by the North Central Forest Experiment Station. The item
is recommended for academic and
public libraries.

Item 88-B
A77.708: Family economics review.
    June 1957-   LC 65-67252
    This quarterly reports research

about various economic aspects of
family living, some of which research comes from the Consumer and
Food Economics Institute. Articles
cover agriculture, poverty, energy,
home economics, real estate, employment, and other subjects which bear
on household economics. Some articles provide consumer advice although Family economics review differs from commercial publications in
that it does not compare competing
brand names. Other articles make
annual or long-range projections,
and some include statistics. Regular features include a list of new
U.S. Department of Agriculture publications and ordering information,
a consumer price report, and cost of
food for the home table. Articles
are 3 to 5 pages in length; each
quarterly is about 25 pages long.
The publication is issued by the
Agricultural Research Service and
prepared primarily for home economics agents of the Cooperative Extension Service. However, it is a useful consumer guide and is recommended for public libraries.
Academics should consider it if it
fulfills a program need.

Item 90
A21.2: DEPARTMENT OF AGRICULTURE.
    OFFICE OF COMMUNICATION. Gen-
    eral publications.

Issued specifically to inform
the public of the advancements and
importance of agriculture in the nation's economy, these publications
are public relations materials.
They are usually pamphlets on one or
more selected themes. The following
are representative:
    Agriculture USA, no. Ag8/15
    Is the world facing starva-
        tion?, no. St2
    What farm exports mean to you,
        no. F22/17
    What makes U.S. farm trade
        grow?, no. F22/10.
Three or four titles are issued annually. Recommended for academic
and public libraries.

Item 91
A21.9/8: DEPARTMENT OF AGRICULTURE.

OFFICE OF INFORMATION.  List of available publications and congressional lists.

The only regularly issued and revised list of this series is Popular publications for the farmer, suburbanite, homemaker, consumer, no. 5.  It lists publications available free to individuals and describes conditions under which they may be available free in bulk.  Ordering information is included.  Arrangement is by subject.  Recommended for public libraries.

Item 95-D
A17.18/2:  NATIONAL AGRICULTURE LI-
BRARY.  Bibliographies and lists of publications.

These titles are infrequent but useful.  They are prepared by the library and its cooperating institutions.  Subjects may have academic as well as popular appeal.  A recent bibliography is Rural development literature, no. R88/969-75.  It is annotated and gives adequate information for locating materials cited.  Recommended for academic and public libraries.

Item 102
A57.38:  SOIL CONSERVATION SERVICE.
Soil survey reports.

Since 1899, the Department of Agriculture and the state agriculture experiment stations have cooperated in producing soil surveys.  The surveys contain maps as well as interpretations and descriptions of soil use and management, formation and classification.  These data provide farmers and ranchers with assistance in soil management and in solving technical problems.  Soil surveys are also useful in planning educational programs and research.  Surveys published since 1957 contain more interpretations of types of soils in a county.  Beginning in 1957, maps were printed on a photomosaic base.  Interpretations commonly included since 1957 vary with the needs of the area, but the following generally occur:  estimated yields of crops, support of recreation, capa-

bility as range land, interpretations for community planning, engineering uses of soils, and support of wildlife habitat.  Older surveys are still useful but their maps and interpretations sometimes need to be updated.  Surveys cover one or more counties or parts of counties.  Soil surveys are issued as paperbound books, usually under 100 pages in length.  Frequency varies, but the reports are published as work for a soil survey area is completed.  Because only the surveys for local areas will be of any great use in most libraries, these should be identified and added.  Depository libraries can select the states for which coverage is desired, thereby placing an element of control on the quantity.

Item 102-A
A57.38:list  SOIL CONSERVATION SER-
VICE.  List of published soil surveys.  LC 72-601470

This list is published irregularly and contains a list by state of all geographical areas which have had soil surveys completed.  Information about availability and ordering is included.  This is a useful reference source for academic and public libraries regardless of whether Soil survey reports (A57.38, item 102) is held.  It enables the user to determine the existence of such a report.  It is small, infrequent, and recommended.

Item 122
A57.9:  SOIL CONSERVATION SERVICE.
Soil conservation.  v.1-
1935-   LC Agr. 35-403

This monthly publication is about 25 pages in length and contains articles of 2 to 6 pages.  Frequent features in the magazine include a column recognizing soil conservation activities around the country, notes of recently completed surveys, and lists of approaching meetings.  Articles are of major interest to persons working in conservation, but the publication has established itself as being of interest to a wide audience.

Articles report conservation projects around the country and include pictures, environmental activities, educational programs, and position statements on conservation projects. Because of the close relationship of conservation to environmental concerns, the monthly is recommended for public and academic libraries.

Item 152
　　BUREAU OF THE CENSUS.  Census of Agriculture.
C3.31/5:  Special reports.
C3.31/12:  Final reports, other than area and special reports.
　　Special Reports may contain data from supplemental surveys in addition to agriculture census information.  Designated as volume 5 of the agriculture census, this series for the 1969 agriculture census is divided into sixteen parts, including one each for nine major types of farm operations, farm finance, ranking agricultural counties, and horticultural specialties.
　　The Final Reports group includes volumes 2, 3, 4, and 6 (in multiparts) of the census of agriculture.  The General reports, volume 2, presents statistics by subjects such as type of farm, irrigation and drainage, livestock, and farm management.  The nation, regions, and states are treated under each topic.  Nine individual chapters of volume 2 average about 300 pages each.  Agriculture services, volume 3 of Final Reports, is a new title reporting data related to services by state and county.  Irrigation, volume 4, is a 200-page volume for the 1969 census, reporting on drainage basins, water conveyed, crop production, and land irrigated.  Drainage of agricultural lands, volume 6, includes data on drainage on individual farms and from public projects.
　　The foregoing descriptions are based on the 1969 census of agriculture.  (In that census, Special Reports were classified C56.227/2, and Final Reports, C56.227/3.  The 1974 census of agriculture, and future

censuses, are expected to be classified in C3.)  The publishing program remains relatively stable from one census to the next, but librarians should watch for preliminary materials which describe the series planned for upcoming censuses.  Agriculture censuses are conducted in years ending in 4 and 9.  Libraries which treat agriculture topically find this useful for reference, although it consumes quite a bit of space.

Item 152-A-1 to A-39
C3.31/4:  BUREAU OF THE CENSUS.
　　Census of agriculture, area reports.
　　A census of agriculture is conducted every five years, in years ending in 4 and 9.  The Area Reports include a state map, highlights of the state's agriculture, charts, summary data, and detailed data for counties.  An appendix provides explanatory text and definitions.  Designated as volume 1 of the census of agriculture, these reports average about 300 pages in length.  For most libraries, this is the basic agriculture census reference tool, but some may also want to consider the series found in item 152:  statistical pictures of various topics as opposed to data organized by state.
　　The foregoing descriptions are based on the 1969 census of agriculture.  (The 1969 census of agriculture was classified in C56; the 1974 census is in C3.)  Depository libraries have the option of electing to receive all or part of these reports because the item numbers distinguish state and two-state areas.

Item 611-F
C55.320:  NATIONAL MARINE FISHERIES SERVICE.  Fishery market development series.
　　The focus here is on cooking.  Recipes appear infrequently in federal documents, but these titles include both cooking instructions for fish and recipes.  Quick oyster pickup, salmon paysanne, sesame catfish, and hush puppies are all

there.  These booklets are issued at a
rate of one each year.  The item is
recommended for academic and public
libraries.

## ARCHAEOLOGY AND ANTHROPOLOGY

Item 646-A
I29.59:  NATIONAL PARK SERVICE.
    Archeological research series.
    Specialized topics explored in
relation to various areas of the National Park system are the subjects
of these articles.  The remains of
prehistoric and historic structures
are being preserved in many areas of
the system.  The studies serve both
as scientific reports and as references for visitors to the areas.
Recent numbers include:
    Big Juniper House, Mesa Verde
    National Park, Colorado, no.
    7C
    Ruins stabilization in the
    Southwestern United States,
    no. 10
    Investigations in Russell Cave,
    Russell Cave National Monu-
    ment, Alabama, no. 13.
Each publication, attractively designed, includes bibliography,
plates, and an index.  The studies
are issued irregularly and are 100
to 200 pages in length.  Recommended
for academic and public libraries.

Item 646-E
I29.77:  NATIONAL PARK SERVICE.
    Anthropological papers.
    Since 1945 the National Park
Service, the Smithsonian Institution, the Army Corps of Engineers,
and the Bureau of Land Reclamation
have cooperated to recover prehistoric and historic materials threat-
ened by dams built by the federal
government on rivers of the nation.
Known as the Inter-Agency Archaeo-

logical Salvage Program, the work
has preserved significant archaeo-
logical data which are written about
in this series.  Other studies focus
on cultures which have been all but
erased by the construction of lakes
and dams on these rivers.  The series began in 1971 and is irregular.
Papers are scholarly interpretations, but they have some popular
appeal because of their origin in
the salvage program and the prevalence of anthropology and archae-
ology as interests of the American
public.
    The two initial papers of the
series are
    Middle Missouri Archeology,
    no. 1
    Like-a-fishhook Village and
    Fort Berthold, Garrison
    Reservoir, North Dakota,
    no. 2.
Both of these focus on the Missouri
River valley of North and South Da-
kota.  Recommended for academic and
public libraries.

Item 921-A
SI1.33:  SMITHSONIAN INSTITUTION.
    Smithsonian contributions to
    anthropology.  v.1-   1965-
    LC 65-52299
    Various museums and bureaus of
the Smithsonian Institution provide
anthropological research for these
publications.  Articles are also accepted from persons outside the institution.  Reports of Western Hemisphere anthropology, and therefore,
of native Americans are predominant.

An exception is The long sword and scabbard slide in Asia, no. 17. Other recent studies are Anthropology of the Numa, no. 14, and Notebook of a Cherokee Shaman, vol. 2, no. 6. Other subjects include the Navaho, Pueblo, and Seneca Indians, and cultures of Guatemala, Ecuador, and Panama. The monographs, varying in length from a few pages to a few hundred pages, have bibliography, indexing, plates, charts, and illustrations. Five to eight titles are issued annually. Recommended for academic and public libraries serving a clientele with an interest in the subject.

## ART AND ARCHITECTURE

Item 432
FA1. COMMISSION OF FINE ARTS. Reports and publications.

A small number of titles have been published in this series, but the quality is high. Massachusetts Avenue architecture, no. M38, and Washington architecture, 1791-1861, no. W27/4/791-861, are beautiful books. The commission has a long history which is recorded in The Commission of Fine Arts, 1910-1963: A brief history, no. H62/910-63. Recommended for academic and public libraries.

Item 648-B
I29.74: NATIONAL PARK SERVICE.
Historic American building survey.

Begun as an attempt to present historically and architecturally important buildings in each state in a book for each state, the series has issued only a few titles. The first one, Wisconsin architecture, no. 1, is the only one to date which focuses on a state. It is designed for the historian, architect, traveler, and general reader, its sources being records in the Library of Congress. In addition, five volumes have been issued on Washington's Georgetown architecture. If the projected series of state guides is continued, they will be important additions. Recommended for academic and public libraries.

Item 831-B-2
NF2. NATIONAL ENDOWMENT FOR THE ARTS. Reports and publications.

NF2.1 is the annual report of the endowment. It contains standard annual report information, names and numbers, but it lacks a narrative.

NF2.2 contains more varied titles. A single subseries seems to emerge:
Museums USA: Art, history, science, and others, no. M97/2
Museums USA: Highlights, no. M97
Museums USA: A survey report, no. M97/3.
Other typical titles include:
The Alvarado School art workshop, no. A18
Artists in the schools, no. Ar7/3.
Opera program, no. Op2
NF2.8 is program guidelines recurring more or less annually for the Artists in schools series, no. Ar7. Examples include:

Architecture and environmental
 arts, no. Ar2
Crafts, no. C84
Dance touring, no. D19.2
Literature, no. L71
Expansion arts, no. Ex7
Music, no. M97.
 These titles will be particularly useful for higher education,
secondary education, and civic
groups interested in funding for
programs, or in program aids. The
titles are usually pamphlets; three
or four are issued a year. The item
is recommended for academic and public libraries.

Item 916
S16.2:  NATIONAL COLLECTION OF FINE
 ARTS, WASHINGTON, D.C. General
 publications.
 Primarily catalogs from exhibitions at the National Collection of
Fine Arts, this series is as broad
in scope as the exhibitions themselves. Each publication is well
designed, softbound, and easily com-
petes with those commercially published. Catalogs from recent exhibitions are
 Alfred H. Maurer, 1868-1932,
  no. M44
 Pennsylvania Academy moderns,
  1910-1940, no. P38/910-40
 American art in the Barbizon
  mood, no. B23
 Craft multiples, no. C84.
Recommended for academic and public
libraries.

Item 917
 NATIONAL GALLERY OF ART, WASH-
 INGTON, D.C.
S18.2:  General publications.

S18.8:  Handbooks, manuals, guides.
 Pamphlets are issued in these
series at a rate of one or two a
year. They are usually public information materials which are useful
to people not presently touring the
National Gallery. The Extension
Service loans slide lectures, films,
and audio-visual programs, the catalogs of which are included in this
series. These titles, whether catalogs, museum guides, or discussions
of style, are all vital links between the population and its National Gallery. Recommended for all
libraries.

Item 922-B
S111.2:  NATIONAL PORTRAIT GALLERY,
 WASHINGTON, D.C. General publications.
 These publications are generally catalogs of exhibitions at the
National Portrait Gallery. The exhibitions have a tendency to be organized thematically and the resul-
tant catalog is quite an interesting
book. Recent releases are
 'If elected ...' Unsuccessful
  candidates for the presidency, 1796-1968, no.
  P92/2/796-968
 The black presence in the era
  of the American Revolution,
  1770-1800, no. B56/770-800
 Portraits of the American stage,
  1771-1971, no. St1/771-971.
 These publications are hand-
somely designed and inexpensive by
comparison with commercially produced catalogs. They are usually
softbound. Recommended for public
and academic libraries.

# BIOLOGICAL SCIENCES

Item 609-C-1
C55.302: NATIONAL MARINE FISHERIES
    SERVICE. General publications.
    Typical subjects of this group
are grants for fishery activities,
seafood purchase and cooking, and
ocean life. The focus is both on
the people who earn their living by
the sea and on the beneficiaries of
that livelihood, the general population. Examples include:
    Shrimp--A new picture for 1974,
    no. Sh8
    A seafood heritage, no. Se1/2
    Our living oceans, no. Se1.
One or two titles are issued annually in pamphlet format. Recommended for academic and public libraries.

Item 610
I49.36/2: FISH AND WILDLIFE SER-
    VICE. Conservation note.
    No. 1- 1959- LC 65-1525
    Numbered pamphlets are issued
infrequently about subjects of interest to conservation. The American buffalo, no. 12, and Migration
of birds, no. 8, are among the recent ones. They have potential use
as teaching aids. Recommended for
public libraries.

Item 612
I49.2: FISH AND WILDLIFE SERVICE.
    General publications.
    Beautiful nature guides, career
materials, conservation pamphlets,
and public relations materials are
included in this series. A few administrative reports are issued, but
most titles acquaint the public

either with programs of the agency
or with wildlife. Representative
titles include:
    Duck plague in waterfowl,
    no. D85/3
    Fifty birds of town and city,
    no. B53/4
    To have and to hold: Alaska's
    migratory birds, no. Aℓ1s.
    About one title a year is
issued. The format is pamphlet.
Recommended for academic and public libraries.

Item 612-A
I49.30: FISH AND WILDLIFE SER-
    VICE. North American fauna.
    No. 1- 1889- LC Agr.
    6-1826
    Scientific reports on birds,
mammals, reptiles, and amphibians
are included in this series. Individually titled numbers are usually
50 to 100 pages. They are written
for the professional but are comprehensible by students. Titles
are issued infrequently. Recent
titles include:
    The distribution and occur-
    rence of the birds of Jack-
    son County, Oregon, no. 70
    The screech owl, no. 71
    The sea otter in the Eastern
    Pacific Ocean, no. 68
    Natural history of the Swain-
    son's warbler, no. 69.
Recommended for libraries supporting biology programs.

Item 613-B
I49.66: FISH AND WILDLIFE SERVICE.
    Resource publications.

Individually numbered reports issued from this series are similar in subject matter and level of specialization to reports in the Special Scientific Reports series, I49.15/3, item 614-C. The Resource Publications series contains reports of research carried out by persons working at various wildlife refuges around the country. Some are leaflets of a few pages which would be of interest to refuge visitors, but most are scientific reports. Some describe techniques and others are reviews of the literature. Recent titles include:

> Key to nematodes reported in waterfowl, no. 122
> Review of the literature on the endangered masked bobwhite, no. 108
> Trapping techniques for sandhill crane studies in the Platte River valley, no. 107
> Characteristics of the black-footed ferret, no. 109
> Common marsh plants of the United States and Canada, no. 93.

Three or four titles are issued annually. They are usually less than 100 pages in length. Because of their broad scope, they are recommended for academic and public libraries.

Item 614-C
I49.15/3:   FISH AND WILDLIFE SERVICE. Special scientific report: Wildlife. LC 59-60429
Several recurring series are issued here. These reports tend to be studies which have comparative value when undertaken annually or periodically. Note particularly:

> Mammals imported in the United States in (year)
> Birds imported into the United States in (year)
> Mourning dove status report, (year)
> Waterfowl status report, (year).

Other papers are studies of individual species and their habits. Examples include:

> Bibliography of the North American land tortoises, no. 190
> Breeding and wintering areas of canvasbacks harvested in various states and provinces, no. 185
> Bird damage to blueberries in the United States, no. 172.

The studies are scientific and require special knowledge to be used satisfactorily. Six to eight are issued annually. Most are under 100 pages in length. Recommended for academic and public libraries.

Item 614-D
I49.47/4:   BUREAU OF SPORT FISHERIES AND WILDLIFE. Wildlife research report.
Subject bibliographies and research papers about birds, mammals, other wildlife, and their ecology are issued in this series. They are specialized scientific papers of value to ecologists and biologists and to trained naturalists, with portions of each paper appealing to the nonspecialist. Numbers are issued irregularly and infrequently. Length varies from 100 to 300 pages. Various research-report series associated with wildlife and its agencies have existed in the past. This one began in 1972. The two initial reports are

> An analysis of the population dynamics of selected avian species, no. 1
> Population ecology of migratory birds, no. 2.

Recommended for academic and public libraries.

Item 615-A
I49.68:   BUREAU OF SPORT FISHERIES AND WILDLIFE. Technical papers. 1-  1966-  LC 73-640195
Brief research reports about some subject related to fish and wildlife and averaging about 30 pages in length are issued here. They are more specialized than those reports cited in Special Scientific Reports series (I49.15/3, item 614-C), and Resource Publications series (I49.66, item 613-B),

and therefore appeal to a more limited audience.  Recent issuances are
representative titles:
> Biology of the pile perch,
> Rhacochilus vacca, in Yaquina
> Bay, Oregon, no. 57
> Thermal characteristics of Lake
> Michigan, 1954-55, no. 69
> History of salmon in the Great
> Lakes, 1850-1970, no. 68
> Atlantic salmon (Salmo salar):
> An annotated bibliography,
> no. 83.

Four or five titles are issued a
year.  Recommended for academic libraries.

Item 616-B
> FISH AND WILDLIFE SERVICE
> I49.13:  Wildlife leaflets.
> I49.13/3:  Wildlife Service leaf-
> lets.

The two series of pamphlets are
similar in coverage and format; they
are frequently used for reference
and sometimes as teaching aids.
Only one or two titles are issued
per year.  The Selected list of
federal laws and treaties relating
to sport fish and wildlife, no. 489,
is revised periodically, citing various public laws relating to wildlife.  Birds protected by federal
law, no. 494, lists bird names and
cites authorities, such as the Migratory Bird Act of 1918 and the
Endangered Species Conservation Act
of 1969.  Other leaflets are about
specific kinds of wildlife:
> The South American monk, Quak-
> er, or gray-headed parakeet,
> no. I49.13:496
> Diving ducks, no. I49.13/3:D85.

Recommended for academic and public
libraries.

Item 616-C
> I49.71:  BUREAU OF SPORT FISHERIES
> AND WILDLIFE.  Wildlife por-
> trait series.

Reproductions of paintings and
photographs are issued periodically
with accompanying information about
the subjects.  The portraits are
large and suitable for classroom use
or for library display.  The separate descriptions include the size

of the bird or mammal, range of
territory in winter and summer,
community and breeding habits, and
food source.  The accompanying text
is in leaflet format.  Portraits
vary in size, but 14" x 17" is average.  The portraits are issued
in groups of ten to twenty at one
time, once every two or three
years.  Recommended for public libraries.

Item 910-D
> SI1.27:  SMITHSONIAN INSTITUTION.
> Smithsonian contributions to
> zoology.  No. 1-   1964-
> LC 76-604322

These publications are reports
from museums and bureaus involved in
zoological research.  Systematic,
ecological, behavioral, and various
general studies of animal genera
and species are the major portion of
the series.  An occasional bibliographical or methodological paper
is published, such as A new approach
in the analysis of biogeographic
data, no. 107.  Common studies are
> The echinoids of Carrie Bow
> Cay, Belize, no. 206
> Ecology and behavior of the
> giant wood spider Nephila
> maculata (Fabricus) in New
> Guinea, no. 149
> The systematics, postmarsupial
> development, and ecology of
> the deep-sea family Neotan-
> aidae (Crustacea:  Tanaida-
> cea), no. 170.

Monographs vary from a few to a few
hundred pages in length and have indexes, bibliographies, plates, and
charts.  Twenty to thirty titles a
year are issued.  Recommended for
libraries serving scholarly zoological interests.

Item 910-E
> SI1.29:  SMITHSONIAN INSTITUTION.
> Smithsonian contributions to
> botany.  No. 1-   1969-
> LC 72-603821

The science division of the
Smithsonian Institution is comprised
of several museum and institute facilities whose research is the basis
of these publications.  Scientific

colleagues at other institutions may also submit papers. The publications are primarily of two categories: monographs on individual genera and flora studies of particular geographical areas. Recent titles include:

> Flora of the Marquesas, 1:
> Ericaceae-Convolvulaceae,
> no. 23
>
> The genus Thrinax (Palmae:
> Coryphoideae), no. 19
>
> A revision of the lichen genus
> Hypotrachyna (Parmeliaceae)
> in tropical America, no. 25.

Publications include indexes, bibliographies, plates, and illustrations, and they are usually under 100 pages in length. Five to ten titles are issued annually. Recommended for libraries serving botanical interests.

Item 910-G
SI1.30:  SMITHSONIAN INSTITUTION.
Smithsonian contributions to

paleobiology.  No. 1-   1969-
LC 75-605177

Fossil plant and animal studies compose this irregular series. Monographs vary in length from a few pages to a few hundred pages, but shorter ones predominate. Persons working in bureaus in the science division of the Smithsonian Institution are the main contributors, although papers are accepted from outside the institution. Recent paleobiological studies have been:

> Paleoornithology of St. Helena
> Island, South Atlantic Ocean,
> no. 23
>
> Revised Tertiary stratigraphy
> and paleontology of the Wes-
> tern Beaver Divide, Fremont
> County, Wyoming, no. 25

Plates, charts, illustrations, bibliographies, and often indexes accompany the reports. Three to five titles are issued annually. Recommended for libraries supporting paleobiological interests.

## CONSUMER INFORMATION

Item 247-B
C13.53:  NATIONAL BUREAU OF STAN-
DARDS.  NBS consumer informa-
tion series.

The technical research going on at the National Bureau of Standards covers many subjects of potential interest to the general population. By way of this series, such knowledge is shared with the public. Products are neither tested nor recommended, but the research is frequently of practical value. Recent numbers include:

> Care of books, documents,
> prints, and films, no. 5
>
> What about metric?, no. 7

Making the most of your energy
dollars, no. 8.

The reports are often 15 to 30 pages and are issued at a rate of one a year. They are illustrated, informative titles. Recommended for academic and public libraries.

Item 533-A
FT1.3/2:  FEDERAL TRADE COMMISSION.
Consumer bulletins.

These useful guides to consumer awareness are 8- to 10-page pamphlets written in nontechnical language. The series is numbered; issues are irregular and infrequent. Recent titles include:

Freezer meat bargains, no. 5
Look for that label, no. 6
Don't be gyped, no. 8
Protection for the elderly,
    no. 9.
The format provides examples of what
to guard against and also what to
look for. Details about FTC, other
consumer protection groups, and the
action they can take is sometimes
included. They are good supplements
to common sense. Recommended for
public libraries.

Item 558-A-2
GS2.16:  GENERAL SERVICES ADMINIS-
    TRATION. Consumer information
    series.
    Four or five titles are issued
a year in this series which is a response to Presidential Executive Order 11566 directing federal agencies
to provide knowledge of consumer
products to the public when the
knowledge is available. These 8-
to 12-page reports are nontechnical,
graphic, and descriptive. The information provided is that which has
been learned from buying products
for the government. This is a popular item in public libraries. Recent titles include:
    Household cleaners, no. 18
    Portable humidifiers, no. 19
    Car care and service, no. 20
    Pots and pans, no. 22
    Everyday hand tools, no. 23.

Item 580-B
GS11.9:  GENERAL SERVICES ADMINIS-
    TRATION. CONSUMER INFORMATION
    CENTER. The consumer informa-
    tion catalog.
    This quarterly index of se-
lected federal publications of consumer interest began in 1970 in
response to a Presidential Order to
encourage federal agencies to develop and make available information
of interest to consumers. The Consumer Information Center was established as a disseminating point for
this material.
    Publications are listed by sub-
ject. Some titles discuss products,
others services. Basic bibliographic information is included as

is an order from. All publications
listed can be ordered from the center. Recommended for academic and
public libraries.

Item 857-I-1
HE1.509:  OFFICE OF CONSUMER AF-
    FAIRS. Consumer news. v.1-
    April 1971-
    Published on the first and fif-
teenth of each month by the Office
of Consumer Affairs, Department of
Health, Education, and Welfare, the
newsletter reports to consumers on
programs of the federal government.
Specifically, it includes reports on
legislation, public policy forums,
energy saving discoveries, recalls
of products, and reminders of proposed federal laws of consumer interest on which consumers may wish
to comment officially. Information
is pertinent and timely. A back
file of a few months is adequate.
Recommended for all libraries.

Item 857-I-5
HE1.502:  OFFICE OF CONSUMER AF-
    FAIRS. General publications.
    The chief title issued here is
Directory: Federal, state, county,
city government consumer offices,
no. St2. Issued annually, this
guide helps the individual consumer
to find where complaints should be
directed. It is organized by state
and includes the name of the official and address of the office.
In addition, publications have been
issued on consumer education. Other
directories of services have appeared occasionally. Two or three
publications are issued annually.
Recommended for academic and public
libraries.

Item 982-D-6
TD8.14:  NATIONAL HIGHWAY TRAFFIC
    SAFETY ADMINISTRATION. Con-
    sumer information series. v.1-
    1970-
    Designed primarily to assist
the car buyer in comparing items of
safety performance among various
makes and models of vehicles, including motorcycles, publications
in the series are planned to be

compilations of data provided by manufacturers in response to the Safety Administration's regulations. Three areas of performance are covered in the only title issued to date, Performance data for new (model year) passenger cars and motorcycles: Stopping distance, acceleration and passing ability, and tire reserve load. These safety features are explained and the data given for each make and model of vehicle sold in this country. The title has been annual. The publication is prepared for the consumer and is therefore nontechnical. The volume is a companion to the Consumer Aid series, no. TD8.14/2, item 982-D-9. Recommended for reference in academic and public libraries.

Item 982-D-9
    NATIONAL HIGHWAY TRAFFIC
    SAFETY ADMINISTRATION.
TD8.14/2:  Consumer aid series.
    v.1-    1970-
TD8.14/3:  Consumer affairs fact
    sheet.
    Designed to assist the individual in comparing aspects of the motor vehicle's safety performance, the Consumer Aid series provides annual booklets containing manufacturer's data for the consumer. The series is in three parts:
    Brakes--A comparison of braking
        performance for (model year)
        passenger cars and motor-
        cycles, part 1
    Tires ..., part 2
    Acceleration and passing abil-
        ity ..., part 3.
These booklets contain similar information to that found in the Consumer Information series, no. TD8.14, item 982-D-6. The Consumer Aid series is more up-to-date at the present time and for that reason is

the more desirable of the two, if a choice is to be made. Each part explains the performance feature and the Department of Transportation's regulation in regard to it. The publication is designed for the consumer and is nontechnical.
    The Consumer affairs fact sheet focuses on consumer protection in general; it is issued infrequently.
    The item is recommended for academic and public libraries.

Item 1062-C
Y3.C76/3:2  CONSUMER PRODUCT SAFETY
    COMMISSION.  General publica-
    tions.
    Yet another consumer watchdog of the government, the Consumer Product Safety Commission establishes product safety standards and may ban hazardous consumer products. To meet this function, the agency carries out extensive research on products and provides information and education programs for the consumer and for industry. The result is a series of publications with broad appeal to library users. Examples include:
    Hazardous analysis:  Play-
        ground equipment, no. H34/4
    Hazardous analysis:  Bottles
        for carbonated soft drinks,
        no. H34/3
    Gasoline is made to explode,
        no. G21
    Bicycles:  Buy right, drive
        right, no. B47
    Look at it this way, it's a
        cutting machine, no. C98.
Some are research reports and others are leaflets for nonspecialists. Most are easily comprehended. The titles are issued at a rate of four or five a year and are good additions to academic and public libraries.

Item 191-A
I19.65: Earthquake information bulletin. v.1- 1969-
    The publication provides current information on earthquakes for both the casual and specialized reader. Published six times a year by the Geological Survey, issues contain six to eight articles of 20 to 30 pages in length. Seismological activities around the world are reported, but the emphasis is on the United States. Regular features include the earthquake history of a state, an annotated list of publications, and notices of conferences. Recent earthquakes are also reported. Recommended for academic and public libraries.

Item 250-E-1
C55.14: NATIONAL OCEANIC AND ATMO-SPHERIC ADMINISTRATION. NOAA. v.1- 1971-
    Published quarterly to acquaint readers with programs and responsibilities of the agency, this periodical is somewhat technical, yet it may appeal to the popular scientist. Issues are about 20 pages in length with ten to twelve brief articles in each. Subject matter deals with coastal zone management and preservation, the climate, marine environments, outer space, and wildlife. Regular features include news and legislation in the field, and a few recipes for sea fare. A few years of holdings may be desirable. Recommended for academic and public libraries.

Item 250-E-2
C55.2: NATIONAL OCEANIC AND ATMO-SPHERIC ADMINISTRATION. General publications.
    The goals of this agency are monitoring conditions in the atmosphere and preparing the public for them, planning use of the ocean and space resources, and exploring the possibility of environmental modification. Its activities are reflected in the publications:
    The marine environment and oceanic life, no. M33/2
    Earthquakes, no. Ea7/2
    NOAA motion picture films, no. F48
    A federal plan for natural disaster warning and preparedness, no. N21/2.
Two or three titles are issued annually. Recommended for academic and public libraries.

Item 250-E-11
C55.26: NATIONAL OCEANIC AND ATMO-SPHERIC ADMINISTRATION. Bibliographies and lists of publications.
    The bibliographies and catalogs of the Department of Commerce, C1.54 and C1.54/2, item 126-A, provide a measure of this service. In the present series, however, special attention is given to the publications issued by this agency. Subject bibliographies are issued infrequently as are lists of publications. A recent title is Marine ecosystems analysis program: Bibliography of the New York bight, a two-part bib-

liography and subject index of federally and commercially published materials. The bibliographies are good reference sources. Recommended for academic and public libraries serving an audience with some specialized knowledge.

Item 342-B
D103.48: Water spectrum. v.1-
    Spring 1969-
    Issued by the Army Corps of Engineers, this quarterly intends to be a major forum for the written discussion of water resources. Each contains about seven articles of 3 to 10 pages each, written by professionals in the corps and in other state and federal agencies concerned with water resources. Topics have included inland waterways, waste water irrigation, groundwater, wildlife management, state plans, land management, and water processing of coal. Articles are written in a relatively popular style and should have broad appeal. The quarterly is attractively designed. Recommended for academic and public libraries.

Item 434-A-1
FE1.2: FEDERAL ENERGY ADMINISTRA-
    TION. General publications.
    Assessment of the national energy situation is one of the activities of the FEA. That responsibility along with public information programs is evident in the publications of this series. Reports of workshops, energy industry reports, forecasts, facilities, and career guides are all in the province of this item. Some reports are technical but many have broad appeal. Recent titles, accumulating at a rate of about ten to twelve annually, include:
    The relationship of oil companies and foreign govern-
        ments, no. Oi5
    Fact sheet: Solar energy,
        no. So4
    Directory of state government
        energy-related agencies,
        no. St2
    Energy conservation: Under-
        standing and activities for

young people, no. Y8.
As the series continues, revisions may be required. Recommended for academic and public libraries.

Item 434-A-2
FE1.17: Monthly energy review.
    LC 75-640927
    Energy information previously incorporated in the PIMS monthly petroleum report and Monthly energy indicators is now collected and analyzed in the Monthly energy review. Although the latter contains some textual material, a major portion of the content is tabular and statistical. Sources of energy on which the world is dependent are presented individually in terms of consumption, resource development, price, and international implications. The publication reflects the mission of the Federal Energy Administration and is important to libraries as it assesses current energy resources. Issues are 60 to 80 pages in length. It contains appended definitions and explanatory notes. Recommended for academic and public libraries.

Item 434-A-3
    FEDERAL ENERGY ADMINISTRATION
FE1.15: Energy information reported to Congress as required by Public Law 93-319.
FE1.15/2: Report to Congress on the economic impact of energy actions.
    Energy information reported to Congress is a quarterly report providing the summary text and tabular series necessary to describe the use of energy resources. Some of the data appear in the Monthly energy review (FE1.17, item 434-A-2) in a slightly different form. Resource development, production, consumption, and environmental concerns are among the many subjects of discussion.
    The Report to Congress on the economic impact of energy actions, required by law, is an annual assessment of the economic impact of energy factors on the nation during the particular period. It discusses

consumption, employment, prices, industry impacts, balance of payments, and energy actions. It does not make recommendations. The Report to Congress is an important summary and analysis and is for academic and larger public libraries.

Item 434-A-8
FE1.19: Energy reporter. 1-
    1975-
    This 8-page newsletter is issued about ten times a year by the Federal Energy Administration's Office of Communications and Public Affairs. It transmits topical and timely information to the general public. Recent Reporters have covered such topics as the national energy plan, progress on the Alaskan pipe line, the popularity of wind-powered electric generators, and the impact of OPEC prices. The information varies from reports to ideas to news. Recommended for academic and public libraries.

Item 434-A-15
FE1.24: FEDERAL ENERGY ADMINISTRA-
    TION. Energy information in
    the federal government, a di-
    rectory of energy sources
    identified by the Interagency
    Task Force on Energy Informa-
    tion.
    This annual compendium is a new title. It is developed from the data base of the Federal Energy Information Locator System. Use of the volume allows one to identify federal agencies collecting specific kinds of energy data and to locate this data. The volume is a directory only, but it is a valuable reference source. In some cases, a depository publication is the source of an agency's information on energy. Recommended for academic and public libraries.

Item 474-A-1
ER1.2: ENERGY RESEARCH AND DEVEL-
    OPMENT ADMINISTRATION. Gen-
    eral publications.
    This is the only ERDA group of publications annotated here because all others appear too technical at this time. Other series will undoubtedly be initiated later, and those should be scrutinized. Career materials, research notes, and general ERDA public education titles compose the series. They are attractively designed, and it appears that four or five are issued annually. Recommended for academic and public libraries.

Item 600-A
I1.89: DEPARTMENT OF THE INTERIOR.
    Bibliographies and lists of
    publications.
    Lists of publications are issued infrequently, sometimes as subject bibliographies, such as A listing of 1974-75 conservation publications ..., no. C76/974-75, or as a list of available department publications. The series is a useful reference item and important to bibliographic control. Recommended for academic and public libraries.

Item 601-A
I1.95: DEPARTMENT OF THE INTERIOR.
    Conservation yearbook. No. 1-
    Recent issues of this are among the most attractive printed materials available from the government; they contain glossy pictures on almost every page. Text accompanies the illustrations and the general theme is the necessity of conserving natural resources and of acting quickly to formulate such national policy. There is emphasis upon recycling, preserving natural beauty, clean energy, international cooperation, and other related goals which have arisen in popular concern in the past decade. The beauty of the publication combined with the urgency of the theme seems yet another attempt to alert citizens to the crisis in our natural resources. The Conservation yearbook corresponds to an annual report, and like the Department of Agriculture Yearbook (A1.10, item 17) generates individual yearbooks:
    Our environment and our natural

resources:  Indivisibly one,
1972

In touch with people, 1973

Our natural resources:  The
choices ahead, 1974.

Recommended for academic and public
libraries.

Item 603

I1.2:  DEPARTMENT OF INTERIOR.
General publications.

Energy, water, trust territories, careers in the department,
environmental statements, ocean resources, and land use planning are
all within the publishing responsibility of this miscellaneous series.
Titles vary in length and in format.
Some are scientific reports, but
most are brief and easily understood.  Three or four titles are
issued a year, and recent ones include:

Marine resources development,
no. M33

Guam, no. G93

Energy perspectives, no. En2/6

Resource and land information
for South Dade County, Flor-
ida, no. D12

Alaskan natural gas transportation systems, no. Aℓ1/15.

Recommended for academic and public
libraries.

Item 619-C

I19.56:  DEPARTMENT OF THE INTERIOR.
River basins of the United
States.

Leaflets about major rivers of
the country are issued in this series.  They appear infrequently but
are useful teaching aids.  Information on any given basin includes
the early exploration, headwaters
and mouth, tributaries, course, and
other basic data as well as pictures
and maps.  Recommended for academic
and public libraries.

Item 619-D

I19.61:  GEOLOGICAL SURVEY.  Journal
of research.  v.1-  1973-
LC 72-60024

Published bimonthly, the Journal contains papers by the survey
staff and persons working elsewhere

in the field on geologic, hydro-
logic, topographic, and other projects.  Papers are scientific and
technical summaries of research.
They are 8 to 10 pages long in Journal issues of over 100 pages.  The
Journal compares favorably with
those of the profession published
commercially.  Each issue is sub-
divided by broad subject categories
and contains a geographic index.
Recommended for academic libraries
serving earth science and geologic
interests.

Item 620

I19.3:  GEOLOGICAL SURVEY.  Bulletin.  No. 1-  1883-  LC GS
14-290

Reports on geological problems
and developments compose this
series.  Issues are individually
titled and appear at a rate of ten
to twenty a year.  They report research and geological administration
both in and out of the survey.  Some
issues are scientific papers, others
are bibliography, reports on methodology, and appraisals of some activity of interest to the nonspecialist.  The following are examples of
reference titles:

Changes in stratigraphic nomenclature by the USGS, 1972,
no. 1394-A

Lexicon of geologic names of
the United States, no. 1350.

Other recent titles include:

A summary of oil and gas production and reserve histories
of the Appalachian basin,
1859-1972, no. 1409

New and refined methods of
trace analysis useful in geo-
chemical exploration, no.
1408

Latin America's petroleum pros-
pects in the energy crisis,
no. 1411.

Length runs from 30 to 100 pages.
Recommended for academic libraries
supporting physical, geological, or
earth science programs.

Item 620-A

I19.4/2:  GEOLOGICAL SURVEY.  Circular.  1-  1933-  LC 33-28329

Titles in this numbered series are issued irregularly but frequently. Fifteen to twenty appear a year, but most issues are between 20 and 100 pages and therefore are not serious space users. The spectrum of activity of the survey is covered by the titles. Minerals, energy, geographic areas, seismology, research models, bibliography, earth history, etc., are topics found among the individual publications. With few exceptions they are scientific reports prepared by the survey or by an agency working closely with the survey. Occasionally, a Circular may be a directory. Recent titles include:

> Worldwide directory of national earth science agencies, no. 716
> Alaskan mineral resource assessment program, no. 718
> National stream quality accounting network, no. 719
> Geological estimates of undiscovered recoverable oil and gas resources in the United States, no. 725.

Recommended for academic libraries supporting physical, geological, or earth science curricula.

Item 621
GEOLOGICAL SURVEY
I19.2: General publications.
I19.42/5: Catalog of information on water data.
  The range of activity of the survey is reflected in its General Publications issued in this category. The formats vary from brochure to technical research reports, but most require only an average understanding of the subject. All aspects of mineral resources and the physical and historical geology of the country are featured here. Career guides, public information materials, and some reference titles are issued in the series. Typical titles include:
> Tree rings: Timekeepers of the past, no. T71
> Active faults of California, no. F27
> Water of the world, no. W29/19

Topographic maps, no. T62.
  Issued for each of twenty-one Water Resources Regions, the Catalog of information on water data is a file of information about water data available in federal agencies. It is not a catalog of actual data. Neither is it essential to libraries, but it is useful as it accompanies the General Publications.
  The item is recommended for academic and public libraries.

Item 622
I19.14/4: GEOLOGICAL SURVEY. New publications of the Geological Survey.
  Issued monthly by the agency, the list provides basic bibliographic information, some annotations, and ordering information. The monthlies are cumulated into an annual compilation, Publications of the Geological Survey, I19.14, item 623. Recommended for academic and public libraries.

Item 623
I19.14: GEOLOGICAL SURVEY. Publications of the Geological Survey. 1893-  LC GS 11-221
  An annual cumulation of New publications of the Geological Survey, I19.14/4, item 622, this list contains a general index and an author index. Major cumulations issued are Publications of the Geological Survey, 1879-1961, and the Supplement, 1962-1970. These are essential to the bibliographic control of the department's publications. Recommended for academic and public libraries.

Item 624
I19.16: GEOLOGICAL SURVEY. Professional paper. 1-  1902-  LC GS 14-289
  Individually titled and numbered reports are issued at a rate of twenty-five a year. Written for the specialist, the papers report investigations of interest to the survey by professional geologists working, for the most part, independently of the survey. Length is usually 20 to 100 pages, although an

occasional large reference volume is issued. Papers include inserted maps and diagrams as necessary. Recent titles include:

> Channel changes of the Gila River in Safford Valley, Arizona, 1846-1970, no. 655-G
>
> Stratigraphy and ammonite fauna of the Graneros shale and Greenhorn limestone near Pueblo, Colorado, no. 645
>
> Mineral resources of Glacier Bay National Monument, Alaska, no. 632.

Recommended for academic libraries supporting earth science or geologic curricula.

Item 625
I19.13:  GEOLOGICAL SURVEY.  Water-supply paper.  1-   1896-
LC GS 14-291

A long-standing series, these papers are technical reports on all aspects of hydrogeology and allied disciplines.  Recent titles include:

> Quality of surface waters of the United States, 1970 (various numbers according to region)
>
> Ground water levels in the United States, 1969-1973, no. 2171.

They are issued irregularly at a rate of ten to twenty a year and are a few hundred pages in length.  Most are prepared in cooperation with other federal or state agencies. Because they are space-consuming, they are recommended only for academic libraries with special interests in water and its accompanying data.

Item 636
I28.3:  BUREAU OF MINES.  Bulletin.
No. 1-   1910-   LC 33-911

Reports of research in and out of the bureau, the information in the Bulletin series is related to minerals, mining, and the technology of the industry.  Three or four individually titled issues appear annually.  They are 20 to 100 pages in length and usually are written for the specialist.  Recent titles include:

> Storage stability of gasoline, no. 660
>
> Coal composition, coal plasticity, and coke strength, no. 661
>
> Microseismic techniques for monitoring the behavior of rock structures, no. 665
>
> Chemical thermodynamic properties of hydrocarbons and related substances, no. 666.

Recommended for academic libraries supporting physical, geological, or earth science programs.

Item 637-A
BUREAU OF MINES
I28.23:  Reports of investigation.
I28.26/6:  Technical progress reports.
I28.27:  Information circulars.

Individually titled Reports of Investigation are issued at a rate of twenty to thirty a year.  The research is administered by the bureau and conducted by its staff. Reports are 20 to 30 pages in length and written for the specialist.  Recent Investigations include:

> Characterization studies of Florida phosphate slimes, no. 8089
>
> Evaluation of refractories for mineral wood furnaces, no. 8090
>
> Selected geologic factors affecting mining of the Pittsburgh coalbed, no. 8093
>
> Tilt precursors in rock before failure, no. 8101.

The major difference between Technical Progress Reports and the other two series under this item is the length.  These are 6- to 8-page reports on some technological advance in one of the bureau's programs.  For example, in the oil shale program:

> Usable gas from oil shale during retorting, no. 85.

In the solid waste program:

> Effect of increasing plastics content on recycling of automobiles, no. 79.

Research carried out at mining research centers around the country,

usually under the administration of
the bureau, is reported in Information Circulars. Papers are usually
technical, 30 to 300 pages in
length, and issued at a rate of ten
to twenty a year. Individually
titled, they cover the range of mining interests. Recent titles include:

Long distance coal transport
   unit trains or slurry pipe-
   lines, no. 8690
The reserve base of U.S. coals
   by sulfur content, no. 8693
Mine power distribution, no.
   8694.

The item is recommended for libraries supporting a program in
physical, geological, or earth
sciences.

Item 637-F
I28.115: BUREAU OF MINES.
   Bureau of Mines research.
   Published annually to summarize
the significant results in mining
research, the publication reveals
the role of the bureau in developing
technology sufficient to increase
recovery of mineral products
necessary to economic growth and development. Projects and studies
summarized here are conducted at research facilities throughout the
country under the administration of
the bureau. The volume is organized
by broad subjects: energy, metal-
lurgy, mining, and mineral supply.
A directory of research installations is included, as is a bibliography of recent publications.
   Recommended for academic libraries supporting physical, geological, or earth science programs, and
for public libraries serving mining
interests.

Item 638
I28.5: BUREAU OF MINES.
   Lists of publications. LC 29-
   26048
   These lists are compiled annually from the monthly New publications, I28.5/2, item 642. The annual includes a subject and author
index. Recommended for academic and
larger public libraries.

Item 639
I28.37: Minerals yearbook. 1932/
   33- LC 33-26551
   This annual report of the
worldwide mineral industry is one of
the longest running document series.
Three volumes make up the current
report which provides statistical
data and textual information on the
year's developments. The volumes
are organized by minerals and by the
geographic unit in which they are
found. One section includes a summary chapter for each mineral commodity important to the national
economy. In the second section,
there is a report by each state in
the United States on the local mineral industry, and a report of the
data available from many foreign
countries. The importance of the
minerals to the economies of these
political units is discussed, statistical summaries abound, and a
discussion of minerals in the world
economy is a concluding point. The
Minerals yearbook is comprehensive
and increasingly important to the
study of natural resources; it is a
valuable reference source. The volumes are large. Recommended for academic and public libraries.

Item 642
I28.5/2: BUREAU OF MINES.
   New publications.
   A monthly leaflet lists new
printed material, including reports
of investigations, information circulars, and technical reports. Bibliographic data, a lengthy annotation, and ordering information are
included. The monthly issues are
compiled annually into the List of
Bureau of Mines publications and articles, I28.5, item 638. Recommended for academic and larger public libraries.

Item 663
I27.5: BUREAU OF RECLAMATION. The
   reclamation era. 1908-
   LC 9-35252
   Published quarterly, issues
deal with water in a broad spectrum.
Articles deal with water as a source
of energy, for municipalities, and

industry, as a recreation source, in flood conditions, and as a part of the ecosystem. The periodical is the official publication of the agency; thus the contents reflect its projects--dams, reservoirs, and canals. Problems and solutions of water conservation and development are the focus. Regular features include a water quiz and notes about publications. The material is non-technical. Recommended for academic and public libraries.

Item 818-A-1
LC33.9: Antarctic bibliography.
     v.1-   1965-   LC 65-61825
     Issued by the Science and Technology Division of the Library of Congress, each annual contains about 2,000 abstracts, arranged by 13 subjects. Indexes are appended for author, subject, geographic, and grantee names. Most materials abstracted are held by the Library of Congress although a few are borrowed from other institutions. The bibliography is essential to the study of cold regions but of limited use otherwise. Recommended for academic libraries.

Item 834-Y
NS1.26: Antarctic journal of the
     United States. v.1-   Jan/Feb.
     1966-   LC 66-9856
     The journal reports United States activities in Antarctic and related programs. Published quarterly, the journal contains about 40 pages per issue. Numerous brief reports containing references and charts are included. Recommended where there is study of or interest in Antarctica.

Item 910-B
SI1.26: SMITHSONIAN INSTITUTION.
     Smithsonian contributions to
     the earth sciences. No. 1-
     1969-   LC 79-5267
     The research for this series is generated at museums or bureaus of the Smithsonian Institution or by individuals working outside the government. Each number is usually a single monograph, but occasionally a group of papers is published under one title. Mineral sciences investigations, 1972-73, no. 14, for example, contains articles covering mineralogy, petrology, lunar studies, meteorites, chemical analyses standards, and polished section techniques. In addition to these subjects, other papers cover regional geology, marine geology, and volcanic ash. Some numbers are individually indexed; all contain bibliography, plates, and illustrations. Three to five titles are issued annually. This series is recommended for libraries with strong earth science needs.

Item 1090
Y3.W29: WATER RESOURCES COUNCIL.
     Reports and publications.
     The council conducts a continuing study of the water supply of the nation and its adequacy in meeting the requirements of the people. The council also administers a program of financial aid to states for developing their land and water resources. Some specific areas of focus have been in flood regulation and flood losses, the use of water in attaining energy self-sufficiency, and observations of sedimentation activities. One recent multivolume publication is notable. A joint effort of the Office of Business Economics, Department of Commerce, and the Economic Research Service, Department of Agriculture, it is titled OBERS projections: Economic activity in the United States, no. 20b2/972/ser.E. Projections are based on the Series E, 1972 census projection of the national population. The report is useful for economic planning of the nation's water and related resources.

     Titles are issued at a rate of two to ten a year. Publications may be lengthy. The work of this council and its publications should be of interest to undergraduate students and to the public. The item is recommended for academic and public libraries.

Item 126
C1.1:  DEPARTMENT OF COMMERCE.  Annual report.  1913-   LC 14-
   30030
   Typically this report includes
a description of the department's
activities during the previous year.
The publication for 1975, issued in
early 1976, is a special Bicentennial edition which summarizes the
history of the department since
1790.  In other years, the report
analyzes the events of the fiscal
year as they affect the administration of the department and programs
of economic development, and describes developments in domestic and
international business, tourism, minority enterprise, science and technology, oceanic and atmospheric activities, and maritime affairs.
This is an attractively designed and
well-written annual report.  Recommended for academic and public libraries.

Item 126-A
   DEPARTMENT OF COMMERCE
C1.54:  Bibliographies and lists of
   publications.
C1.54/2:  Publications: A catalog
   and index.  LC 73-645569
   Subject bibliographies and
lists of publications, sometimes annotated, are issued periodically on
topics relevant to the affairs of
the department.  They include both
commercial and federal publications,
monographs and articles, and, of
course, basic bibliographic data.
One example is Minority business
enterprise--A bibliography, no. M66,

which contains 1400 annotated citations, is organized by format of material, and is indexed.  Bibliographies and publications lists are
irregular and infrequent.
   The basic volume of the Department of Commerce's publications
Catalog lists department publications from 1790 to 1950 and is no
longer in print.  Cumulative supplements are issued annually.  These
catalogs include lists of depository
libraries for federal documents, and
lists of department district offices.  Publications of the year are
arranged by issuing agency.  Papers
and articles from major periodicals
of the department are cited.  A subject index concludes the volume.
This annual publication is a cumulation of the Business service checklist (C1.24, item 127), which is
published every two weeks and lists
publications of the Department of
Commerce.
   Together the two series provide
excellent bibliographic and subject
control for the publications of the
department.  Recommended for academic and public libraries.

Item 126-C
C1.57/4:  Access.  LC 73-644997
   Access is published six times
a year by the Department of Commerce, Office of Minority Business
Enterprise.  Its goal is to serve
minorities, but it also informs
others about the programs and assistance in this area.  Issues are
about 15 pages in length.  Each contains several short articles, some

of which are analyses of minority enterprises, news, and spotlights on particular enterprises. Most communities and colleges have minority populations; these people should have access to this periodical. Recommended for academic and public libraries.

Item 127
C1.24: DEPARTMENT OF COMMERCE. Business service checklist. v.1-  July 5, 1946-
LC 52-35963
The Checklist lists Department of Commerce publications by agency and also serves as an order blank for them. It is a newsletter published every other week. "Key business indicators," is a table of about twelve indicators with dollar units for several time periods. The Checklist includes U.S. population to date, and what it was one year ago. The Checklist is useful in reference rooms with business activity as it is an additional means of maintaining bibliographic control over department publications. Checklists are cumulated into the annual Catalog, C1.54/2, item 126-A. Recommended for academic and public libraries.

Item 127-A
C1.58/2:  Commerce America.  v.1-
Jan. 1976-
Formerly known as Commerce today, this periodical is published every two weeks. It reports on domestic and international commerce both in and out of the Department of Commerce. Articles are usually supported by statistical and tabular material. Issues are about 40 pages in length and contain many brief economic articles, of which some typical subjects are business-consumer trust, international technology transfer, solar heating and cooling units, airport development in Africa, and the Canadian economy. Regular features are news notes, economic highlights, energy management briefs, a calendar of business events, a calendar for world traders, recent publications, and col-

umns on investments abroad. The audience for this magazine is the business community at large, whether student or professional. A few years of back files are desirable. Recommended for academic and public libraries.

Item 128
C1.2:  DEPARTMENT OF COMMERCE.  General publications.
Statistical reports, economic analyses, conference proceedings, and titles which serve to inform the public about the activities and responsibilities of the Department of Commerce compose this series. The work of component agencies is also reflected here, but for more specific publications about these activities, it is advisable to consult the general publications of the particular agency. Six or eight titles in varying formats are issued annually; some are updated periodically. A variety of reading and reference interests are met by these. Typical titles include:
Marketing priorities and energy, no. M34/5
Commerce management has a management internship for you, no. M31/3
National directory of minority manufacturers, no. M66/14
Science and technology fellowship programs, no. Sci2/4.
Recommended for academic and public libraries.

Item 128-A
DEPARTMENT OF COMMERCE
C1.8/3:  Handbooks, manuals, guides.
C1.8/4:  Federal meteorological handbooks.
Some of the titles in the Handbooks series are administrative in their focus, while others have broad application to the general population. They vary in length and format; about one is issued annually. Subject matter varies in accordance with the affairs of the department. Typical titles include:
Energy conservation handbook for light industries and commercial buildings, no. En2

Ocean freight-rate guidelines
   for shippers, no. F88
Federal and state Indian reservations and Indian trust areas, no. In2.
Large libraries will find some of
these titles useful in reference
service. Other publications supplement the general collection. Revisions are occasionally issued.

   The Federal meteorological
handbooks are a multivolume series
which sets forth standardized codes
and practices used in meteorological
observations. The compatible observations are desirable nationally,
among federal and state agencies, as
well as internationally as set forth
in the conventions of the World Meteorological Organization. The volumes are revised periodically and
they are not lengthy. Nevertheless,
they have little pertinence in the
libraries under consideration.

   The item is recommended with
some reservations because of the
usefulness of the first series and
the relative specialization of the
second.

Item 130-C
C46.8: ECONOMIC DEVELOPMENT ADMIN-
   ISTRATION. Handbooks, manuals,
   guides.
   As the agency promotes the revitalization of economically dis-
tressed areas, it publishes various
guides for use by local people. Regardless of the economic state of
one's community, these may be useful
locally. In recent years, they have
appeared infrequently, but one is
worth noting: How to improve your
community by attracting new industry, no. In2/2. Persons who govern
small municipalities are not usually
professional government people; they
may find some of the titles useful.
Recommended for public libraries.

Item 130-D
C46.2: ECONOMIC DEVELOPMENT ADMIN-
   ISTRATION. General publications.
   The economic redevelopment of
communities without enough jobs and
with too little income is a goal of

EDA. These publications reveal the
careful examination of the possibilities for revitalization in various
areas of the country. Recent studies and general releases include:
   An updated evaluation of EDA-
      funded industrial parks, no.
      P23
   EDA--Building communities with
      jobs, no. C73/3
   Zoning for small towns and ru-
      ral counties, no. Z7
   The potential of handicrafts
      as a viable economic force,
      no. H19/2.
Some of this information is not
readily available commercially or
else it is in the form of specialized
analyses. These agency titles are
written in generally popular style
to be used by lay groups in need of
them. Two or three are issued annually. Length and format vary. Recommended for academic and public libraries.

Item 130-F
C46.1: ECONOMIC DEVELOPMENT ADMIN-
   ISTRATION. Annual report.
   1st-   1965/66-   LC 67-60452
   The Economic Development Administration is one of the more people
oriented of those in the Department
of Commerce. The EDA's function is
to aid communities in their planning
and carrying out of projects that
will encourage commercial development by private enterprise. In this
manner jobs are created and unemployment is relieved. These conditions are accomplished by grants and
loans, working capital guarantees,
and technical assistance. The public works program and research activities of the EDA are described in
this report, in both textual material and pictures and in a tabular
form by state and program. Recommended for academic and public libraries.

Item 130-K
C46.18: ECONOMIC DEVELOPMENT ADMIN-
   ISTRATION. Bibliographies and
   lists of publications.
   Publications lists are infre-
quent but useful when available.

The only recent one is Economic research studies of the Economic Development Administration: An annotated bibliography, no. R31. Some subjects included in this bibliography are American Indians, education, tourism, recreation, urban planning, location theory, and income distribution. Recommended for academic and public libraries.

Item 130-L
C46.27: ECONOMIC DEVELOPMENT ADMIN-
ISTRATION. Urban business pro-
files series.

Bearing some resemblance to publications of the Small Business Administration, these 20-page booklets provide business people with some understanding of the opportunities available in small businesses. Each publication focuses on selected urban-oriented businesses such as furniture stores, beauty shops, machine shops, contract dress manufacturing, and convenience stores. Each discusses the guidelines, requirements, and problems of the venture. Guidance on the business' potential as a minority operation is also included here. Other discussions include advice on establishing the market, determining the size of the operation, and securing capital. Revisions will probably be issued as necessary. The series now includes about twelve profiles. Recommended for academic and public libraries.

Item 131-A
C59.9: Business conditions digest.
Jan. 1972- LC 72-621004

Issued monthly by the Bureau of Economic Analysis, this publication compiles approximately six hundred monthly and quarterly statistical time series. Tables and graphs present data on national income and production, cyclical indicators, anticipations of business and intentions of consumers, foreign trade, price movements, analytical measures, international comparison, and details of these features of the economy. Explanation of the method of presentation of the data, how to locate and read the charts, summa-

ries and changes for each issue are included for the user. Business analysts and forecasters use this information in predicting the course of the nation's economy. Much of the data has been published elsewhere by the agency which produced it; however, this is the single monthly summary and comprehensive analysis of the data. Each issue is about 130 pages in length.

Item 134
C3.24: BUREAU OF THE CENSUS.
Census of manufactures. Final
volumes.

The permanent edition of the census of manufactures is three multipart volumes which assemble and reissue earlier paperbound reports. This item is the only product of that census which is included in this guide. (The series which precede it in paperbound form are the Special Report series, no. C3.24/15, item 135; Industry series, no. 3.24/4, item 136; Area series, no. 3.24/3, item 137; Subject series, no. C3.24/2, item 135. They total about 150 reports.) Data collected include information on related industries, manufacturing by state, and details on industries by subject. This publication is one of the more general of the economic census materials, but librarians should note that data are also available for retail trade, wholesale trade, selected service industries, construction industries, mineral industries, and enterprise statistics in various other series issued by the bureau.

These observations are based on the 1972 census of manufactures, which was classified in C56.244. (The 1977 census of manufactures, and future censuses of manufactures, are expected to be classified in C3.) These censuses are conducted in years ending in 2 and 7. Although there is not a considerable amount of change in the publishing pattern from one census to the next, librarians must be attentive to the variations in series, formats, and classifications as announcements are

made.  It was announced in early
1976 that the Final volumes for the
1972 manufactures census would be
issued and sold by a commercial publisher.  This plan was changed after
protest from various groups, particularly librarians, and the volumes
were distributed by GPO as has previously been the case.

The item is recommended for academic and public libraries.

Item 142-E
C59.10:  Defense indicators.  Jan.
1972-    LC 72-621003

The principal time series of
defense activities are published by
the Economic Analysis Bureau in this
monthly analysis.  The prospective
impact of the defense order-
production-delivery process on the
economy may be assessed by charts
and tables which present obliga-
tions, contracts, orders, shipments,
inventories, expenditures, employment, and earnings.  The focus is
clearly on short-term changes in the
economy as influenced by defense activity.  The subject does not have
broad appeal, but citizens should be
aware of the availability of the
data.  Issues are about 30 pages in
length, and they provide an explanation for use of the charts and
tables.  Recommended for libraries
serving business people and students.

Item 160-D
    BUREAU OF THE CENSUS.  Census
    of transportation.
C3.233:  General publications.
C3.233/2:  Final reports.
C3.233/3:  Final reports, permanent
    edition.

General Publications are issued
infrequently and usually serve to
amplify the transportation census.
Fact sheets describing the publication program and the computer summary tape program have been issued
recently.

Final Reports include individual reports in these series:  National travel survey, Truck inventory and use survey, and Commodity
transportation survey.  Approxi-

mately one hundred reports present
data characterizing the nation's
private and commercial transportation activities.  Travel trips by
state of origin, type of trip, season, group size, etc; truck inventory by model, registered weight,
state of registration, area of operation, etc.; and commodity trans-
ported by length of haul, weight of
shipment, destination, etc., are
some of the statistics available in
these reports.  These three surveys
are independent of each other and
their reports are distinctive series.

The Final Reports are issued in
paperbound form as they are completed.  They are cumulated into the
permanent volumes, C3.233/3, when
all reports have been completed.
Additional explanatory material and
graphics may be included in the volumes which make up the bound, permanent edition.  For the 1972 census
of transportation, there are three
volumes in this edition.

A transportation census is conducted in years ending in 2 and 7,
and it is part of what is generally
known as the economic censuses.
These observations are based on the
1972 census, but the publishing organization does not vary greatly
from one census to the next.  Series
may be added or discontinued and
some classification numbers change.
(The series in this item were classified C56.246, C56.246/2, and
C56.246/3, respectively, in the 1972
census of transportation.  The 1977
census is expected to be classified
in C3.)  Librarians should watch for
advance information about the publications generated by each census.
These series are recommended for academic and public libraries.

Item 212-A-1
C57.402:  BUREAU OF EAST-WEST TRADE.
    General publications.

Nonstrategic trade between the
United States and the Soviet Union,
Eastern Europe, and the People's Republic of China is assisted by this
agency.  Products and technologies
with implications for national secu-

rity, short supply, or foreign policy are also controlled by it. Two or three titles a year report economic data from socialist countries, describe the agency's work, and suggest procedures for those commercial institutions wishing to consider East-West trade. Recommended for academic and public libraries.

Item 215-L
C57.18:  DOMESTIC AND INTERNATIONAL BUSINESS ADMINISTRATION. U.S. industrial outlook. 1960-

The developments in more than two hundred industries during the current year are discussed in this volume. Recent trends of the years immediately preceding are also reviewed because of the essential role they play in projections for the future, which are also included in the volume. Organized by type of economic activity, the publication discusses the following categories of industry: building and forest products, materials, transportation, distribution and marketing, consumer goods, communications, machinery, instrumentation, power and electrical equipment, and business and consumer services. The range of individual enterprises is from mobile homes to funeral parlors to shoe repair shops. Although the volume is a useful reference source, it is written without technical data. Issued annually, it contains projections for eight to ten years hence. Two or three previous editions may prove useful for reference and comparison. Recommended for academic and public libraries.

Item 228
BUREAU OF ECONOMIC ANALYSIS
C59.11:  Survey of current business. v.1-  Aug. 1, 1921-
C59.11/3:  Business statistics; biennial supplement. 1951-
C59.11/4:  Special supplements. LC 21-26819

The primary publication in this item is the monthly Survey of current business. It is about 50 pages in length and carries a summary article on the business situation. It includes a section of current business statistics which update the biennial statistical supplement, Business statistics, and two or three articles on the nation's business trends. Statistics and tabular material are dominant throughout each issue, but adequate explanation and text accompany them. A certain comprehension of econometrics is essential for use of this periodical; it is written for the student and professional business person.

Special Supplements to the Survey are issued infrequently on subjects of special interest. United States direct investment abroad and Interindustry transactions are subject surveys produced in this series in the past.

Business statistics is a biennial volume which serves as a basic reference volume for historical data. These data are updated by the statistics section in the monthly issues of the Survey of current business. Statistical tables are organized by subject, and sources of the data are credited. Explanatory notes constitute over one third of the volume. The volume is indexed. Most libraries under consideration will not need a large back file. Librarians should note the "Reference to earlier data" in each volume. At present, annual data from 1929-38 is in the 1959 edition, from 1939-46 in the 1969 edition, and from 1947 to date in the current edition. For use of monthly data, most previous editions may be necessary, but historical data by years is available with only a few volumes.

The item is recommended for academic and public libraries making use of business and economic references.

Item 229
C59.11/2:  BUREAU OF ECONOMIC ANALYSIS. Survey of current business. Weekly supplements. March 14, 1927-  LC 21-26819

Headed Weekly business statistics, this 4-page leaflet provides

charts and tables which update selected data that are published in
the monthly Survey of current business, C59.11, item 228. Recommended
for libraries subscribing to the
monthly.

Item 231-A
C57.102: INTERNATIONAL COMMERCE
    BUREAU. General publications.
    Reports on the participation of
the United States in international
expositions, basic facts about ex-
porting U.S. products, markets
abroad for consumer goods, and the
Commerce Department's assistance to
exporters are typical subjects of
the bureau's publications. Its
function is to encourage and promote
the exportation of consumer goods by
conducting trade center expositions,
trade missions, world trader data
reports, mailing lists, business
counseling, and specific promotional
events. Four or five titles a year
describe the services and provide
data on the markets. Length and
format vary. Recommended for academic and public libraries serving
students and business professionals.

Item 231-E
C57.108: INTERNATIONAL COMMERCE
    BUREAU. Handbooks, manuals,
    rules.
    Guides to exporting, such as
Trade missions: A handbook for
trade mission members, no. T67, and
A guide to financing exports, no.
Ex7, may be more specific than the
general needs of the business community. However, students of marketing and international economics
find these of interest. The Export-
Import Bank, Overseas Private Investment Corporation, and the balance of payments are of interest to
exporters and to academics as well.
Business collections in public libraries should also include some of
these. Recommended for academic and
public libraries.

Item 231-I
C57.111: Foreign economic trends and
    their implications for the
    United States. 1969-
    LC 73-643039

A textual and statistical summary of key economic indicators in
countries throughout the world, this
publication is prepared by the embassy staff in the country under
consideration. A revision is issued
annually for each country. The issues are 10 to 12 pages in length
and focus on current economic situations and trends in regard to pros-
pects for United States investments
and sales in the particular country.
Some political data are inevitable.
The publication is aimed at the
business community but is interesting reading for a wide audience. It
is published by the International
Commerce Bureau. Recommended for
academic and public libraries.

Item 283
CC1.1: FEDERAL COMMUNICATIONS COM-
    MISSION. Annual report. 1936-
    LC 35-26977
    In addition to including the
information required by law, the report contains a comprehensive summary of activities falling under the
commission's concern: the regulation of broadcast services, cable
television, common carrier services,
safety and special radio services,
emergency communication, and frequency use. Statistics are appended
and include some historical series.
The publication is well designed
and is relatively interesting reading. There is a detailed table of
contents but no index. Of all FCC
publications, this annual has greatest potential for general use by library clientele. Recommended for
academic and public libraries.

Item 290
CS1.1: CIVIL SERVICE COMMISSION.
    Annual report. 1st-    1883/
    84-    LC 4-18119
    The general population has some
concern for the Civil Service Commission if for no other reason than
that most citizen contacts with the
federal government are through its
employees. One of the obvious ways
to learn more about the system and
its practices is through its annual
report. It includes a summary of
the year's activities, information

about new policies, the work force, and data on federal civilian employment by state, salary, agency, and other categories. Recommended for academic and public libraries.

Item 290-C
CS1.66:  Civil service journal.
    v.1-  LC 64-55636
    The quarterly is of course of major interest to persons employed by the federal system. The management of the federal civilian work force is of interest to persons working in the private sector as well. The concerns of both employees and management are similar, as evidenced by articles about equal employment opportunity, the status of women, incentive awards, job recruitment, labor relations, and adult education. Regular features include columns about recent court decisions, legislation, benefits, and other notes of special interest to all employees. Articles are brief; each issue is about 35 pages long. Long back files are not necessary. Recommended for academic and public libraries.

Item 290-E
CS1.61:  CIVIL SERVICE COMMISSION. Bibliographies and lists of publications.
    Only a few titles have been issued in this series, but one title is updated occasionally and is a useful reference. Guide to federal career literature, no. C18, lists and describes hundreds of recruiting brochures published by the government. Entries, organized by agency, give title, date of publication, number of pages, college majors applicable, geographic location of positions, summary of contents, and where to obtain copies. Much of the material cited in the discussion of the General Publications series in this book will be indexed in the Guide to federal career literature. Recommended for academic and public libraries.

Item 291-C
CS1.76:  EEO spotlight.  1968-

    Issued by the Civil Service Commission, this bimonthly is not of major significance, but it provides information about equal employment opportunities. The newsletter contains notes of training programs for women and minorities such as the Upward Mobility program now in operation. Tributes to minority groups, such as "Spanish heritage days," and honors to federally employed women are described. An additional use the Spotlight may have is as an example to private enterprise of the kinds of steps being taken in the federal sector to comply with the Equal Employment Opportunity Act of 1972 and Executive Order 11478 of August 1969. Long back files are not necessary. Recommended for libraries serving urban readers or people with access to federal employment.

Item 292
    CIVIL SERVICE COMMISSION.  Examination announcements:
CS1.26:  Nationwide.
CS1.26/3:  General amendments.
CS1.26/4:  Local areas.
    Printed material issued here includes job announcements as well as examination announcements. Receipt of these titles ensures one of a wealth of data on federal employment. Many titles include location of positions to be filled, descriptions of the work, requirements and qualifications, and details for making application. Most grades of Civil Service jobs are covered by some publication; guides to summer employment are issued seasonally. Separate titles usually cover a particular skill or profession. For example:
    Careers in therapy, no. CS1.26/
        4:WA-8-03
    Professional positions in Indian education, no. CS1.26/4:
        DM2-02
    Summer jobs, CS1.26:(year)
    Journeyman trades and crafts,
        no. CS1.26/4:CH-3-02.
Most are revised periodically. Because the series issues titles often, usually in pamphlet form, it is

important to keep the file current. Older and out-of-date publications should be discarded. This is an essential tool for career and placement collections. Recommended for academic and public libraries.

Item 295
CS1.2:  CIVIL SERVICE COMMISSION.
General publications.
Information for employees of the Civil Service (and therefore of less general interest) is issued here. In addition, however, one finds a range of titles and references useful to libraries. The publications accumulate at a rate of six to eight a year and are nontechnical. They do not conform to a particular format. Subjects such as benefits, workshops, career planning, the handicapped, and development are typical. Examples:

Scientists and engineers in the federal personnel system, no. Sci2
An 8½-year record:  Mentally retarded workers in the federal service, no. M52/2
Managing employee development, no. M31/13
Information to consider in choosing a health plan, no. H34/22
Q and A about temporary intergovernment assignments, no. In8/7.

Some subseries emerge:
State salary survey, no. Sa3/4, revised annually
Directory of state merit systems, no. M54/2, revised periodically.
Recommended for academic and public libraries.

Item 299
CS1.48:  CIVIL SERVICE COMMISSION.
Pamphlets.
The commission is responsible for the recruitment, examination, and management of employees in the federal civil service at grades GS-1 through GS-15. It provides leadership for equal employment opportunity and in placement of mentally and physically handicapped people. In support of these activities, the commission publishes a variety of titles in this series which is of general interest to citizens. Examples include:

Working for the U.S.A., no. 4/19
The federal government as an employer of the unskilled and undereducated, no. BRE-40.

Several annuals fall into the series:

Pay structure of the federal civil service, no. SM33
Employee training in the federal civil service, no. T-7
Federal civilian employment, women, no. SM62.

Recommended as a component of career collections in academic and public libraries.

Item 300-A-1
CS1.61/3:  CIVIL SERVICE COMMISSION.
Personnel bibliography series.
This numbered bibliography series is prepared by the Civil Service Commission's library, and reports items received in the library. Topics are management- and personnel-related:

Employee benefits and services, no. 47
Labor management relations in the public service, no. 44
Improving employee performance, no. 45.

These topics are divided into subjects. Entries contain basic bibliographic information and are annotated. Journals, federal publications, and commercial publications are all included. Accumulation is not rapid. Recommended for academic libraries serving business and management programs and for public libraries supporting a similar professional clientele.

Item 430-J-1
FCA1.1:  FARM CREDIT ADMINISTRATION.
Annual report. 1934-   LC 34-26507
Agriculture has attained greater prominence in recent years as farmers and ranchers have been

pressed harder in the production of food and fiber. This fact combined with the increasing costs of land and the inherent threat to the family farm lend attention to the mission of the agency. The providing of adequate and dependable credit to persons involved with the agriculture industry and the supervision of such activity are the main goals of the agency. The report summarizes the annual activity of the several components of the agency. At least half of the 100-page publication is financial data. A large back file is not necessary. Recommended for academic and public libraries in areas where agriculture is practiced or taught.

Item 433
FM1.1:  FEDERAL MEDIATION AND CON-
        CILIATION SERVICE. Annual re-
        port. 1st-    1947/48-
        LC 49-45739
    Useful as a chronicle of collective bargaining, the report is written in good style and is less than 100 pages in length. Brief summaries of strikes in the private sector mediated by the FMCS are given as are illustrative cases of public employee bargaining. The agency also serves to promote smoother daily relations between management and labor and thereby reduce work stoppages. These activities are chronicled by the report, and the features detailing them make it an important document in labor history, of interest to both public and academic library patrons.

Item 434
FM1.2:  FEDERAL MEDIATION AND CON-
        CILIATION SERVICE. General
        publications.
    Titles here do not have broad appeal, but they are of concern to patrons interested in collective bargaining activity. Seldom is more than one issued a year. Some pamphlets provide career information. Typical titles include:
        Federal Mediation and Concilia-
            tion Service:  Taking on
            tomorrow's problems today,

no. 94
Employment opportunities:  Fed-
    eral mediator positions, no.
    Em7
Securing labor-management peace
    through mediation, no. L11/5.
Recommended for public libraries.

Item 437-A-1 to A-50
FP1.18:  FEDERAL POWER COMMISSION.
         National electric rate book.
         LC 40-26159
    One of the functions of the FPC is exhibited in this publication of electric rates for each state. These pamphlets may be purchased for individual states or subscribed to individually by depository libraries. They contain rate schedules for electric service in communities of 2,500 or more people for residential, commercial, and industrial electric services. Revisions are made about every two years, but one previous issue might be retained for comparison. Similar data in greater detail are found in the Rates series, FP1.10, item 438-A, Typical electric bills. A public library should probably obtain the issue for the state in which it is located, and, in the case of larger libraries, perhaps for states of the region as well. It is unlikely that the collection of rate books for all states will be needed by most libraries.

Item 438-A
FP1.10:  FEDERAL POWER COMMISSION.
         Rates.
    Annual surveys, Typical electric bills, published by the FPC are useful to consumers who need comparative information. Comprehensive coverage of the cost to consumers for representative amounts of electricity used per month for home, business, and industry in all areas of the country is provided. No attempt is made to analyze the reasons for variations of rates--such as the proximity of fuel sources or customer population. The data are provided in tables, charts, and maps. An additional annual, All electric homes in the United States, gives

data for this category in cities of 50,000 or more. The series is of interest to the consumer and should be kept for a few years for comparisons. The publications may be useful in conjunction with the National electric rate book, FP1.18, item 437-A-1 to 437-A-50. Recommended for public libraries.

Item 442
FR1.2: BOARD OF GOVERNORS OF THE FEDERAL RESERVE SYSTEM. General publications.

This is the most interesting of the Federal Reserve items available to depository libraries. It contains nontechnical titles of broad interest on credit, banking, and money. Examples:

Federal Reserve System, purposes and functions, no. F31/2
Lending functions of the Federal Reserve banks: A history, no. L54
Monetary policy and United States economy, no. M74
Trust assets of insured commercial banks, no. T77.

Only three or four titles a year are issued. Length and format vary. The item will support economics and business curricula in academic libraries and the business community of public libraries.

Item 526
NCU1.2: NATIONAL CREDIT UNION ADMINISTRATION. General publications.

The business of regulating federally chartered credit unions, chartering new ones, supervising those in operation, and insuring member accounts is the responsibility of this independent agency. A few of these publications are administrative, but most are related to the public's association with credit unions. Career materials, explanations of the system, and information on starting credit unions are all regularly issued titles. Typical examples:

Federal credit unions, no. F31
National Credit Union Adminis-

tration, no. R24
Development of federal credit unions, no. F31/2
Federal credit union bylaws, no. B99.

Publications are revised periodically. Titles are brief pamphlets or booklets and accumulate at a rate of five to eight a year. Recommended for academic and public libraries.

Item 527-B
NCU1.10: NATIONAL CREDIT UNION ADMINISTRATION. Research report. No. 1-  LC 73-644757

Published periodically for the interests of credit union officials, the reports are also of interest to persons in banking careers or courses. Their purpose is to provide information of use in formulating policy and is not to promote NCUA policies. Recent titles include:

Credit unions and the money crunch, no. 7
Credit union liquidity and share insurance: A new dimension, no. 8
Changes in federal credit union common bond policy: A policy analysis, 1965-74, no. 9.

Reports are brief and issued three or four times a year. Charts and tables illustrate the text. The publications may not have broad appeal, but they are of interest to patrons using business and investment collections.

Item 545
GA1.2: GENERAL ACCOUNTING OFFICE. General publications.

Of all the publication series of the GAO, this one is of greatest interest to general readers. It is probably not essential to any library, but if one is attempting to maintain a collection representative of the government activity, a GAO series is desirable. Some interesting titles occur:

United States General Accounting Office needs graduates in statistics, finance, mathematics ..., no. St2

Can federal productivity be
measured? no. P94/3
Federal-State election law surveys, numerous numbers.
Four or five publications are issued
a year. Other titles are copies of
news releases, explanations of the
functions of GAO, guides to auditing
and accounting. Recommended for
consideration by some libraries.

Item 596
FHL1.2:  FEDERAL HOME LOAN BANK
BOARD. General publications.
These titles do not have broad
appeal but they are written in a
popular style. They will be of interest to patrons of business and
banking concerns. About one a year
is issued. Typical titles are
FSLIC=Safety, no. F31/4
The Federal Home Loan what?,
no. F31/3
Step up to a Federal Home Loan
Bank Board career, no. C18
List of member institutions:
Federal Savings and Loan Association Insurance Corporation, no. F31.
The career literature is useful for
vocational collections. Recommended
for public libraries.

Item 597-A
FHL1.27:  FEDERAL HOME LOAN BANK
BOARD. Journal. v.1-   June
1968-
Published monthly for banking
interests, the periodical carries an
interesting variety of articles
about the economy and ultimately has
broad public appeal. A recent issue
included articles on economic recovery, home buyers' difficulties, and
a quarterly review. Statistical series and features of rules, regulations, and opinions appear regularly. Mortgages, money, and banking are dealt with here with the
thoroughness desired by academics,
yet in a nontechnical style appreciated by the public. Recommended for
academic and public libraries.

Item 611-D
C55.322:  NATIONAL MARINE FISHERIES
SERVICE. Fishery facts.

Written by scientists and other
employees of the NMFS, these 20- to
50-page booklets document research
in the fishing industry. They are
suggested materials for public libraries which serve sport fishers
and commercial fishers. Three or
four are issued annually on such
subjects as smoking and preserving
salmon, Pacific herring, inshore
lobster fishing, and constructing
marine artificial reefs.

Item 674-A
IC1.31:  INTERSTATE COMMERCE COMMIS-
SION. Public advisories.
Because these leaflets contain
information useful to shippers and
receivers of small quantities of
merchandise located in small or iso-
lated communities, they have special
importance for patrons of smaller
libraries. Other areas of public
interest should be dealt with eventually, but arranging transportation
for small shipments, shippers'
rights, and alternatives are subjects of the most recent publications to be issued. Publications
appear infrequently and may be revised. Recommended for public libraries.

Item 744
L1.1:  DEPARTMENT OF LABOR. Annual
report of the Secretary of Labor. 1914-   LC 14-30221
The work of the Labor Department commands a great deal of attention at the present time because of
concern about unemployment and
equal opportunity for workers.
Therefore, activities of the U.S.
Employment Service, the Equal Opportunity Employment Commission, and
many other divisions are of note as
they seek to solve problems in both
areas. New legislation and national
developments affecting workers constantly interact in ways to cause
changes in the department. The 75-
to 100-page report is a succinct,
though thoughtful, account of the
many divisions of labor's activities. It is a good record of the
year and inevitably documents numerous cultural and societal conditions

within the jurisdiction of this department. Tables of statistics are appended. Recommended for academic and public libraries.

Item 744-A
L1.34: DEPARTMENT OF LABOR. Bibliographies and lists of publications.

A more active series in publications-listing than that of several government organizations, this one has a few distinct sub-series:

Publications of the U.S. Department of Labor, subject listing, January 1969 to June 1974 (and succeeding cumulations), no. P96/969-74
Index to publications of the Manpower Administration, January 1969 through June 1973 (and succeeding cumulations), no. M31/4/969-73
New publications, a quarterly listing.

In addition, an occasional subject bibliography is published. Recommended for academic and public libraries.

Item 745
DEPARTMENT OF LABOR
L1.2: General publications.
L1.39/8: Seminars on manpower policy and programs.

The scope of the General Publications series is as broad as that of the activities of the department. Subjects include the area of careers in the department and careers in general, collective bargaining, department programs, work-related problems, benefits, etc. Some are special studies, reports of the Secretary of Labor, symposia, and public information activities. Typical titles include:

Often-asked questions about the Employee Retirement Income Security Act of 1974, no. Em7/11
Directory of Job Corps centers, no. J57/12
The Job Bank: Using a computer to bring people and jobs together, no. J57/14

Collective bargaining in public employment and the merit system, no. C68/4
Apprentice training, no. Ap6
Immigration from Latin America, no. R11
What about a career in labor law?, no. C18/4.

Four to six titles a year are issued. Recommended for academic and public libraries.

In recent years, no titles have been issued in the Seminars on Manpower Policy and Programs series.

Item 745-A
L1.7/2: DEPARTMENT OF LABOR. Handbooks, manuals, guides.

Many of these publications serve as guides to programs of the Labor Department and are, to some extent, in-house guides. Nevertheless, they serve as a means of informing the public about programs and their regulations. The usefulness of the series is best revealed by some titles:

Summer youth employment: A reference, no. Y8
How to train workers on the job, no. W89
Merchandising your job talents, no. S57/3
Relating general educational development to career planning, no. C18
Complaint filing guide, no. C73
CETA coordination with WIN, no. C73/3.

Four or five titles are issued a year, and they are revised as necessary. Materials should be discarded as revised or as deemed obsolete. Recommended for academic and public libraries.

Item 746-C
L1.42/2: PRESIDENT. Employment and training report of the president, and a report on the labor requirements, resources, utilization, and training, by the U.S. Department of Labor. 1963-   LC L63-45

This annual report analyzes broad areas of labor concern. From it one can assess the impact of current economic developments on the level of employment. The Comprehensive Employment and Training Act of 1973, the Emergency Unemployment Compensation Act of 1974, and the Emergency Jobs and Unemployment Assistance Act of 1974 are examples of legislation which have generated substantial activity in the department, not the least of which is felt in the employment requirements, resources, utilization, and training of the nation. The 1975 report focuses on these developments. Unemployment, wages, women, minorities, implementation of legislation, and program response to employment needs are current concerns and subjects of discussion. The Department of Health, Education, and Welfare cooperates to provide for this report details which fall under the authority of that department. Tables and statistics are present throughout as well as appended to the report. This feature may result in the discontinuation of Statistics on manpower: Supplement to the manpower report of the president, L1.42/2-2, also contained in item 746-C, which has not been issued since the 1969 edition. An index to the report was published for the years 1963-72 and issued in this series. The report is recommended for academic and public libraries.

Item 746-C-1
L36.2: DEPARTMENT OF LABOR. EMPLOYMENT STANDARDS ADMINISTRATION. General publications.
Titles in this miscellaneous series are similar to some found in the Bulletin series, L2.3, item 768. Pamphlets and book-length statistical studies make up the item. The following are examples of recent publications, of which there are four to eight a year:
Black lung medical benefits, no. B56
Questions and answers on the OFCC testing and selection order, no. Of2
Private household workers, no. H81
Wages and hours of work of non-

supervisory employees, no. N73/3.
Some have reference value. Recommended for academic and public libraries.

Item 746-H
L37.14: EMPLOYMENT AND TRAINING ADMINISTRATION. Research and development monographs.
Reports of research carried out under contract from or funds provided by the Employment and Training Administration research grants, this numbered series covers topics related to all aspects of work. Dual careers, minorities, retirement, automation, welfare, youth, and the disabled are likely subjects of one or another monographs. Reports vary in length from 25 pages to a few volumes and may include some bibliography, methodology, and statistical data. Three or four a year are issued. Recent titles have included:
Youth and the meaning of work, no. 32
Jobs for veterans with disabilities, no. 41
Negro employment in the South, no. 23
Abstracts of seven doctoral dissertations completed under Manpower Administration grants, no. 34.
Several years of back files are desirable and useful because the reports represent trends in labor history. Recommended for academic and public libraries.

Item 746-M
L1.56: EMPLOYMENT AND TRAINING ADMINISTRATION. MDTA research and development findings.
The reports are similar in nature to, though more comprehensive than, the Research and Development Monographs, L37.14, item 746-H. Both report research projects which have been carried out under the authority of the Manpower Development and Training Act of 1962. This series issues titles which may serve as manuals for a particular labor problem or situation. Analyses are

presented and specific behavioral
objectives are provided, as well as
case studies and examples.  Recent
titles, which appear at a rate of
one a year, are
> Handbook for upgrading low-
> skilled workers, no. 13
> Methods of assessing the dis-
> advantaged in manpower pro-
> grams, no. 14
> Productive employment of the
> disadvantaged: Guidelines
> for action, no. 15.
Recommended for academic and public
libraries.

Item 746-N
L37.10: Worklife. v.1-  1976-
    Worklife was until recently en-
titled Manpower.  The change follows
the name change of the Manpower Administration to Employment and
Training Administration and the resulting removal of a sex reference
in the title.  Worklife contains
about six articles per 30-page issue
on the relationship between economic
developments and the labor force.
Programs supported by ETA are featured, as are the groups of people
affected.  Because laws such as the
Comprehensive Employment and Training Act (CETA) have played a significant role in job availability, articles frequently focus on this and
other legislative developments.  The
monthly journal is attractively designed and provides good reading.
Recommended as a popular Labor Department item for academic and public libraries.

Item 748
L37.102: BUREAU OF APPRENTICESHIP
    AND TRAINING.  General publica-
    tions.
    It sometimes seems that the in-
formation for the key to career
planning lies in the wealth of federal document material on the subject.  Accordingly, this item includes guidance for various training
programs.  For the most part, publications, three or four a year, conform to "National standards
for ...," as evidenced by these examples:

> National apprenticeship and
> training standards for the
> Graphic Arts International
> Union, G75
> National standards of appren-
> ticeship for the lathing in-
> dustry, no. L34
> National apprenticeship and
> training standards for paint-
> ing and decorating and dry-
> wall finishing, no. P16.
The various appropriate labor union
groups have consulted in the preparation of these publications.  Recommended for public libraries.

Item 752-C
L37.13: EMPLOYMENT AND TRAINING AD-
    MINISTRATION.  Area trends in
    employment and unemployment.
    Sept. 1957-  LC L65-306
    This tends to be a monthly pub-
lication.  The official list of areas of high unemployment is provided
by this bulletin.  The "Highlights"
of each issue includes the labor areas of the country added to or
dropped from the list of areas of
substantial unemployment, with a
brief explanation as to the industry
concerned.  Additional explanation
describes legislation which assists
these areas; other compilations of
tabular data related to the subject
are included.  Three or four years
of back files are adequate.  Recommended for academic and public libraries.

Item 766
PrEx1.10/3: Performance, the story
    of the handicapped.  v.1-
    July 1950-  LC 59-30059
    The brief, monthly magazine
published by the President's Committee on Employment of the Handicapped, reports progress in employment opportunities for the handicapped.  It contains several short
articles about the activities and
problems of the handicapped.  The
handicapped themselves are interested in this magazine, and its
presence in libraries attracts the
attention of prospective employers
and others in positions to allevi-
ate some of the difficulties faced

by the handicapped.  Two or three years of back files are adequate. Recommended for public libraries.

Item 768
L2.3:  BUREAU OF LABOR STATISTICS.
Bulletin.  No. 1-  Nov. 1895-
LC 15-23307
This series treats a broad scope of labor statistics and includes a few subseries.

Area wage survey is a publication of annual wages for all standard metropolitan statistical areas in the U.S. and for some other individual areas.  Information may be used for wage and salary information, for collective bargaining, and for determining plant locations. Two summary bulletins are issued at the end of each year.

Handbook of labor statistics is an annual volume of all major statistics produced by the bureau.  The 1975 volume is the last which will contain a complete series of historical data.  It should be retained as a reference volume.  Beginning with 1976, the volume will include data for 1967 to the present.

Occupational outlook handbook is a biennial reference tool providing employment information for all levels and areas of jobs.  Each position is described by nature of the work, places of employment, training required, earnings, and outlook. Addresses of professional organizations and unions are usually included as sources of additional information.  It is supplemented by Occupational outlook quarterly, L2.70/4, item 770-A.

Analysis of work stoppages is an annual detailed statistical presentation.

Directory of national unions and employee associations is a continuation of the Directory of national and international labor unions in the United States.  The new Directory is issued irregularly.

National survey of professional, technical, and clerical pay is an annual, detailed survey of the occupations indicated in private industry.

Wage calendar is an annual summary identifying companies and unions whose contracts will change for some reason in the given year.

Wage chronology highlights individual employers, or employers and unions, and traces changes in wage scale and benefits over several decades.  Separate Bulletins are issued for each employer or group.

Industry wage survey selects a category of employers (hotels, auto repair shops, department stores) and surveys wages and benefits.  Separate Bulletins for each category are issued.

Union wages and hours selects specific crafts and jobs in a variety of industries for its survey. Separate Bulletins are issued for each industry.

In addition, numerous individual statistical publications on a variety of labor issues are issued:
> Directory of data sources on racial and ethnic minorities, no. 1879
> Library manpower:  A study of of supply and demand, no. 1852

U.S. working women, no. 1880.
Annotated bibliographies are occasionally published.  Many items are updated.  Librarians should determine a reasonable period of time for holding annuals and have a systematic withdrawing policy if space demands.  The entire Bulletin series is prodigious, accumulating at a rate of over two linear feet a year. Yet it is an essential item for all libraries.

Item 768-B
L2.41/2:  BUREAU OF LABOR STATISTICS.  Employment and earnings.
v.1-  July 1954-  LC 56-102
Data for this monthly are collected by the Bureau of the Census, the Employment and Training Administration, state employment security agencies, and state departments of labor, all in cooperation with the Bureau of Labor Statistics.  Each issue includes regular features, tables of incomes, and other characteristics of the employed and unem-

ployed.  Librarians should note that
this information is summarized in
the annual Handbook of labor statistics, L2.3, item 768.  A brief written account of current developments
is also included.  Special statistical features occur in most issues,
such as household and establishment
data used for bench marks.  As is
characteristic of BLS publications,
there are several pages of explanatory notes appended to each issue.
Each issue is about 150 pages long.
Recommended for academic and public
libraries.

Item 768-D
L2.44:  Current wage developments.
       No. 1-  Jan. 1948-   LC L48-43
    This monthly publication of the
Bureau of Labor Statistics reports
on employee compensation.  It notes
selected wage and benefit changes
resulting from collective bargaining agreements and management decisions.  Also included is a statistical summary and extensive tabular
data.  Issues are about 50 pages
long.  Retention of the publication
for three to five years may be desirable; the information eventually
appears in summary form in some
other BLS publication.  Recommended
for academic and public libraries.

Item 768-E
    BUREAU OF LABOR STATISTICS
L2.34:  Catalog of publications.
L2.34/2:  Bibliographies and lists
       of publications.
    Issued semiannually and some-
times annually, the Catalog features
annotations for bulletins, reports,
press releases, reprints, and periodicals issued by the bureau during
the given period.  It is organized
by subject; bibliographic data and
ordering information are available
for each entry.  Material emanating
from the BLS is of some concern to
libraries and should be followed.
This title is a source of bibliographic control.
    The Bibliographies and Lists of
Publications are directories issued
periodically for the purpose of
listing groups of studies or surveys

conducted under a common program.
Bibliographic data and ordering information accompany listings.  Recent titles include:
       Directory of industry wage sur-
       veys and union wages and
       hours studies, 1960-73, no.
       W12/960-73
       Directory of area wage surveys,
       January 1973-December 1974,
       no. W12/4/973-74.
    The item is recommended for ac-
ademic and public libraries.

Item 768-F
L2.38/3:  BUREAU OF LABOR STATIS-
       TICS.  CPI detailed report.
       LC 75-641423
    This monthly statistical publi-
cation keeps people informed of
price movements.  One can readily
locate the percentage rise (or fall)
in the consumer price index each
month.  The change is analyzed, and
selective components are discussed.
Appropriate tables and statistics
are included.  Librarians should
note that this information is summarized in the annual Handbook of labor statistics, L2.3, item 768.  Of
particular use are three or four
pages at the end which explain what
the consumer price index is, how
changes are calculated, and the role
of seasonally adjusted data.  These
topics, along with a system for determining the reliability of the index, are ideal sources of explanations for patrons.  Each issue is
about 30 pages long.  Recommended
for academic and public libraries.

Item 768-I
L2.37:  BUREAU OF LABOR STATISTICS.
       Estimates retail food prices
       by city.
    This publication carries data
which the Bureau of Labor Statistics
has assembled for computing the consumer price index.  Included is a
note that the primary use of the
data should be in making comparison
from time-to-time rather than from
place-to-place because prices are
estimated from certain bench mark
averages, and differences in prices
between areas may not represent true

differentials. The series is probably more interesting to students of
economics than to the general patron. However, to the extent that
one is interested in consumer affairs and the rate of inflation, it
may be desirable for public library
clientele. Librarians should note
that this information is summarized
in the annual Handbook of labor statistics, L2.3, item 768.

Item 768-0
L2.102/2: BUREAU OF LABOR STATIS-
     TICS. Chartbook on prices,
     wages, and productivity. v.1-
     June 1974-   LC 74-648393
     Charts and tables are used to
present current changes in prices,
wages, and productivity in the national economy. Historical data of
five to twenty years ago may be
charted to show change in perspec-
tive. The publication is a monthly
and is about 40 pages in length.
Librarians should note that this information is summarized in the annual Handbook of labor statistics,
L2.3, item 768. Recommended for academic and for public libraries with
an aggressive business group.

Item 769
L2.2: BUREAU OF LABOR STATISTICS.
     General publications.
     Many of these titles sound fa-
miliar and may show up in other Department of Labor series as well.
The series is typical of the general publications line and includes
titles related to programs of the
agency. Its strength may be in its
career materials and in its issuance
of publications which explain some
of the statistical work. Examples:
     Jobs for which a high school
          education is preferred, but
          not essential, no. J57/2
     Social science and your career,
          no. So1/2
     The consumer price index:  A
          short description, no. P93/19.
Only one or two titles are issued a
year. Recommended for academic and
public libraries.

Item 770
L2.6:  BUREAU OF LABOR STATISTICS.
     MLR, monthly labor review.
     v.1-   July 1915-   LC 15-26485
     Articles focus on working Amer-
icans and their benefits, working
environment, training, satisfaction,
and productivity. Coverage is also
given to labor trends, research,
government regulation, and arbitration. Issues frequently contain articles of international scope. Articles are scholarly and documented.
Monthly features include book reviews, current labor statistics,
significant decisions in labor
cases, major agreements expiring
next month, research summaries, etc.
A monthly issue is over 100 pages in
length. The journal has a long-
standing reputation as an outstanding publication; it is quite readable. Recommended for academic and
public libraries.

Item 770-A
L2.70/4:  Occupational outlook quar-
     terly. v.1-   Feb. 1957-
     LC 58-100
     Published by the Bureau of La-
bor Statistics, this quarterly carries 4- to 6-page articles on trends
in the job market. It can be used
in conjunction with Occupational
outlook handbook, L2.3, item 768,
because it provides updated career
guidance. A recent issue contained
three articles on the field of law
and the prospect of employment in
the future. Other recent topics
have included computer industry employment, transition from school to
work, high unemployment among black
teenage girls, and careers in music
therapy. The periodical is attractively designed and readable. It
should provide good reading for persons in counseling and others who
follow employment trends. Recommended for college and public libraries.

Item 781
L36.103:  WOMEN'S BUREAU.  Bulle-
     tins.

Titles issued in the Bulletin series in the previous decade have generally been on the subject of women's careers. The series has been inactive until recently. A recent and periodically revised title is the Handbook on women workers, no. 297. This book is pertinent and an excellent reference source for such topics as women's employment by occupations and industries, income and earnings, education and training, federal and state labor laws, civil and political status, etc. A recommended series for all libraries.

Item 782
L36.102: WOMEN'S BUREAU. General
     publications.
     Statistical and public information titles compose this series. It is at present the most varied and prolific of bureau items; it issues three or four publications a year. A few subseries have emerged:
     Women workers today, no. W89,
          a periodic leaflet
     Brief highlights of major fed-
          eral laws and orders on sex
          discrimination, no. Se9
     Facts on women workers of mi-
          nority races, no. M66.
Other single titles include:
     Nontraditional occupations for
          women of the hemisphere: The
          U.S. experience, no. Oc1
     Laws on sex discrimination in
          employment, no. Em7.
     The item is recommended for academic and public libraries.

Item 783
L36.110: WOMEN'S BUREAU. Leaflets.
     Brief pamphlet material of general interest to women is issued here. Examples include:
     Get credit for what you know,
          no. 56
     A working woman's guide to her
          job rights, no. 55
     Who are the working mothers?,
          no. 37
     Publications of the Women's
          Bureau, no. 10.
Leaflets are occasionally revised. One or two a year are issued. Recommended for academic and public libraries.

Item 783-A
L36.112: WOMEN'S BUREAU. Pamphlets.
     These provide more substantive information for women than does the Leaflet series. Education and day care have been the main subjects of concern in the series of late:
     Continuing education programs
          and services for women, no.
          10
     Guide to conducting a consul-
          tation on women's employment
          with employers and union rep-
          resentatives, no. 12
     Federal funds for day care pro-
          jects, no. 14.
One or two a year are issued; titles are revised. Recommended for academic and public libraries.

Item 827
LR1.2: NATIONAL LABOR RELATIONS
     BOARD. General publications.
     The NLRB is an independent agency responsible for administering the National Labor Relations Act, which serves to reduce interruptions in commerce caused by industrial strife and provides for secret ballot elections to be held among employees to determine whether they wish to be represented by a labor organization. The general public will be more interested in this than in other series of the board. Publications issued in this series explain the board's functions, and they describe careers:
     The NLRB ...what it is, what it
          does, no. N21/4
     Your government conducts an
          election, no. El/2
     A career in labor-management
          relations, no. C18/2
     Where the action is ...labor-
          management relations exam-
          iner, no. Ac8.
Publications are brief and infrequent. They are usually pamphlets. Revisions are issued occasionally. Recommended for academic and public libraries.

Item 837
P1.2: POSTAL SERVICE. General
     publications.
     This series has a few titles of an in-house and regulatory nature,

but most of them serve to instruct
or inform the general user of the
Postal Service.  Examples include:

> Addressing for the optical
>     character reader, no. Ad2
> How to wrap and send parcels,
>     no. P21/14
> Stamp collecting for the fun of
>     it, no. St2/6
> A new look at zip code, no.
>     Z6/4
> Selling to the Postal Service,
>     no. Se5.

Four to six titles appear a year.
Most material is in pamphlet or
leaflet form.  Recommended for public libraries.

Item 839
POSTAL SERVICE
P1.10/4:  Directory of post offices.
    1954/55-  LC 55-61389
P1.10/5:  Directory of international
    mail.  1955-   LC 55-61157
P1.10/8:  National zip code direc-
    tory.  1965-   LC 66-60919
    The first list in the Directory
of post offices is by state; it includes the name of each post office,
its county and zip code.  The next
list is by name of post office, and
the final one is numerical by zip
code.  Other information of special
use to the Postal Service is included, such as discontinued names,
military installations, and Postal
Service agency addresses.  The directory is published annually and
kept up to date by the weekly Postal
bulletin, which is not included under this item.
    The Directory of international
mail includes specific detail on
rates and conditions governing mail
to individual foreign countries.  It
is updated by supplements and cumulated irregularly.
    The annual National zip code
directory is a handy reference.  It
is arranged alphabetically by state
and provides zip codes for each post
office.  Zip codes for cities with
several are listed by street so that
the code for a particular address
can be determined.
    The item is recommended for ac-
ademic and public library reference

collections.  If the series are
purchased, P1.10/5 is not essential.
Purchase of P1.10/4 in alternate
years may be adequate for most libraries.  P1.10/8 need be purchased
only once; in following years, it
may be exchanged for the new edition.  Discard old editions of the
other two.

Item 840
P4.10:  POSTAL SERVICE.  Description
    of United States postage stamps.
    Published irregularly, the
guide contains illustrated descriptions of all U.S. postage and special service stamps since July 1,
1847.  In addition it includes such
philatelic aids as how to obtain
first-day covers, a history of the
use of postage stamps in this country, and various statistics.  The
title is a useful reference for both
academic and public libraries.

Item 848
Pr39.9:  PRESIDENT.  The economic
    report of the president to the
    Congress.  Jan. 1947-
    LC 47-32975
    The Employment Act of 1946 re-
quires that this report be made annually to Congress.  The responsibility for the preparation of the
report is assumed primarily by the
Council of Economic Advisors, whose
annual report is also included in
these editions.  The combination of
the two reports provides a summary
of the progress of the economy over
the past year, as well as an outline
of the administration's policies and
programs.  The annual is an important historic record:  the tone of
the 1974 report is one of controlled
optimism about the course of the
economy, while the 1975 report som-
berly describes a severe recession.
The volume is about 250 pages of
text and extensive tabular material.
Emphases vary with the course of the
economy.  A back file may be justi-
fiable for some libraries.  Recommended for academic and public libraries.

Item 901-B
SBA1.2:  SMALL BUSINESS ADMINISTRA-
    TION.  General publications.
    The functions of counseling,
protecting, and assisting the interests of small businesses are exercised by this agency.  The agency
seeks to ensure that small businesses get their share of government
contracts, purchases, and loans.
Aid is available in time of disaster
and economic injury.  In this atmo-
sphere of assistance, numerous publications are issued annually to inform and instruct persons running
small businesses.  Recent titles include:
    Developing Indian-owned busi-
        ness, no. In2/2
    SBA disaster loans, no. L78/4
    Lease guarantee, no. L48
    Loans to local development com-
        panies, no. L78/18
    Management assistance, no. M31/
        13
    SBA:  What it is ...what it
        does, no. Sm1.
They are in brief pamphlet or booklet format.  Recommended for public
libraries.  Some academic libraries
may acquire these for particular
student needs.

Item 901-C
SBA1.12:  SMALL BUSINESS ADMINISTRA-
    TION.  Small business manage-
    ment series.  No. 1-
    LC 59-37013
    Many titles have been in this
series during the two previous decades, and some of them have now been
revised.  A recent title is Management audit for small service firms,
no. 38.  Subjects covered are in the
areas of materials, management, community relations, capital, auditing,
retailing, technical aids, and insurance.  Publications are 50 to 100
pages in length, readable and certainly of interest to the public
library patrons.  Some academics
will also find the subject matter
relevant to student needs.

Item 901-J
    SMALL BUSINESS ADMINISTRATION
SBA1.14:  Small marketers aids.

SBA1.14/2:  Small marketers aids an-
    nual.
    These series have recently sur-
faced after a few years of dormancy.
Outwitting bad check-passers, no.
137, is an 8-page leaflet which discusses the problem, its detection
and control.  Other pointers are
found in other numbers which have
special importance for the small
business person.
    The Small marketers aids annual
collects the separate numbers which
were issued during the year, and it
serves as a permanent copy.  Individual numbers may be discarded upon
its receipt.
    The series are recommended for
academic and public libraries.

Item 901-K
SBA1.3:  SMALL BUSINESS ADMINISTRA-
    TION.  Small business bibliog-
    raphies.
    This series was dormant for
several years but has recently been
reactivated.  Individual numbers of
about 8 pages each focus on such
topics as pet shops, marketing, manufacturing, training, and purchasing
for operators of small businesses.
No. 79, Small store planning and design, discusses the design process,
consumer behavior, store location,
personnel management, etc.  Recommended for academic and public libraries.

Item 901-N
    SMALL BUSINESS ADMINISTRATION
SBA1.18:  Publications.
SBA1.18/2:  Bibliographies and lists
    of publications.
SBA1.18/3:  Classification of man-
    agement publications.
    Basic bibliographic data and
order information are given for
printed materials issued by the
agency.  One or more of the lists
appear annually.  Recommended for
libraries serving patrons with interests in small business or management problems in general.  This is
an important tool for bibliographic
control.

Item 903-A
SE1.27:  SECURITIES AND EXCHANGE
    COMMISSION.  DIVISION OF TRAD-
    ING AND EXCHANGES.  Directory
    of companies filing annual re-
    ports with the Securities and
    Exchange Commission.  LC 59-
    61379
    Companies are listed alphabeti-
cally and by industry in this annual.
It is useful to the business community at large and to students of
business.  Securities traded on exchanges (SE1.16, item 907-B) may be
used in conjunction with this.  Recommended for libraries supporting
business and investment interests.

Item 904
SE1.2:  SECURITIES AND EXCHANGE COM-
    MISSION.  General publications.
    The overall nature of this se-
ries is technical.  The majority of
the publications will be of interest
only to members of the business community.  There are, however, a few
publications relating to the small
investor and general public.  Examples of both kinds follow:
        Report of the Real Estate Ad-
        visory Committee to the Se-
        curities and Exchange Com-
        mission, Washington, D.C.,
        October 12, 1972, no. R22
        Cost of flotation of regis-
        tered issues, 1971-72, no.
        F66/7
        Future structure of the secu-
        rities market, no. Se26/11
        The work of the Securities and
        Exchange Commission, no. Se26.
Recommended for academic libraries
serving business curriculum and for
public libraries serving a business
and investment community.

Item 907-B
SE1.16:  SECURITIES AND EXCHANGE
    COMMISSION.  Securities traded
    on exchanges under the Security
    Exchanges Act.  1936-  LC 41-
    23651
    This annual is an alphabetical
list of all securities currently being traded on stock exchanges, except for some which were exempted
under the Security Exchanges Act.

It also does not include bank securities, which are subject to the jurisdiction of other federal agencies.  This list can be used in conjunction with Directory of companies
filing annual report with the Securities and Exchange Commission,
SE1.27, item 903-A.  Recommended
for libraries supporting business
and investment interests.

Item 925
T1.2:  TREASURY DEPARTMENT.  Gen-
    eral publications.
T63.102:  TREASURY DEPARTMENT.  FIS-
    CAL SERVICE.  General publica-
    tions.
    The breadth of finance, bank-
ing, and services administered
through the Department of the Treasury is found here.  Publications of
interest to the consumer, the traveler, tourist, accountant, employee, and taxpayer are issued frequently.  Specific subjects include
revenue sharing, information and reports of payments, careers in the
department, pension plans, foreign
exchange, gold markets, taxes, and
legislation affecting these responsibilities.  Six or eight titles are
issued a year.
    Two subseries are issued annu-
ally by the Fiscal Service series
and have some reference value:
        Federal aid to states, no. Ai2
        Foreign currencies held by the
        U.S. government, no. C93.
Other titles are infrequent.
    The item is recommended for ac-
ademic and public libraries.

Item 955
T22.1:  INTERNAL REVENUE SERVICE.
    Report of the Commissioner of
    Internal Revenue.  LC 9-4972
    Policies and procedures of IRS
for collecting money and administer-
ing the tax system are the substance
of these annual reports.  The agency
is responsible for providing some
assistance to taxpayers in the form
of publications and other communications.  It is responsible for ensur-
ing compliance, international programs, legal activities, and planning and research, all of which are

reported here annually.  The appendix contains useful information to taxpayers.  The report will not help one file a tax return, but it is good information about the services available and the functions of the IRS.  Recommended for academic and public libraries.

Item 956
T22.2:  INTERNAL REVENUE SERVICE.
General publications.
An occasional title here is a specific guide to some phase of taxation, but for the most part all publications provide information about the agency or about a service to taxpayers.  The series includes an extensive group of titles about careers with the agency:
A new dimension in taxation,
no. T19/14
Estate tax attorney, no. Es8/4
Internal auditor, no. Au2/3.
Publications which provide other guidance are
Retirement planning, no. R31
Tax administration advisory
staff, no. Ad6/3
U.S. Jaycee volunteer, no. V88.
All are in brief pamphlet or booklet form, are issued at a rate of six to eight a year, and are revised frequently.  Recommended for academic and public libraries.

Item 956-A
INTERNAL REVENUE SERVICE
T22.19/2:  Handbooks, manuals,
guides.
T22.19/5:  Tobacco tax guide.
A guide series for the taxpayer, these titles are more specialized than the other handbook series annotated here, Your federal income tax, T22.44, and Tax information, IRS publications, T22.44/2, both item 964-B.  These titles are useful for persons paying taxes from a slightly atypical situation.  These examples give one an idea:
Tax guide for U.S. citizens
abroad, no. C49
A guide to federal estate and
gift taxation, no. Es8
Tax guide for small business,
no. Sm1

Teaching taxes program, no.
T19/2.
All are annual editions.  Old ones need not be retained.
The Tobacco tax guide is a compilation of reference materials dealing with tax on cigars, cigarettes, cigarette papers, and related products.  It includes laws, regulations, revenue rules, industry circulars, and miscellaneous materials.  It is not particularly useful to public or academic libraries, but neither is it bulky nor issued frequently.
The item is recommended for academic and public libraries.

Item 964-B
INTERNAL REVENUE SERVICE.
T22.44:  Your federal income tax.
1943-
T22.44/2:  Tax information, IRS publications.
Your federal income tax is the annual guide issued to individuals preparing tax returns.  It is usually available at the end of the tax year or at the beginning of the new one.  Each edition contains many examples, filled-in forms, and schedules to show how income and deductions are to be reported.  It is essential for reference collections.  Only the current guide should be retained.
Other IRS publications, annual leaflets and pamphlets, are issued to supplement Your federal income tax.  Some of the information in the leaflets is contained in the larger guide but issued separately here, while some titles are amplifications or new material.  All patrons find some of these titles useful.  Examples include:
Tax benefit for low-income in-
dividuals, no. 596
Tax information on educational
expenses, no. 508/8
Tax information on condomin-
iums and cooperative apart-
ments, no. 588
Voluntary tax methods to help
finance political campaigns,
no. 585
Interest equalization tax highlights, no. 573/3

Tax benefits for older Americans, no. 554.
Numerous publications are issued but
need not be kept beyond the current
tax year or beyond their revision.
They are important for reference until a new edition is issued.
    The item is recommended for ac-
ademic and public libraries.

Item 966
T28.2:   BUREAU OF THE MINT.   General
    publications.
    The history of our money and
its production is recorded in these
titles.  They are infrequent but
useful reference titles.  Typical
titles include:
    Our American coins, no. C66/8
    How to make a penny, no. D43.
In addition, legislation affecting
coinage and some administrative documents are also found in the series.
Of the Mint Bureau publications,
this is the most useful series.
Recommended for academic and public
libraries.

Item 974
    SECRET SERVICE
T34.2:   General publications.
T34.8:   Handbooks, manuals, guides.
    Three or four titles a year are
issued in this series which publi-
cizes the work of the agency.  The
duties--protecting the president and
his family and suppressing forgery
and counterfeiting--are evidenced in
these materials.  They are brief and
periodically revised.  Recent examples include:
    The Secret Service story, no.
    Se2/2
    Know your money, no. M74
    Use of illustrations, of obli-
        gations and securities of the
        United States and foreign
        governments, no. Il6.
    Handbooks, manuals, and guides
are similar in format and appearance
to the General Publications.  These
titles are administrative in nature,
but nevertheless of interest to the
public.  One or two are issued a
year.  Examples include:
    Physical fitness programs, no.
    P56

Guide to taking palm prints,
    no. P18.
    The item is recommended for
public libraries.

Item 989-B
VA1.34:   VETERAN'S ADMINISTRATION.
    VA fact sheets.
    Federal benefits for veterans
and dependents is a booklet issued
irregularly which details eligibility and benefits.  It provides necessary explanation and referral
for persons subject to these benefits.  Essentially a catalog of assistance to veterans, it is an important public library reference.
Only the latest edition is needed.
Recommended for public libraries.

Item 997
Y4.Ec7:Ec7  CONGRESS. JOINT ECONOMIC
    COMMITTEE.  Economic indicators.
    May 1948-    LC 48-46615
    Prepared for the Joint Economic
Committee by the Council of Economic
Advisors, this monthly publication
includes tabular material on total
U.S. output, income, and spending;
employment, unemployment, and wages;
production and business activity;
prices; money, credit, and security
markets; and federal finance.  Data
for the previous five or ten years
are charted for most categories.
Much of the data appears in other
publications, but Economic indicators is the only publication of
this comprehensive a scope.  It is
an important reference and is recommended for academic and public
libraries.

Item 1050-A
    APPALACHIAN REGIONAL COMMISSION
Y3.Ap4/2:   Reports and publications.
Y3.Ap4/2:2Ap48:   Appalachia.
    The economic, physical, and so-
cial development of the thirteen-
state area, the Appalachian region,
is the subject of this series.
Plans and programs which provide for
highway systems, health projects,
vocational education, housing construction, land reclamation, water
resources surveys, etc., are activities of the commission and also

topics of individual monographs.
Recent examples include:

Appalachian ways:  A guide to
the historic mountain heart
of the East, no. 8Ap4

Impact of mine drainage on recreation and stream ecology,
no. 2M66/App E, F

The future of Appalachian coal,
no. 2C63

Appalachian data book, no. 2Ap4,
available for each state

Annual report, no. 1/year.

Most are nontechnical.  They are
produced at a rate of two or three
titles a year.  All provide some in-
sight into the craft, culture, and
economics of the region.

Appalachia is published six
times a year.  It contains feature
articles on life in the region.  Recent issues have included writings
on flood damage by tropical storm
Agnes, a health maintenance organization, a photographic essay on
Christmas in Appalachia, and the
success of the Foxfire enterprises.
Of course, economics of the region
plays a central role in the journal.
Compassion and feelings of kinship
are aroused by this reading material, regardless of the geographic
location of the reader.

Item 1059-A-1
Y3.Eq2:  EQUAL EMPLOYMENT OPPORTUN-
ITY COMMISSION.  Reports and
publications.

Printed materials available
from the commission are related to
its responsibility for ending discrimination based on race, color,
religion, sex, or national origin
in hiring, promotion, firing,
wages, testing, training, and other
terms of employment; and to encourage programs in the private sector
which put equal employment opportunity into action.  Publications
also amplify the provisions of the
Civil Rights Act of 1964, and the
Equal Employment Opportunity Act of
1972.  Titles are of interest to employees and employers.  Recent examples:

Employment problems of women,
no. 11

Affirmative action and equal
employment:  A guidebook for
employers, no. 8Em7/3

Spanish surnamed American employment in the Southwest,
a directory of resources for
affirmative recruitment, no.
2R24.

Most are reports of studies or directories and are in book form.
Three or four titles a year are issued.  Recommended for academic and
public libraries.

Item 1067-I
Y3.In8/21:  INTERDEPARTMENTAL COM-
MITTEE ON THE STATUS OF WOMEN.
Reports and publications.

The status of women in federal
agencies is the concern of this commission.  It monitors women's advancement and provides for some information exchange between public
and private organizations.  Publications include:

The Equal Rights Amendment and
alimony and child support
laws, no. 2Eq2/2

Need for studies of sex discrimination in public schools,
no. 2Se9

Women, no. 2W84, which is similar in purpose and content to
an annual report.

One or two publications a year are
issued.  It is an interesting, pop-
ularly written body of information.
Recommended for academic and public
libraries.

Item 1070-K
Y3.N21/16:1 NATIONAL ADVISORY COUN-
CIL ON INTERNATIONAL MONETARY
AND FINANCIAL POLICIES.  Annual
report.

It is the work of the council
to coordinate the activity of international financial institutions and
U.S. government agencies involved in
foreign financial exchange.  This
report cites these transactions by
way of describing the multilateral
economic assistance to other nations,
trade policies, foreign investment
policies, and foreign indebtedness.
The appendixes list, among other
things, reconstruction and develop-

ment loans provided by the World Bank, the Inter-American Development Bank, and the Asian Development Bank. Statistical tables cover features of United States balance of payments and foreign assistance, the Agency for International Development, and much other data relevant to international finance. Recommended for academic libraries and for larger public libraries.

Item 1082
Y3.T25:2  TENNESSEE VALLEY AUTHORITY. General publications.
     This agency is regional and of little direct benefit to a large number of citizens, but it is exemplary of an unusual phenomenon in the history of this country. It is a government program--U.S. owned and operated--of resource conservation and electric power. Printed material resulting from this facility is related to the production of energy, a river control system, flood problems, dams, outdoor recreation, and conservation education. Examples include:
> Douglas Reservoir:  Fish and fishing, no. D74
> Facts about electric rates, no. Eℓ2/8
> Fertilizer marketing in a changing agriculture, no. F41/10
> Summer and fall wildflowers of Land between the Lakes, no. L22/3.

The format varies from leaflet to booklet. Three or four titles a year are issued. Recommended for academic and public libraries.

## EDUCATION

Item 445-N-2
HE1.462:  BUREAU OF CHILD DEVELOPMENT SERVICES. General publications.
     These titles are devoted primarily to the Head Start program. They are of interest to parents, planners, and community program planners. Examples include:
> Films suitable for Head Start development programs, no. F84
> Using Title XX to serve children and youth, no. C43
> Directory of full-year Head Start programs, no. H34/5.

Three or four publications are issued annually. Publications are revised as necessary. Recommended for public libraries.

Item 449
HE1.459:  Children today.  v.1- Jan./Feb. 1972-  LC 72-620933
     Published six times a year by the Child Development Office, this magazine is about 34 pages in length and includes six or seven articles in each issue. Some issues focus on special themes, such as day care or autism. Others contain articles on various topics aimed at families and persons who work with children professionally. Recent subjects have included childhood leukemia, play therapy, reading to young children, and youth advisory services. Regular features include news in the field, book reviews, letters, and notice of government publications.

Articles are written by teachers, psychologists, pediatricians, parents, and social workers. The magazine is a superb publication. Recommended for academic and public libraries.

Item 452
HE1.452:  CHILDREN'S BUREAU.  General publications.
Titles are on the subject of children and are of general interest to parents, educators, and researchers. They are issued infrequently and do not require special knowledge for use.  Typical titles include:
> Families for black children: The search for adoptive parents, no. F21
> Handicapped children in Head Start programs, no. H19
> Tips on the care and adjustment of Vietnamese and other Asian children in the United States, no. V67.

Four or five are issued annually. Recommended for academic and public libraries.

Item 454-C-3
HE1.410:  OFFICE OF CHILD DEVELOPMENT.  Day care USA.
Essentially a series of handbooks on day care practices appropriate for infants, preschool, and school-age children, these publications are individually numbered and issued irregularly.  Each one is devoted to a particular topic, such as children with special needs, family day care, and health services, providing guidance to parents and to other persons responsible for the administration of day care programs. The emphasis is on practical ideas. Recommended for academic and public libraries.

Item 455
OFFICE OF EDUCATION
HE19.101:  The Commissioner's annual report.  1971-  LC 77-26233
HE19.101/2:  Administration of Public Laws 81-874 and 81-815, annual report of the Commissioner of Education.

Because the Department of Health, Education and Welfare no longer issues a depository edition of its annual report, it is necessary to collect reports from some agencies within the department.  The Office of Education report is a chronicle of the condition of education in the nation, the agency's program objectives, equality of education and opportunity, quality, management, and nonprogram activities. It lacks the imaginative format of some reports but is well written.
Known as an appendix to the Annual Report of the Commissioner of Education, the report on the administration of the two laws is not an essential title, but it is useful if the item is selected for acquisition.  The laws, enacted in 1950, authorize federal payments directly to local school districts financially burdened as a result of federal activity.
The item is recommended for academic and public libraries.

Item 455-B
HE19.115:  American education.  v.1-Jan. 1965-  LC 65-9862
Editorial policies of this periodical reflect the federal interests in education at all levels. Published ten times a year by the Office of Education, it is aimed at professional educators and concerned citizens.  Readers are kept up to date on significant trends in education and typical educational practice.  Special emphasis on the assistance provided by federal programs and legislation, teacher training, career education, research results, and administrative practice is found in the contents.  Recent issues have included articles on training students for the job demands of local industries, programs for giving teenagers the basics for becoming good parents, and college theater troupes.  Issues are 30 to 40 pages in length and carry six to ten short articles.  Regular features include news in the field, statistics, and recent federal publications of interest.  The period-

ical is attractively designed and compares favorably with commercial publications. A few years of back file are desirable. Recommended for academic and public libraries.

Item 455-D
HE19.128:  OFFICE OF EDUCATION. Bibliographies and lists of publications.
HE19.317:  NATIONAL CENTER FOR EDUCATION STATISTICS. Bibliographies and lists of publications.

Three or four publications are issued annually from this item on subjects pertinent to the interests of the agency. The bibliographies are usually annotated and include materials issued privately and by the government. Recent bibliographic subjects include education in the U.S.S.R., education of ethnic groups in the U.S., outdoor education, and booklists for young people. Supplements are sometimes issued as additional materials become available. The Educational Resources Information Center (ERIC) is the source of material for many of these publications, while some are compiled by program specialists or other professional educators. Occasionally a list of publications containing information on their availability from one of the HEW agencies is issued. This series makes a significant contribution to the reference literature of education. Recommended for academic and public libraries.

Item 455-F
NATIONAL CENTER FOR EDUCATION STATISTICS
HE19.321:  Schools for careers: An analysis of occupational courses offered by secondary and postsecondary schools.
HE19.337:  Directory of postsecondary schools with occupational programs, public and nonpublic.
HE19.337/2:  Enrollments and programs in noncollegiate postsecondary schools.

Schools for careers is an analytical report developed and issued in response to the national atten-

tion being focused on career education. The volume is useful in conjunction with the directories of vocational institutions issued under this item. The information from these directories is analyzed and compared in a format which is both textual and tabular.

The Directory of postsecondary schools provides a comprehensive listing of career-related programs. It provides guidance to students and to persons planning educational programs. Organized by state, the directory lists the name and address of the school, telephone, enrollment, notes on accreditation, relationship to the Office of Education if any, established eligibility, control or affiliation of school, program offerings, and type of school. Information for the directory is supplied by the schools in their response to a questionnaire. Index is by program and by name of school or institution. Enrollments and programs provides statistics for these institutions.

These three titles are ideally annuals, but some years have been skipped. Another limitation of their usefulness is the time lag between collection of the data, their publication, and their analyses. These three series promise to be valuable references in guidance and career planning, in both academic and public libraries. Schools for careers has permanent reference value for purposes of comparison; the other two are not likely to be needed beyond the current edition.

Item 460
OFFICE OF EDUCATION
HE19.113:  Education directory: Education associations.
NATIONAL CENTER FOR EDUCATION STATISTICS
HE19.324:  Education directory: Colleges and universities.
HE19.324/2:  Education directory: Public school systems.

Education associations is an annual volume of information compiled from questionnaires returned from education organizations and associations. Issued annually, it contains national and regional education associations, college professional fraternities, honor societies, recognition societies, state education associations, foundations, religious education associations, and international education associations. It is indexed by name of association and by subject. For each entry, the name and address is given, as is the chief officer, and titles of official publications.

Colleges and universities, some sometimes called Higher education, is issued annually for the academic year. It lists institutions in the United States which offer a two or more year program of college level studies. It is organized by state and city and includes for each institution, the telephone number, address, congressional district, county, enrollment, tuition and fees, calendar system, control or affiliation, type of program, degree offered, accreditation, and names of officials. Several appendixes are included, as is an index by name of institution.

Public school systems is also issued annually for the academic year. It provides a current listing of local public school systems, but it does not include area vocational-technical training schools. The name, mailing address, county, grade span, number of pupils, and number of schools is given for each system.

The three directories have many uses and in some cases provide information which is not available in commercial publications. They are recommended reference titles for academic and public libraries.

Item 460-A-10
    NATIONAL CENTER FOR EDUCATION
    STATISTICS
HE19.315:  Digest of education statistics.
HE19.320:  Projections of educational statistics.
    This 200-page annual, Digest of education statistics, covers American education from preschool through graduate school. The

sources of the data are both government and otherwise. Data are available on schools, colleges, enrollments, teachers, graduates, educational attainment, finances, federal funds, libraries, international education, and research and development. Some textual material accompanies the tables. Historical series are available for some categories of data. Retaining the volume for every fifth year may be an alternative to a complete back file.

Projections of educational statistics to ten years hence are data desired by many administrators in their plans for a cost-effective educational system. This publication is issued annually and projects anticipated enrollments, graduates, earned degrees, teachers, expenditures, and student charges to ten years ahead. The figures are based on current estimates. Sources and estimation methods are explained. Some textual material accompanies the tables. The 200-page volume is essential to educational planning.

The item is recommended for academic and public libraries.

Item 460-A-14
    OFFICE OF EDUCATION
HE19.109:  Education around the world.
HE19.112:  Opportunities abroad for teachers.
    Issued irregularly, Education around the World is a series of 20-page booklets about the educational systems of individual countries. The booklets contain information about the country, its people, and the basic organization of the system. A glossary and a suggested reading list are included.

Opportunities abroad for teachers is an annual pamphlet describing the teacher exchange program carried out by the Office of Education and the Department of State. Details of the opportunities available for American teachers and teachers from other countries are included.

This item is recommended for academic and public libraries.

Item 460-A-20
> NATIONAL CENTER FOR EDUCATION
> STATISTICS

HE19.318:  Statistics of public
schools, advance report.

HE19.318/3:  Statistics of state
school systems.

HE19.318/4:  Statistics of local
public schools.

HE19.326:  Statistics of public elementary and secondary day
schools.

HE19.327:  Preprimary enrollment.

Various categories of data for
elementary and secondary education
are found here.  These miscellaneous
statistics, similar to those found
in the financial series in item
460-A-22, cover enrollment, staff,
instruction, population, attendance,
and graduation data.  Most are compiled from reports submitted by
school administrators.  The statistical titles are designed to be issued annually although most lag several years behind.  Individually,
they are 20 to 30 pages in length,
except for HE19.318/4, which is
about 300 pages.  Much of the data
is summarized in the annual Digest
of education statistics (HE19.315,
item 460-A-10), and for many libraries this summary is adequate.
Recommended for academic and public
libraries.

Item 460-A-22
> OFFICE OF EDUCATION

HE19.126:  Public school finance
programs.
> NATIONAL CENTER FOR EDUCATION
> STATISTICS

HE19.313:  Revenues and expenditures
for public elementary and secondary schools.

HE19.318/2:  Statistics of local
public school systems' finance.

HE19.323:  Bond sales for public
schools.

This group of statistical publications on elementary and secondary education is of interest to
teacher-training programs and to
local communities.  These financial
statistics are similar to those
found in the miscellaneous series
in item 460-A-20, except for the

subject detail.  Use of these statistical publications makes it possible to compare programs and expenditures throughout the country.
There is frequently a lag of three
or four years between collection of
the data and issuance.  In the meantime, the Digest of education statistics, HE19.315, item 460-A-10,
provides annual summaries.  In some
cases, the Digest is adequate reference.  Librarians should evaluate
the need for detail before making
this additional selection.  These
annual reports are about 20 pages
in length except for the Statistics
of local public school systems finance, which is 300 to 400 pages.
Recommended for academic and public
libraries.

Item 460-A-54
> NATIONAL CENTER FOR EDUCATION
> STATISTICS

HE19.325:  Fall enrollment in higher
education.

HE19.325/2:  Post secondary education:  Fall enrollment in
higher education, institutional
data.

HE19.329:  Earned degrees conferred.

HE19.330:  Students enrolled for advanced degrees.

HE19.333:  Associate degrees and
other formal awards below the
baccalaureate.

These five series are sources
of data on degrees and enrollments
in higher education, issued annually
and several years after the collection of data.  The data, compiled
from questionnaires filed by the
institutions, are organized by curriculum, subject field, and specific
institution.  The series provide
comprehensive reference for educational planning and administration.
The volumes are bulky.  An extensive back file is not necessary for
most collections.  Recommended for
academic and public libraries.

Item 461
> OFFICE OF EDUCATION

HE19.9:  Fund for the Improvement
of Postsecondary Education publications series.

HE19.102:  General publications.

An annual, Program information and application procedures is issued from the Fund for the Improvement of Postsecondary Education publications series.

The General Publications series consists of surveys, statistical summaries, research reports, and the recommendations of task forces on the education of Americans.  Four or five titles are issued annually, of which the following are examples:

A study of the attitude toward life of our nation's students, no. St9/4

Progress of education in the United States of America, no. P94

Higher education prices and price indexes, no. P93.

All are of potential interest to educators and the general community.

The item is recommended for academic and public libraries.

Item 461-A-1

HE19.302:  NATIONAL CENTER FOR EDU-
CATION STATISTICS.  General
publications.

The agency gathers data from various educational programs and institutions around the country and tabulates it to reveal various trends in enrollments, student characteristics, attitudes, and finances. Some of the studies are contracted by the agency to private individuals and institutions.  The result is a variety of studies of which the following are examples:

Vocational plans of full-time community and junior college students, no. V85

Status report on public broad-casting, no. B78

Profiles in school support, no. Sch6.

Adult education, educational technology, and national longitudinal studies are general concerns of the agency.  Much of the data is specialized and the analyses detailed, yet the publications have some bearing on the work of most educators.  Two or three titles are issued annually.  Recommended for

academic libraries and for public libraries serving the educational community.

Item 466-A

HE19.210:  Resources in education.
v.1-  Nov. 1966-  LC 72-
216727

The journal is sometimes referred to as ERIC, the acronym for the agency from which it is issued, Educational Resources Information Center.  The monthly journal is an abstracting service.  Each issue consists of the resumes (an abstract with basic bibliographic information) and separate subject, author, and institution indexes.  Information for ordering the ERIC document is also included.

The purpose of the journal is to announce recent report literature related to the field of education. It makes possible the early identification and acquisition of educational literature.  The Educational Resources Information Center is a national network for acquiring, abstracting, indexing, storing, retrieving, and disseminating education information.  Reports cited in the journal are available from the ERIC Document Reproduction Service and in some cases, in published sources.

Two semiannual, cumulative indexes are issued.  Beginning with the 1975 volume, the only annual index available is through a commercial publisher.

The abstracting journal is recommended for academic libraries and for public libraries supporting research in education.

Item 717-L

J1.43:  DEPARTMENT OF JUSTICE.  List
of participating institutions.

Published by the Law Enforcement Assistance Administration, this annual lists institutions of higher education participating in the Law Enforcement Education Program. Known as LEEP, the program provides education grants and/or loans to public law enforcement and criminal justice personnel and students who

have selected careers in these
fields.  This list is organized by
state, and includes the name and address of the institution, the congressional district, and the crime-
related degree program  and degree
level.  An important element in
career literature, the list is recommended for academic and public libraries.

Item 724
J21.9:  IMMIGRATION AND NATURALIZA-
        TION SERVICE.  Federal text-
        books on citizenship.
    These are textbooks for educat-
ing foreigners who wish to become
citizens of the United States.  Designed to help them read, write, and
speak English, the books resemble
elementary social studies exercises
in content and level.  Some are
about life in this country; others
are about history and government,
and the rights and responsibilities
of becoming a citizen.  They are
used in citizenship classes and
serve as preparation for the citizenship examination.  Two or three
different series, along with teachers' guides, are revised periodically.  Persons interested in naturalization for whatever reason will
be attracted to these texts in libraries.  Only current editions
need to be retained.

Item 806-I
LC2.11:  LIBRARY OF CONGRESS.  GEN-
         ERAL REFERENCE AND BIBLIOGRAPHY
         DIVISION.  Children's books.
         LC 65-60014
    An annual list of children's
titles, the publication is brief but
provides basic bibliographic data
and a short annotation for some notable books of the year.  The age
range is preschool through junior
high.  About six hundred books are
included and divided into age, format, and subject categories.  Compiled under the direction of
Virginia Haviland, this is recommended as a librarian's tool in all
libraries.  Retain as long as referred to, or about five years.

Item 1049-F
DEPARTMENT OF STATE
S1.67/4:  Directory of contacts for
          international educational, cul-
          tural, and scientific exchange
          programs.
ADVISORY COMMISSION ON INTERNA-
TIONAL EDUCATION AND CULTURAL
AFFAIRS
Y3.Ad9/9:  Reports and publications.
    An annual list, the Directory
of contacts includes private and
governmental agencies, and their
contact persons, active in the international exchange of persons and
programs.  It is organized by type
of agency:  federal, intergovernmental, and private.  These listings
include address, personnel, and a
statement about the scope of activity and interests.  This is a useful
reference in all libraries and com-
plements the quarterly (below).
    The only regular publication
series of the Advisory Commission on
International Education and Cultural
Affairs is the quarterly International educational and cultural exchange.  Interest in foreign educational exchanges has escalated in
this country during the last decade.
The commission was created to provide educational and cultural exchange as a means of increasing understanding between peoples in foreign countries and in the United
States.  The quarterly publication
provides a forum for the communication of ideas and experiences in
cultural and educational affairs.
Each issue is stimulating and creatively inspired with articles about
college foreign study programs,
teaching internships, traveling
performance groups, graphic arts exchanges, accounts of experiences,
and human factors which sometimes
impede achievements.  Articles are
brief; contributors are usually from
outside government.  Regular features include news about funding,
resource materials, announcements of
international conferences, and letters from readers.  Long back files
are not necessary.
    The item is recommended for ac-
ademic and public libraries.

Item 1062-B
Y3.Ex8:  NATIONAL ADVISORY COUNCIL
ON EXTENSION AND CONTINUING
EDUCATION.  Reports and publications.
    The council reports annually to
the Department of Health, Education
and Welfare on all federally supported continuing and extension education programs.  Publications resulting from this activity include
in addition to the annual report,
research reports, and surveys.  Subjects of these reports are the
Higher Education Act, women, and educational institutions.  Titles are
issued infrequently and are usually
brief.  Recommended for academic and
public libraries.

## ENGINEERING

Item 320-B-2
D14.9:  DEFENSE CIVIL PREPAREDNESS
AGENCY.  Technical report series.
    This group of publications with
potential for use by the average
citizen deals with the subject of
protecting the public from disaster.
Reports, which provide both information and instruction, are technical
but they are not beyond the comprehension of patrons with this concern.  Three or four publications
a year of 30 to 50 pages in length
compose the series.  Examples include:
    Wind resistant design concepts
        for residences, no. 83, a
        book of guidelines for home-
        owners and builders
    Protecting mobile homes from
        high winds, no. 75/2, an in-
        formative and instructive
        publication for owners and
        users of mobile homes
    A case for protective design,
        nuclear, and otherwise, no.
        72, a reprint from another
        publication describing the
        changing responsibility of
        the civil defense agency.
Publications in this technical series are examples of the increasing
concern of federal civil defense
about preparedness for peacetime
emergency.  Publications are superseded from time to time; older editions should be discarded.  Recommended for academic and public libraries.

Item 337
D103.2:  ARMY CORPS OF ENGINEERS.
    General publications.
    The Army Corps of Engineers has
attracted a substantial amount of
publicity over the past decade, and
this series is a useful one to describe its activities.  It contains
career information and some historical material about the corps, but
the focus is primarily upon projects
and control activities.  Attractive
tourist brochures include maps, pictures, and recreational information
for most of the areas of corps projects.  Examples include:
    Lower Granite Lock and Dam,
        Snake River, Washington,
        no. Sn1/3
    Oregon coastal harbors, no. Or3
    Lakeside recreation in New
        England, no. N42e.
Some are descriptions of projects in
nontechnical language:
    Mississippi:  1973, no. M69/5

Meet the Rock Island District
Corps of Engineers, no. R59/2.
Many are comprehensive studies and
surveys of a geographical area.
They are of a technical nature and
include:

Tropical storm Agnes, June 1972,
no. Ag6/5
Impact of tropical storm Agnes
on Chesapeake Bay, no. Ag6/6
Development of the Lower Mekong
Basin, no. D49x
Aquatic macrophytes of the Columbia and Snake River drain-
ages, no. C72/3.

Size and format vary.  Length
runs from a few pages to a few hundred pages.  Three to ten publications are issued annually.  Recommended for academic and public libraries.

Item 857-D-8
DEFENSE CIVIL PREPAREDNESS
AGENCY
D14.8:  Handbooks, manuals, guides.
D14.8/6:  CPG series.

A total of three or four titles
a year are published in each of
these series.  They are potentially
interesting to various citizen
groups as their focus is on emergency preparedness.  Occasionally
one is highly technical but in general they are useful to the user
lacking special knowledge.  Recent
examples include:

Disaster planning guide for
business and industry, no.
D14.8:D63/2
Disaster operations:  A hand-
book for local governments,
no. D14.8:D63
Civil preparedness exercise
program guidance, no. D14.8:
Ex3
Guide for crisis relocation
contingency planning, no.
D14.8/6:2-8-D-1.

A closer look at these publications
reflects the changing nature of federal civil defense from concern with
nuclear attack to peacetime hazard
and disaster.  Riots, tornadoes,
earthquakes, and other severe emergencies also demand immediate attention.  Recommended for academic and
public libraries.

Item 857-D-10
D14.8/3:  DEFENSE CIVIL PREPAREDNESS
AGENCY.  Handbook series.

Few titles occur in this series,
but one of them is worth noting and
certainly worth acquiring.  In time
of emergency:  A citizen's handbook
on disaster, no. 14-B, is published
periodically.  It is a 40- to 50-
page handbook of guidance and instructions for reacting to peacetime disasters and should supplement
specific instructions issued by local governments on emergency preparedness.  Another recent publication is Home shelter, no. 12-1,
which gives construction detail on
building a fallout shelter outside
and underground.  Previous editions
may be discarded as newer ones are
available.  Recommended for academic
and public libraries.

Item 982-D-1
TD8.2:  NATIONAL HIGHWAY TRAFFIC
SAFETY ADMINISTRATION.  Gen-
eral publications.

A significant portion of the
department's work is in the area
of transportation safety.  These
titles include not only research
reports on safety which are relatively technical, but also a large
group of public information and
consumer-related titles.  State
licensing, law enforcement, pupil
transportation, collision analyses,
etc., are frequent topics.  Typical
titles include:

Emergency medical services,
no. Em3
Tips on car care and safety,
no. C18
Alcohol safety countermeasures
program, no. Al1/2.

Formats and lengths vary.  The four
or five titles issued a year frequently include a revised edition
of an earlier title.  Recommended
for public libraries.

Item 982-D-2
NATIONAL HIGHWAY TRAFFIC SAFETY
ADMINISTRATION
TD8.9:  Motor vehicle safety defect
recall campaigns.  1970-
LC 73-645352
TD8.9/2:  Safety-related recall cam-

paigns for motor vehicle equipment, including tires.

In response to the agency's numerous requests for information on defects in motor vehicles, these summaries are published quarterly. Cumulative editions are issued annually. Manufacturers are required to furnish the Secretary of Transportation with copies of all communications to dealers or purchasers regarding defects in their equipment. These reports are compiled from that data. Organization is by manufacturer. Date of company notification, make, model, model year, description of defect, number of pages on file, and number of vehicles recalled are included for each recall campaign. Consumer advocate groups and alert individuals will be attracted to these publications. Recommended for public libraries.

Item 982-D-7
NATIONAL HIGHWAY TRAFFIC SAFETY ADMINISTRATION
TD8.12: Report on activities under the National Traffic and Motor Vehicle Safety Act. 1970-
LC 73-615480
TD8.12/2: Report on activities under Highway Safety Act. 1970-
LC 74-615483
TD8.12/3: Report on activities of National Highway Traffic Safety Administration under Highway Safety Act and National Traffic and Motor Vehicle Safety Act. 1970- LC 79-615602
TD8.12 and TD8.12/2 are both annual reports required by law. They focus primarily on progress made during the year in carrying out the purpose of legislation. Vehicle safety is central to the programs and research designs of TD8.12, and highway safety, to the other. Defects investigations, crash avoidance, crash survival, enforcement of standards, highway environment, and traffic engineering are described by program. State and local community accomplishments are discussed, as are the persistent problems which delay achievements. Consumer assistance is a basic assumption in these

laws and is reported upon here. Congressional regulation and enforcement of safety having increased rapidly in recent years, this item may continue to incorporate new legislation. Appendixes include tables and charts, lists of publications, research grants, and contracts. TD8.12/3 is an inactive series at present.

The item is recommended for academic and public libraries.

Item 982-D-12
TD8.16: NATIONAL HIGHWAY TRAFFIC SAFETY ADMINISTRATION. Report on International Technical Conference on Experimental Safety Vehicles.

These are proceedings of a conference which has met on several occasions since the late 1960s. It is sponsored by the United States Department of Transportation and held in cities around the world. The technical features and engineering of vehicles are often too complex for the comprehension of the average consumer; nevertheless this series should be noted. The publication confirms the widespread cooperation among governments and among competitive companies in the area of research and development for road safety. Technical papers include such topics as accident analysis, human factors, vehicle structural properties, environmental and energy factors. Some papers deal with research conducted by several manufacturers while others document the progress made in the research on an individual make of vehicle. Some library patrons will find this of interest, and engineering students who deal with safety problems will find this series particularly pertinent. A lengthy back file is not necessary.

Item 982-G-2
TD2.8: FEDERAL HIGHWAY ADMINISTRATION. Handbooks, manuals, guides.

Titles here are generally administrative, but most have applicability to local transportation

planning as well.   Representative
titles include:

> User documentation for the FWHA
> carpool matching program, no.
> C22/2
> A manual for planning pedes-
> trian facilities, no. P34
> Urban origin-destination sur-
> veys, no. Url/2
> How to pool it, no. P78.

The three or four titles issued a
year average 100 to 200 pages in
length.  Recommended for public libraries.

Item 982-G-3
FEDERAL HIGHWAY ADMINISTRATION
TD2.14:  Highway beauty awards competition.
TD2.14/2: Annual highway awards competition series.
The competition has been conducted annually for several years,
and these publications announce the
awards, which go to the state,
county, or local highway agency responsible for the aesthetic blending
of the highway into the environment.
Occasionally civic organizations or
industrial groups are responsible
and noted as well.  "The outstanding
example of motorist service station"
is also included.  The photography
is beautiful and attests to the jus-
tification for the award.  The publications are 30 to 40 pages in
length and are an important contribution of the agency in the recognition of progress in highway design.
Recommended for public libraries.

Item 982-G-5
TD2.2:  FEDERAL HIGHWAY ADMINISTRA-
TION.  General publications.
Both popular materials and research reports compose this series
which is as broad as the scope of
the agency itself.  Publications include the topics of the federal highway construction program, road and
vehicle safety, urban transit, preservation of natural beauty, public
parks, and recreation lands along
highways.  Titles include:

> Double up, American:  Car pool
> kit, no. C17
> European experience in pedes-

trian and bicycle facilities,
no. B47/2
Cost of operating an automobile,
no. Au8
Accidents on main rural highways, no. Ac2/2
Interstate system route log and
finder list, no. In8/3.

Some titles are potential reference
items.  Many include survey data
about road use, accidents, finance,
and energy; they accumulate at a
rate of eight to ten a year.  Recommended for academic and public libraries.

Item 982-I-1
TD1.115:  NATIONAL TRANSPORTATION
SAFETY BOARD.  Publications.
The pamphlet is published annually.  It is a catalog of printed
material which may be useful to the
general public and to the transportation industry.  It includes ordering information and blanks, along
with basic bibliographic data for
each title.  This is a useful reference aid and increases the bibliographic control over the subject.
Retention of older lists is not necessary.  Recommended for academic
and public libraries.

Item 982-I-5
DEPARTMENT OF TRANSPORTATION
TD1.20:  DOT-TST series.
TD1.20/2:  DOT- TSC series.
Most titles issued here are
highly technical.  They will not
appeal to a large number of patrons,
but they are included because they
support physics programs, and because the reports are about transportation issues which constantly
confront Americans.  Further,
TD1.20/2 contains several volumes of
statistics which have reference
value.  Six or eight publications
are issued a year and average 100 to
200 pages in length.  Representative
titles include:

> Increased fuel economy in trans-
> portation systems by use of
> energy management, no.
> TD1.20:75-2
> Awards to academic institutions
> by the Department of Trans-

portation, no. TD1.20:75-89
Energy statistics, no. TD1.20/2:
   74-12
Summary of national transporta-

tion statistics, no. TD1.20/2:
   73-36.
Recommended for academic libraries.

ENVIRONMENTAL SCIENCES

Item 207-B-1
C55.502:  NATIONAL ENVIRONMENTAL
   SATELLITE SYSTEM.  General publications.
   The agency operates one of the
nation's two civil satellite systems
and concentrates on developing ways
of using environmental data for general benefit.  This series issues
about one title a year.  The titles
vary from pamphlets to monographs,
but they are all written to inform
the public.  Typical titles include:
   Environmental satellites:  Sys-
      tems, data interpretation,
      and applications, no. En8/2
   The polar-orbiting, operational,
      environmental satellite, no.
      N21
   Geostationary, operational,
      environmental satellite, no.
      G29.
These materials have potential use
for high school and college class-
rooms.  Recommended for academic and
public libraries.

Item 207-C-1
C55.602:  ENVIRONMENTAL RESEARCH
   LABORATORIES.  General publications.
   Research in the physical environment, an activity shared with
many other federal agencies, is the
work of the Environmental Research
Laboratories.  There are several
predecessors to this bureau, including the former Coast and Geodetic
Survey.  Description, simulation,

modification, prediction, and monitoring the environment are the
broad subjects of inquiry.  Specific
environmental situations are also
dealt with in the literature, such
as the New York bight project and
San Francisco earthquakes.  Two or
three titles are issued annually in
various formats.  Recommended for
academic and public libraries.

Item 273-D-1
C55.202:  ENVIRONMENTAL DATA SERVICE.
   General publications.
   Three or four titles here are
issued annually as descriptive brochure, bibliography, or research report.  They are written in a popular
style and serve to advise the public
of the agency's activity and services rendered.
   NCC--The National Climatic
      Center, no. N21c
   Seismological publications and
      services, no. Se4
   Earthquake history of the
      United States, no. Ea7.
Recommended for academic and public
libraries.

Item 273-D-4
C55.213:  ENVIRONMENTAL DATA SERVICE.
   Daily weather maps.  Weekly
   series.
   Maps are issued by week in one
publication which includes one page
of explanatory material and seven
pages of maps and charts.  Those
used are the surface weather map,

the 500-millibar height contours
chart, the chart for highest and
lowest temperatures, and the chart
for precipitation areas and amounts.
These four charts for each day are
arranged on a single page. The
weekly is issued two or three weeks
after the fact. Undergraduate programs in meteorology are served by
weather maps, and many public library patrons observe weather patterns.

Item 275
C55.102:  NATIONAL WEATHER SERVICE.
    General publications.
    Four or five titles a year de-
scribe the activity of the bureau.
Some are technical reports, but most
are appropriate for the reading and
reference needs of the general public.  Typical titles include:
    High seas storm information
        service, no. St7/73
    Severe local storm warning ser-
        vice, no. St7/2
    The National Weather Service
        and water management, no.
        W29.
Recommended for academic and public
libraries.

Item 275-F
C55.109:  NATIONAL METEOROLOGICAL
    CENTER, SUITLAND, MARYLAND.
    LONG RANGE PREDICTION GROUP.
    Average monthly weather outlook.
    LC 74-642183
    Issued twice a month, the 4-
page leaflet is an estimate of the
average rainfall and temperature for
the next thirty days in the United
States.  Meteorological observations throughout the Northern Hemisphere are analyzed, and from these
estimates, predictions are made.
The outlook does not, however, provide a detailed forecast because the
weather events throughout the world
affect those in other areas in ways
not entirely understood.  Recommended for academic and public libraries.

Item 278-A
C55.106:  NATIONAL WEATHER SERVICE.
    Regulations, rules, and instruc-
    tions.

Safety rules in formats appropriate for posting is the norm for
this group of materials.  Tornado
safety rules in schools, no. T63/2;
and Winter storm safety rules, no.
St7, are examples.  They are good
educational publications, for file
or display.  Recommended for academic and public libraries.

Item 278-B
C55.111:  NATIONAL WEATHER SERVICE.
    Operations of the National
    Weather Service.
    Meteorological, hydrological,
and oceanographic programs and services of the National Weather Service are described in this annual
volume.  It is intended to serve
other governmental units, and it
will inform a general audience of
the many public and specialized programs.  In addition to those programs named above, data acquisition,
overseas operations, space support,
communications and dissemination,
climatology, and education and
training are covered.  The volume is
attractively designed and includes
many maps for locating various NWS
installations.  The current edition
is adequate for general reference.
Recommended for academic and larger
public libraries.

Item 431-I-1
EP1.2:  ENVIRONMENTAL PROTECTION
    AGENCY.  General publications.
    This group of titles is very
useful to the average patron, and
it is one of the few EPA series
which is nontechnical.  Some of its
titles are administrative or for a
specialized use, but most are written to appeal to a broad spectrum of
readers.  Career materials, conference proceedings, citizen advisory
communications, reports on status of
research, and directories are typical kinds of titles.  Eight to ten
titles a year are issued in varying
sizes and formats.  Recent titles
include:
    Environmental organizations di-
        rectory, no. Or3
    The challenge of the environ-
        ment:  A primer on EPA's
        statutory authority, no. C35

Citizen role in implementation
of clean air standards, no.
C49
Environmental impact of land
use on water quality, no.
W29/16.

This series is probably the
best source of information for the
general reader on activities of the
agency in the areas of water, air,
pesticides, and radiation. Recommended for academic and public libraries.

Item 431-I-9
EP1.21: ENVIRONMENTAL PROTECTION
AGENCY. Bibliographies and
lists of publications.
Recent examples of these general and specialized bibliographies
include:
Selected publications on the
environment, no. En8/4
An environmental bibliography,
no. En8
Bibliography of R and D research reports, no. En8/7.
The bibliographies list both EPA
publications and commercial titles.
Some list those titles published in
the interest of increasing the public's awareness and knowledge of the
environment. Others list technical
studies of interest only to the specialist. Basic bibliographic data
and ordering information are included. Recommended for increased
bibliographic control in academic
and public libraries.

Item 431-I-11
EP1.23: ENVIRONMENTAL PROTECTION
AGENCY. Ecological research
series.
Reports on the effects of pollution on humans, plants, animals,
and materials are published here.
Methodology, ecosystems, short- and
long-term dangers, restoration activities, and detection of pollutants are subjects of investigation.
The reports are technical and seek
to establish criteria necessary for
setting standards to control pollutants in the aquatic, terrestrial,
and atmospheric environments. Representative titles include:

A conceptual model for the
movement of pesticides
through the environment,
no. 660/3-74-024
The fate of select pesticides
in the aquatic environment,
no. 660/3-74-025
Future dredging quantities in
the Great Lakes, no. 660/3-
74-029
Nutrient inactivation as a lake
restoration procedure--labo-
ratory investigations, no.
660/3-74-032.
For various reasons, this series is
prolific. Twenty to forty reports
are issued annually in lengths from
a few pages to a few hundred. If
space is available, and if the library supports rigorous environmental study, this series is recommended.

Item 431-I-12
EP1.23/2: ENVIRONMENTAL PROTECTION
AGENCY. Environmental protection technology.
Research performed to study
programs and systems of technology
that control and treat pollution
sources is published here. Methodology, instrumentation, and equipment are described. Occasionally
bibliographies and abstracts of the
literature are issued. Because environmental quality standards are
established by the government, federal agencies are obliged to support
research which will improve the
technology enabling the private sector to maintain these standards.
Representative studies include:
Demineralization of wastewater
by electrodialysis, no.
600/2-75-047
Scientific irrigation schedul-
ing for salinity control of
irrigation return flows, no.
600/2-75-064
Contributions of urban roadway
usage to water pollution, no.
600/2-75-004.
Like other EPA research series,
this one is prolific, forty to sixty
numbers a year. Length varies from
a few pages to a few hundred. If
space is available and the library

supports a rigorous environmental studies program, the series is recommended.

Item 431-I-19
EP1.23/3: ENVIRONMENTAL PROTECTION AGENCY. Socioeconomic environmental studies series.

Issues such as financial incentives and liabilities, finding a new land ethic by way of land-use planning, standards for quality of life, and the philosophy of resource allocation are broad concerns of this series. The socioeconomic impact of environmental problems also affects the legal system of the country, and consideration of it is found in some of these studies. Representative titles include:

> Environmental management in the Malibu watershed, no. 600/5-75-018
> Secondary impacts of transportation and wastewater investments, no. 600/5-75-013
> Used oil law in the United States and Europe, no. 600/5-74-025.

Six to eight titles are issued annually. The studies are technical and vary in length. Recommended for libraries supporting rigorous environmental studies interests.

Item 431-I-23
EP1.23/4: ENVIRONMENTAL PROTECTION AGENCY. Environmental health effects research.

Physiological and psychological studies are issued here. Toxicology and other medical specialities, including biomedical instrumentation and methodology are within the scope of the subjects dealt with. Most research is designed from a medical viewpoint and is directly concerned with human tolerances for unhealthy environments. Much of the research utilizes animals with application intended for human health. Representative titles include:

> Molybelenum--A toxicological approach, no. 600/1-75-004
> Health consequences of sulfur oxides, no. 650/1-74-004
> Bibliography of the cat, no. 600/1-76-007.

Four to six studies in varying lengths are issued annually. Where a degree of interest and specialization in biomedical topics exist, this series is recommended.

Item 431-I-24
EP1.23/5: ENVIRONMENTAL PROTECTION AGENCY. Environmental monitoring series.

The technology for the identification and quantification of pollutants in the environment at their lowest conceivable concentrations is the subject of research in this series. Developing new and improved methods of monitoring these pollutants is one of the responsibilities of EPA. Other research deals with the strength of pollutants as a function of time and atmospheric considerations. Representative titles include:

> Tritium fractionation in plants, no. 680/4-75-006
> Monitoring disposal-well systems, no. 680/4-75-008
> Handbook of radiochemical analytical methods, no. 680/4-75-001.

Ten to twenty titles are issued annually. Lengths vary. Recommended for libraries supporting environmental studies with strong emphasis on quantification.

Item 431-I-66
EP1.67: ENVIRONMENTAL PROTECTION AGENCY. EPA journal. v.1-Jan. 1975-

The journal is a monthly printed on recycled paper, and it includes about ten articles in each issue. Typically, articles focus on activities and concerns of the agency, its legislated responsibilities, and current developments. Recent articles cover such subjects as solid waste disposal, junk car recycling, and the changing seasons. New publications and other materials on the environment are noted. Individual issues are about 25 pages in length. The journal is designed for public use and is not highly technical. Recommended for all libraries.

Item 496-C
EP2.24: ENVIRONMENTAL PROTECTION
AGENCY. Fish kills caused by
pollution.

There are many kinds of environmental catastrophes, some of which
are discussed in publications issued
by this agency. Oil spills, emis-
sion violations, open burning, and
chemical pollutants are covered in
various EPA series, but these publications are usually highly technical. The average reader can easily
relate to and comprehend the fish-
kill annual. It is about 30 pages
in length, written in popular style,
and attractively designed. It consists of texts and tables to provide
information on pollution-causing operations and regional data. One or
two recent editions are adequate for
most libraries. Recommended for
public libraries.

Item 603-G
I1.98: DEPARTMENT OF THE INTERIOR.
Final environmental impact
statements.

Complete reports are issued
here of actions recommended by the
department. The publications are
several hundred pages in length and
are issued frequently. They follow
a regular format, beginning with a
detailed description of a proposal
(which is usually implicit in the
title), and proceed to describe the
environment affected, the environmental impact of the proposed action, a discussion of the relationship between local short-term use of
man's environment and the maintenance and enhancement of long-term
productivity, alternatives to the
action, and numerous tabular data.
In addition, dozens of groups and
organizations are consulted and a
summary of that correspondence is
included. The reports are not
highly technical and, for the most
part, are easily comprehended. They
appear incredibly thorough. Examples include:

Yukon-Kuskokwim National Forest,
no. Y9/2, a recommendation
that 7.3 million acres of
public lands be designated

as national forest by Congress

Proposed federal coal leasing
program, no. C63, a recommendation that the moratorium be
lifted and the Bureau of Land
Management resume coal leasing

Operation of the National Wildlife Refuge System, no. W64,
an examination of the continued operation of the system.

The activity, and therefore the
series, is new; in 1975, about eight
feet of shelf space were used by it.
It is bulky, but it can be of value
to any library supporting environmental and conservation interests.
Recommended for academic and public
libraries.

Item 834-R
NATIONAL OCEANIC AND ATMO-
SPHERIC ADMINISTRATION. OFFICE
OF ENVIRONMENTAL MONITORING AND
PREDICTION.
C55.27: Summary report; weather
modification. LC 74-642944
C55.27/2: Weather modification ac-
tivities report.

A summary of weather-
modification activities conducted in
the United States and other countries during a given year, the Summary Report is an annual of interest
to both the scientific and civic
communities. The effects of legislation on the activities and the
mathematical models in use are described. The scope of the report
is limited only by the modifications
engaged in and has recently included
discussions of fog dissipation, hail
suppression, cloud electricity, coordination of modification, and commercial enterprises.

All nonfederally sponsored
weather-modification activities must,
by law, be reported to the Secretary
of Commerce. Weather Modification
Activities Reports is a brief summary of all activities reported to
the Secretary of Commerce and the
National Oceanic and Atmospheric Administration during a given period

of time, usually several months.

The item is recommended for academic and public libraries supporting meteorological interests.

Item 856-E
PrEx14.2:  COUNCIL ON ENVIRONMENTAL
QUALITY. General publications.

Titles of both a technical and nontechnical nature fall into this series.  Broad subjects of environmental concern, such as land use, waste disposal, natural resources, and water supplies are within the scope of these publications, which are issued at a rate of about five a year.  Typical titles include:

The federal environmental monitoring directory, no. En8/3
Energy in solid waste, no. En2/2
The Delaware River basin, no. D37
Fluorocarbons and the environment, no. F67
Ocean dumping: A national policy, no. Oc2
MERES and the evaluation of energy alternatives, no. M42.

Reports are prepared in the interest of the Department of Housing and Urban Development as well as the Environmental Protection Agency in some cases.  These titles should be compared with those titles available through HUD and EPA.  Recommended for academic and public libraries.

Item 856-E-1
PrEx14.1:  COUNCIL ON ENVIRONMENTAL
QUALITY. Annual report.

Required by the National Environmental Policy Act of 1969, this is a report on the state of the environment and efforts made to improve it.  The volume is comprehensive and contains an index and appendixes.  Subjects of major concern are land use, perspectives on the environment, legislation, international efforts, and major studies undertaken by CEQ.  The Annual Report is essential to the individual's understanding of the federal role in concern for the environment.  Recommended for academic and public libraries.

Item 1061-C
PrEx14.9:  Pesticides monitoring
journal.  v.1-   1967-
Y3.F31/18:  FEDERAL COMMITTEE ON
PEST CONTROL.  Reports and publications.

Technical articles of 3 to 10 pages each compose the quarterly, Pesticides monitoring journal.  It is issued by the Environmental Protection Agency and the Council on Environmental Quality.  Contributors, from both government and independent institutions, are all professionals in the field.  Categories of research published are pesticides in people and water, and residues in food, feed, fish, and wildlife.  Articles include abstracts, bibliography, figures, tables, and charts.  Each issue includes an appendix, "Chemical names of compounds discussed in this issue."  Representatives from the range of federal agencies concerned with pesticides in humans and the environment sponsor the publication and form the advisory groups for it.  While nonscientists will find much of the material too technical, they will be stimulated by the research.  Citizens have a responsibility to know about the effects of pesticides, and most of that data are necessarily technical.  A back file is desirable for some libraries.

The Federal Committee on Pest Control has not issued any publications lately.

The item is recommended for academic and public libraries.

Item 552-A
GP3.22/2: SUPERINTENDENT OF DOCU-
MENTS. Subject bibliographies.
These 4- to 10-page bibliographies are issued eight or ten times
a month, each on a subject of value
to librarians and patrons. The series was added in 1975 and serves,
in a sense, as an advertising service for the Public Documents Division. The bibliography is in itself
an order form and includes shipping
labels. Bibliographic data, the
SuDoc classification, and price are
included for each entry. These publications correspond roughly to the
former Price Lists (GP3.9, item 554),
which have been discontinued. Entries are not annotated and subjects
do not necessarily conform to an issuing agency. For example, a recent
bibliography, National defense and
security, no. 153, included titles
from the Departments of Defense,
State, and Interior; Arms Control
and Disarmament Agency; National
Science Foundation, and from various committees. Other subjects are
Poetry and literature, no. 142; Foreign trade and tariff, no. 123; Marketing research, no. 125; Political
activities, no. 136; and Sanitation
and sewage, no. 134. Bibliographies
are not yet being revised but should
be as the series continues. Decisions about retention should be made
on the basis of timeliness and reliability. Recommended for academic
and public libraries.

Item 552-B
GP3.22/3: SUPERINTENDENT OF DOCU-
MENTS. Publications reference

file in microfiche (48x).
Feb. 23, 1977-
Three sections of microfiche
provide numerous points of access
to the bibliographic tool which con-
stitutes the GPO's books in print
or documents in stock. One section
is arranged by stock number, a second by SuDoc number and the third is
a dictionary index by subject, title,
author, keyword, key phrase, and series. Each entry includes the data
mentioned above, the price, and
other basic bibliographic information. The file is issued monthly,
completely updated. The PRF user's
manual, a pamphlet, accompanies the
microfiche file. The Publications
Reference File also serves as a cataloging tool for individual document
titles. Recommended for academic
and public libraries.

Item 553
GP3.7/2: SUPERINTENDENT OF DOCU-
MENTS. Numerical lists and
schedule of volumes of the reports and documents of the 73d-
Congress ...1933/34-  LC 34-
28260
U.S. Senate and House Reports
and Documents are assigned an individual number for the session of
Congress in which they occur, and
are cumulated into bound volumes and
assigned a serial number to become a
part of the Serial Set. If one
knows the individual report or document number, then he or she can look
in the Numerical lists to determine
the serial number of the bound volume. In addition, the Schedule of
volumes lists the individual reports

and documents in each volume. An important feature for documents librarians is a section which lists documents that are printed as both congressional documents and departmental documents. These documents are distributed to depository libraries in the original departmental edition and not as a part of the Serial Set. Librarians should note this in order to account for outstanding volumes of the Serial Set.

The publication is issued for each session of Congress and is essential for use of the Serial Set. It has permanent reference value and is useful for tracking down specific interlibrary loan information even if a library does not hold the Serial Set. Recommended for academic and public libraries.

Item 554
GP3.9:  SUPERINTENDENT OF DOCUMENTS.
    Price lists.

Periodicals currently sold on subscription by the Government Printing Office are described in the quarterly Price List known as Government periodicals and subscriptions service, no. 36. Organization is alphabetical by title and includes a brief annotation, general ordering and remittance information. The Price List provides access to the subscription service of the GPO, as well as the option of a number of standing orders.

Price Lists for other subjects are no longer issued. Subject Bibliographies (GP3.22/2, item 552-A) have assumed some of this responsibility.

Recommended for academic and public libraries.

Item 556
GP3.17:  SUPERINTENDENT OF DOCUMENTS.
    Selected United States government publications. July 1, 1928-

This publication changes frequency from time to time. At present it is a monthly published in pamphlet form. Recently issued publications of general interest or popular appeal are annotated. Basic bibliographic and order information is provided. Some marketing techniques are apparently employed, as certain new titles are spotlighted by photograph or illustration. This title is one of the few publications in the documents system which resembles a commercial catalog of publications. Librarians make considerable use of it in selection of federal publications for purchase; patrons may also want to order from it. Two years of back files may be desirable. Recommended for all libraries.

Item 557
GP3.8:  SUPERINTENDENT OF DOCUMENTS.
    Monthly catalog of United
    States government publications.
    No. 1-   Jan. 1895-   LC 4-18088

The Monthly catalog is the basic aid for locating documents distributed by the Government Printing Office. It is a monthly bibliography, organized by agency and indexed by subject, author, title and series/report. Until 1977, the February issue contained a list of all periodicals and subscription documents. Beginning 1977, a serials supplement is issued annually to replace the list of periodicals previously found in the February issue. The September issue contains the list of designated depository libraries, and the December issue, a cumulative index for the calendar year.

The Monthly catalog changed its format with the July 1976 issue to reflect the following changes at GPO:  joining the Ohio College Library Center's (OCLC) on-line cataloging network, converting to the Machine Readable Cataloging (MARC) format, and adopting Anglo-American rules for cataloging. These changes represent a landmark in the production of the Monthly catalog and its service to all libraries. The Monthly catalog now purports to be an evolving publication. It is important that librarians observe and respond to the changes. Recommended for all libraries.

Item 803-B
LC3.11: COPYRIGHT OFFICE. Compendium of Copyright Office practices. LC 75-612129
This reference title is made available to the public pursuant to the Freedom of Information Act. The Compendium has been available in the Copyright Office for inspection and copying, but it was not published and distributed through GPO until 1970. Additional portions, amendments, and supplements continue to be issued. The Compendium is a general guide to office practices and is not a book of rules or regulations. It does not cover every situation but offers precedents, and therefore may be of interest to the public. The volume is indexed. Recommended for libraries serving a clientele which might require this kind of copyright information.

Item 806-B
LC2.8: LIBRARY OF CONGRESS. GENERAL REFERENCE AND BIBLIOGRAPHY DIVISION. Handbooks, manuals, guides.
These titles have a tendency to be obscure bibliography, yet the need for them may arise. The following are recent:
French-Speaking Central Africa: A guide to official publications in American libraries, no. Af8/3
Spanish-Speaking Africa: A guide to official publications, no. Af8/4.
Librarians with opportunities for searching out locations of government publications of other countries may welcome these. Recommended for academic libraries.

Item 806-C
LC2.2: LIBRARY OF CONGRESS. GENERAL REFERENCE AND BIBLIOGRAPHY DIVISION. General publications.
Little activity in this series can be found in the last few years, but the series is notable for the serious reference materials found among its titles in the past. The following are examples:
Louisa May Alcott: An annotated

selected bibliography, no. AC1/2
Africa south of the Sahara: A selected, annotated list of writings, 1951-56, no. Af8
Creating independence, 1763-1789, no. In2/5/763-89
Archive of recorded poetry and literature: A checklist, no. P75/5.
The series functions to serve bibliographic and reference needs. Librarians should note the future publications from this division. Recommended for academic and larger public libraries.

Item 806-F
LC24.7: LIBRARY OF CONGRESS. LATIN AMERICAN, PORTUGUESE, AND SPANISH DIVISION. Bibliographical series.
Titles are issued infrequently from this series but they are useful reference titles in libraries where Latin American cultural interests are served. A recent example is Latin America, Spain, and Portugal: An annotated bibliography of paperback books, no. 13. Recommended for academic and public libraries.

Item 807
LC14.6: LIBRARY OF CONGRESS. CONGRESSIONAL RESEARCH SERVICE. Digest of public general bills and resolutions. 74th- Congress; 1936- LC 36-26093
The principal function of the Digest is to summarize public bills and resolutions and the changes they pass through during the process of legislation. Committee action, floor action, and passage in one or both chambers are documented. Indexes are included for sponsors, subjects, titles, and identical bills. The Digest is issued in a series of cumulative issues with supplements and eventually in a final issue for each session of Congress. The Congressional Research Service claims to be functioning exclusively for the legislative branch, but it is providing a valuable service for library patrons as

well. The Digest is also useful in locating numbers and names of bills, and numbers of public laws before going to other sources. Recommended for all libraries collecting legislative publications.

Item 816
LC30.9: LIBRARY OF CONGRESS. PROCESSING DEPARTMENT. Monthly checklist of state publications. v.1-  1910-  LC 10-8924
State documents published in the last five years and received by the Library of Congress are recorded here. Individual titles are listed by state of issuance and are assigned numbers. Complete bibliographic information, price, issuing agency, and Library of Congress card number are included as available. Compilation of the Monthly checklist depends upon the cooperation of state agencies which are responsible for sending copies of all their publications to the Library of Congress. An annual index follows the monthly issues. Periodicals are listed in the June and December issues. The checklist is an important bibliographic tool even for libraries not maintaining collections of state publications. For some states it is the most complete listing of the particular state's publications. Recommended for academic and larger public libraries.

Item 818-B
LC29.2: LIBRARY OF CONGRESS. REFERENCE DEPARTMENT. General publications.

Few titles in this group have appeared in recent years. The series was prolific, however, in the 1950s and 1960s, and titles were useful. They have typically been annotated bibliographies prepared by LC librarians about a subject or an idea. There have also been general guides to libraries and library facilities. This series has potential as valuable reference works. It should be noted by or subscribed to by academic and public libraries.

Item 823-A
LC18.2: LIBRARY OF CONGRESS. UNION CATALOG DIVISION. General publications.
Few titles are being issued in this series at present. However, one of significant reference value should be noted. Newspapers on microfilm, no. N47/2, is issued about every ten years. It is an attempt to list locations of positives and negatives of microfilms of newspapers known to exist by the Microfilming Clearing House of the Library of Congress. Organized by states and countries of newspaper publication, the listing is particularly useful for determining a United States library location of a foreign or a domestic newspaper microfilm for an interlibrary loan request. The most recent edition is adequate. Other reference tools are potentials for publication by the Union Catalog Division.
The item is recommended for academic and larger public libraries.

Item 188-A-1
    NATIONAL TECHNICAL INFORMATION
    SERVICE
C51.11:  Bibliographies and lists of
    publications.
C51.11/3:  Selected reports.
    Occasionally publications lists
call attention to special subjects
or categories of NTIS data and research:
    1970 census of population micro-
        fiche, no. P81
    NTIS special interest publica-
        tions, no. P96
    Information about new techno-
        logical developments in 25
        major subject categories,
        no. T22.
One or two may be issued annually.
    Selected Reports are monthly
bibliographies of NTIS titles varying in subject with each issue.  Recent monthly reports have been:
Bridge the gap, NTIS will improve
your bottom line, Take a monumental
tour through technology with NTIS,
and Two hundred years of progress
thru ...technology.  Issues are
about 16 pages in length.
    The item is recommended for ac-
ademic and public libraries.

Item 238
C13.1:  NATIONAL BUREAU OF STANDARDS.
    Annual report.  1901/02-
    LC 6-23979
    Technological advancement is
possible only when adequate measurement is available.  Technological
progress in this country has been
possible because the National Bureau of Standards has been success-
ful in determining and maintaining
these measurements and in establishing cooperation with government
agencies and private institutions in
the creation of standard practices.
These and other activities are described and presented graphically
in the reports, which average about
30 pages in length.  While not an
essential to any collection, it is
an interesting annual report to
popular and professional scientists.
Recommended for academic and public
libraries.

Item 244
C13.2:  NATIONAL BUREAU OF STANDARDS.
    General publications.
    The work of the bureau is for
public benefit; some of the applications of the work are reflected
in this series of printed materials.
Representative titles include:
    NBS film catalog, no. F48
    Ways to reduce fuel consumption
        in household heating, no. F95
    National Bureau of Standards at
        a glance, no. N21/7
    A directory of standards labo-
        ratories, no. St2/2.
Four or five titles are issued annually.  Some titles are of an administrative nature, but most are relevant to general interests.  Recommended for academic and public libraries.

Item 250
C13.13:  Dimensions.
    The goal of advancing science
and technology and promoting their
effective application for the pub-

lic's benefit is furthered by this monthly periodical. Dimensions reports in a technical, but easily comprehensible style, the results of the National Bureau of Standards research in energy conservation, fire safety, computer applications, environmental protection, materials utilization, consumer product performance and other areas of national concern.

An attractive publication averaging about 30 pages monthly, it has featured recent articles on smoke detectors, preserving historic adobe architecture, and dentistry research. Monthly columns note conferences, news, and publications. The monthly is an important chronicle of federal research in response to national concerns. Recommended for academic and public libraries.

Item 254
C21.2:  PATENT OFFICE.  General publications.

The laws and regulations governing the issuance of patents and trademarks are not formally a part of this series, but the general information necessary for obtaining a patent is available here.  These are typical titles:
   General information concerning patents, no. P27
   Q and A about trademarks, no. T67/2
   Patents and inventions:  An information aid for inventors, no. P27/10
   Engineers, scientists, no. En3.
Other titles describe the agency and its operation.  Two or three publications are issued annually.  Recommended for academic and public libraries.

Item 271
C51.2:  NATIONAL TECHNICAL INFORMATION SERVICE.  General publications.

This agency of the Department of Commerce is the central facility for the dissemination of government-contracted research.  Documents and microfiche of government-contracted research are for sale through the

NTIS within weeks of their release. Much of the research is too technical for the interests of the audience in question, but the General Publications explain the scope of the National Technical Information Service.  Recent examples include:
   NTIS information services, no. N21T
   NTIS goes to college, no. C68
   City games, no. C49/2, an operational simulation game.
Three or four titles are issued annually.  Recommended for academic and public libraries.

Item 818-A
LC33.2:  LIBRARY OF CONGRESS. SCIENCE AND TECHNOLOGY DIVISION.  General publications.

In earlier years this series produced a number of good titles but it has not been active of late. Typically it published works relating to scientific bibliography. Lists of serials in translation, serial locations around the world, or serials in LC were also issued regularly.  Librarians should continue to observe this series because it is likely to continue to produce good reference titles.  Recommended for academic and larger public libraries.

Item 834-B
NS1.1:  NATIONAL SCIENCE FOUNDATION. Annual report.  1st-   1950/51- LC 52-60336

Written and organized in somewhat the same style as Smithsonian year (SI1.1, item 909), this annual is good reading for the grant writer or taxpayer interested in science programs.  National and international programs are described by purpose and subject matter.  Appendixes include publications of the current year, names of members of advisory panels, and criteria for the selection of research projects.  A short back file is adequate.  Recommended for academic and public libraries.

Item 834-C
NS1.2:  NATIONAL SCIENCE FOUNDATION. General publications.

The most noticeable title in this series is the multivolume Initial reports of the Deep Sea Drilling Project, no. D36/2, which continues to report data collected by the University of California in the Atlantic and Pacific oceans. It is of interest to oceanography and marine geology programs. Other publications tend to be reports of NSF contracts, projects supported, and conference and symposia proceedings. Typical titles include:

Young and senior science faculty and engineering faculty, 1974: Support, research participation, and tenure, no. F11

A technology assessment of geothermal energy resource development, no. G29/2

Perspectives on ocean policy, no. Oc2/3

Course and curriculum improvement projects, no. C83.

Four to eight titles are issued a year. Length and format vary. Recommended for academic libraries and for public libraries supporting the scientific community.

Item 834-F-1
NS1.29: Mosaic. v.1- 1970-

Published six times a year by the National Science Foundation, the journal is a source of communication between scientific and educational communities and the NSF. Other articles are about administration of research and participants in research, and science students and facilities. Some issues are thematic, all the articles relate to a subject of broad interest, such as the recent ones of food and the social sciences. Recommended for academic libraries and for public libraries supporting the scientific community.

Item 834-H
NS1.13: NATIONAL SCIENCE FOUNDATION. Bibliographies and lists of publications.

These are issued periodically to include annual reports, descriptive brochures, announcements, science resource studies, special studies, and periodicals of the agency. Basic bibliographic and ordering detail accompanies the titles. Recommended for academic and public libraries as a reference aid for bibliographic control.

Item 834-P
NS1.20: NATIONAL SCIENCE FOUNDATION. Handbooks, manuals, guides.

Persons who write proposals for funding or who are in contact with NSF probably receive this information directly. However, persons in the planning stage of a grant request may find these titles valuable. They are essentially guides to programs:

Guidelines for preparation of unsolicited proposals to research applied to national needs, no. R31

Guide for preparation ...instructional scientific equipment program, no. I68

Guide for preparation ... student-oriented programs, no. S32

Guide to programs, no. P94.

Most are only useful for the current year and should be discarded later. Recommended for academic and public libraries.

Item 834-T
NS1.22: NATIONAL SCIENCE FOUNDATION. Surveys of science resources series.

Reports of varied scientific activities and various characteristics of the scientific community make up this series. Studies look at graduate science education, the national origin of scientists, various analyses of funding, research occurring in state agencies, and research activities at independent nonprofit institutions. These surveys consider a multitude of variables and generate annual data, so that several of the series are issued annually or biennially. The data provide a good reference source. Five or six titles are issued annually. Recommended for academic and larger public libraries.

Item 1061-B
Y3.F31/16:   FEDERAL COUNCIL FOR
     SCIENCE AND TECHNOLOGY.  Re-
     ports and publications.
     The work of the council is to
coordinate activities among federal
agencies in the area of science and
technology.  The council seeks
closer cooperation and improved
planning and management.  Its publications are not of broad appeal but
will be of interest to the scientific community.  Recent examples:

Marine research, no. 2M33/2
The possible impact of fluoro-
     carbons and halocarbons on
     ozone, no. 12/18a
Directory of federal technology
     transfer, no. 2F31
Intergovernmental use of fed-
     eral R and D laboratories,
     no. 2L11.
Most are technical papers or re-
search bibliographies.  Two or three
are issued a year.  Recommended for
academic libraries.

## GEOGRAPHY

Item 811-A
LC5.2:   LIBRARY OF CONGRESS.  GEOG-
     RAPHY AND MAP DIVISION.  Gen-
     eral publications.
     Titles in this series are in-
frequent but of interest.  They are
compiled by persons working in the
division but are sometimes about
subjects or materials located elsewhere.  These publications are usually paperbound and under 100 pages
in length.  Although they may include copies of a few maps, these
titles are generally lists of maps.
Recent examples include:
     Facsimiles of rare historical
          maps:  A list of reproduc-
          tions for sale by various
          distributors, no. H62/3
     Railroad maps of the United
          States, no. R13
     Guide to the history of cartog-
          raphy, no. H62/2.
Recommended for academic and public
libraries.

Item 856-A-1
PrEx3.10/4:   CENTRAL INTELLIGENCE
     AGENCY.  Maps and atlases.
     This series includes a variety

of map materials.  Thematic atlases,
such as USSR agriculture atlas, no.
Un3/2, and Issues in the Middle East,
no. M58/1, are good sources for
teaching aids and general knowledge.
They approach standard atlas size
and contain features comparable to
commercial atlases.  For several
areas of the world, the CIA has access to more geographical data than
are readily available to nongovern-
mental firms, and it is therefore in
a more authoritative position for
publishing atlases.  The People's
Republic of China atlas, no. C44/3,
is an example.  In addition to con-
ventional data, it includes economic,
historical, and cultural data.  Relief maps of individual countries
are issued also.  They include geographical data on population, economic activity, and land utilization.
Recommended for academic and public
libraries.

Item 876-A
S1.119/2:   DEPARTMENT OF STATE.
     Geographic bulletins.
     Various geographical reports of
political units and regional divi-

sions of the world have been issued in this series in the last ten years. The most current and potentially useful reference title to date is Status of the world's nations, no. W89, which is issued regularly to report the nomenclature used by the U.S. government for nations of the world. Since 1943 the number of independent nations has more than doubled and some have changed their names. Unsettled international situations cause names to be in a continuing state of flux. The bulletins list nations, dependencies, and areas of special sovereignty, including their United Nations affiliations, sovereignty, capital, population, and area. A chronological checklist of nations that have become independent since 1943 and a wall-size map are also included. Recommended for academic and public libraries.

## GOVERNMENT AND INTERNATIONAL RELATIONS

Item 125-A-3
AC1.2: ARMS CONTROL AND DISARMAMENT
    AGENCY. General publications.
    These pamphlets are a particularly useful group for libraries with no reason to have a comprehensive collection of original documents. Most make an effort to impart to the public general information about some phase of the agency's activity. Examples include:
    Test Ban Treaty: Questions and
        answers, no. 18
    Arms control achievements, 1959-
        1971, no. AC41959-71
    Salt lexicon, no. Sa3.
Copies of agreements also occur periodically, such as the recent Arms control and disarmament agreements, 1959-1972, no. Ar5/3/959-972, and Arms control and disarmament agreements: Texts and history of negotiations, no. Ar5/3/975. The titles appear at a rate of two to three a year and are recommended for academic and public libraries.

Item 327-J
D101.22:880-nos. DEPARTMENT OF THE
    ARMY. Area handbooks.
    These handbooks are prepared for military personnel by Foreign Area Studies of the American University. However, because they contain social, economic, and political information of interest to the average citizen, they are recommended library additions. They contain maps, extensive bibliography, and an index, and are several hundred pages in length. At present about one hundred countries are each covered by a handbook. The handbooks are revised periodically, and old ones may be discarded.
    Also in the Area Handbook series are bibliographic surveys of literature about strategically significant nations of the world. Recent publications are Communist Eastern Europe, no. 550-8, Africa, no. 550-17, and Latin America and the Caribbean, no. 550-7-1. Organization is by subject and country; entries are annotated. The bibliographies contain extensive maps and are a few hundred pages in length.
    Both the bibliographies and the handbooks contain information about military installations, but it is not the emphasis. These publications purportedly do not attempt to

affect policy nor to express a particular point of view. Recommended for academic and public libraries.

Item 577
GS4.109: United States government manual. 1935-   LC 35-26025
The official handbook of the federal government, the manual describes purposes, function, and legal bases for most government agencies. Of note to librarians and the interested public is the section which accompanies the descriptions of many agencies, called "Sources of information." In this section one can usually find program information, addresses for information on employment, contracts, speakers, films, and publications. The manual formerly included more detail about the publishing programs of agencies but now more often lists only the sources of publications. It is the key to the comings and goings of agencies, commissions, organizations, and their respective personnel. It is revised annually and is useful historically in a larger collection. For many libraries, the current and previous two or three years are adequate. Recommended for academic and public libraries.

Item 577-A
GS4.114: Weekly compilation of presidential documents. v.1-
Aug. 2, 1965-   LC 65-9929
Presidential materials released by the White House during the preceding week are published every Monday in this compilation. The document includes addresses and remarks, appointments and nominations, press releases, communications to Congress, executive orders, letters, memoranda, meetings with foreign leaders, resignations and retirements, and various other statements. Weekly, quarterly, and annual indexes are produced; the cumulation continues with each issue. The publication contains important primary source materials for general information and undergraduate research. This weekly is the source material for the Public papers of presidents of United States (GS4.113, item 574-A), and need not be retained after the receipt of that annual volume. However, the Public papers are edited, and decisions about the disposition of the Weekly compilation should be made with this in mind. Recommended for academic and public libraries.

Item 666
I35.2: OFFICE OF TERRITORIES. General publications.
Information about the territories of the United States is issued here. One title issued periodically is Territorial areas administered by the United States, no. T27/2, which is a useful reference. Other titles are infrequent but usually focus on the territorial responsibilities of the department. Recommended for academic and public libraries.

Item 672-C
IA1.8: Problems of Communism.  v.1-
1952-   LC 54-61675
Published six times a year, the periodical treats world communism by providing analyses and background information. Contributors are persons both in and out of government. Their writing reflects a range of opinion. Each issue contains a few lengthy articles including such recent titles as "The challenge of Eurocommunism," "Soviet counter-imperialism," and "The shifting sands of Arab communism." About one third of each issue is devoted to book reviews. Photographs and documentation are used as necessary to provide an attractive publication. Issues are 60 to 90 pages each. Some curricular and community interests demand back files. Recommended for academic and public libraries.

Item 725
J21.2: IMMIGRATION AND NATURALIZATION SERVICE. General publications.
Titles here vary from being of use to the border patrol to persons entering the country. In either case, knowledge of the operation increases the mobility and security of citizens and visitors. Typical

titles include:
> To visitors entering the United
> States, no. V82
> Naturalization requirements and
> general information, no. N21/4
> A practical Spanish grammar for
> border patrol officials, no.
> Sp2.

Titles are revised as necessary.
They vary in length and format but
tend to be pamphlets. One or two
are issued annually. Recommended
for public libraries.

Item 850
Pr39.2: PRESIDENT. General publications.

Probably the most important
reason for maintaining this series
is its historical value. (The Special Commissions and Committees publications, item 851-J, are more
useful currently.) The general publications contain a variety of materials which are pertinent and sometimes sensitive to the administration in which they occur. Their
presence in a collection will probably be more meaningful historically
than at present. The following
titles are examples:
> Why Vietnam, no. Pr36.2:V67,
> from the Johnson administra-
> tion
> Federal executive branch review
> of the recommendations of the
> 1971 White House Conference
> on Youth, no. Pr37.2:W58/971
> The Conference on Inflation, no.
> Pr38.2:In2, from the Ford ad-
> ministration.

Four to twenty are issued in
each administration, and the classification number changes, as does
that for item 851-J. (See item
851-J for an explanation of the
classification number.) Inaugura-
tion programs, messages to Congress,
task force reports, and various
other presidential reports are included here. Recommended for academic and public libraries.

Item 851-J
Pr39.8: PRESIDENT. Special commissions and committees.

From this series have come a
number of well-known reports from
commissions appointed by the president to study a particular situation
of importance to the nation. Lesser-
known commissions are sometimes appointed, and their reports, while
attracting less attention, are present here. The following are the reports from commission investigations
over the past fifteen years, some of
which are familiar:
> Report of President's Commis-
> sion on Assassination of
> President John F. Kennedy,
> no. Pr36.8:K38/R29
> Report of the President's Com-
> mission on Campus Unrest,
> no. Pr37.8:C15/R29
> Council on International Econ-
> omic Policy: Special report:
> Critical imported materials,
> no. Pr37.8:In8
> Report to the president by the
> Commission on CIA activities
> within the United States,
> no. Pr38.8:C33/C33.

The classification number
changes with each president. Pr is
followed by the number corresponding
to the ordinal number of succession
to the presidency. Pr37 is Nixon;
Pr38, Ford; Pr39, Carter.

Those reports of historical
significance should be retained in-
definitely; others will have little
long-term reference value. Recommended for academic and public libraries.

Item 853
PrEx2.8: OFFICE OF MANAGEMENT
AND BUDGET. Budget of the
United States government. 1971/
72-   LC 70-611049

The Budget contains most of the
fiscal information which users ordi-
narily need. The material is textual as well as tabular, describing
program costs by function and by
agency and account. These various
budgets are listed for the year in
question and for the two previous
years to offer comparison. This
feature generally eliminates the
need for keeping a back file unless
extensive use is being made of budget data.

Accompanying the Budget under this item is the Budget of the United States government: Appendix, no. PrEx2.8/app. It is a large volume of detailed information on the budget of each agency, including individual program accounts. While this volume contains very interesting data and an important record, it is not essential to most research.

The Budget is recommended for larger libraries. United States budget in brief, PrEx2.8/2, item 855-A, is an alternative for others.

Item 855-A
OFFICE OF MANAGEMENT AND BUDGET.
PrEx2.8/2:  United States budget in brief.
PrEx2.8/6:  Budget highlights.
Smaller libraries are well-served by a concise summary of the Budget of the United States government (PrEx2.8, item 853) issued here as United States budget in brief. It includes a variety of tables and a discussion of the federal program by function. Summaries and some historical data are provided by the tables and may eliminate some need for back files. However, because of the limited material included, five years of back files seem reasonable for the sake of comparison.

Budget highlights consists of charts and tables. This title has not been distributed for several years and is not essential to the libraries under discussion.

Item 856-B-2
PrEx15.9:  PRESIDENT. Report on national growth and development. 1972-   LC 72-621794
Among the functions of the Domestic Council is assessing national needs and priorities. The council makes recommendations to the president on such matters and maintains a continuous review of ongoing programs. It follows then that this biennial report is in the purview of the council as it focuses on the effects of growth and development on the quality of life in this country. The Report, required by the Housing and Urban Development

Act of 1970, assumes certain premises which may represent the position of the federal government but are not necessarily accepted throughout the country. One such premise is that the quality of life depends upon sustained economic growth and increased productivity. At any rate, the Report is a summary of the influence of the federal, state, and local governments on the factors affecting the quality of life of Americans. At the present time, the reports are interrelated and it may be wise to hold about ten years of them. Recommended for academic and public libraries.

Item 862-A
S1.116:  DEPARTMENT OF STATE. African series.
Some of these materials may appear in other State Department series, but libraries supporting interests in area studies will find the consolidation useful. One or two titles are issued annually on current issues and foreign policy in Africa. They are extremely important to the fields of current events and to international relations, and are written to appeal to a broad audience. Recent titles include:

Drought damage and famine in Sub-Sahara, no. 58
A look at African issues at the United Nations, no. 50
Southern Rhodesia: The question of economic sanctions, no. 55
The U.S. role in African development, no. 52.
Formats vary; all are generally under 50 pages. Recommended for academic and public libraries.

Item 862-B
S1.123:  DEPARTMENT OF STATE. OFFICE OF MEDIA SERVICES. Background notes. 1965-
LC 66-61561
Eight-page leaflets serve the important function of providing brief and current information about countries throughout the world. Each country is introduced by a pro-

file: data on geography, people, government, and the economy. This material is followed by a textual discussion of the same subjects. A map, reading list, and travel information are included, as is a concluding discussion of the country's relations with the U.S. and other foreign states. Leaflets can be arranged alphabetically and stored in loose-leaf binders. Superseded issues should be discarded when a revision is issued. The series serves as a useful reference tool and may be an alternative to expensive commercial handbooks. The Index, S1.123/2, lists Background Notes currently available and is issued from this item number.

The item is recommended for academic and public libraries.

Item 864
S1.3: DEPARTMENT OF STATE. Department of State bulletin. v.1-July 1, 1939-   LC 39-26945
Called the official weekly report of U.S. foreign policy, the publication includes statements, addresses, and news conferences of the Secretary of State and the president, and press releases from the department. A typical issue includes an interview with the president by several European correspondents, the transcript of the secretary's news conference of the previous week, press releases concerning the secretary's trip to Vienna and other European spots, the president's exchange of toasts with the Shah of Iran at a White House dinner, and various other statements. Articles on foreign affairs also occur, as does a regular section "Current actions," listing the status of various agreements and conventions. Publications of the U.S. government and of the United Nations relating to foreign policy are noted. The weeklies average about 40 pages and are individually indexed. Recommended for all libraries.

Item 865
S1.8: DEPARTMENT OF STATE. Diplomatic list. LC 10-16292
This quarterly directory of foreign diplomatic officials living in Washington is organized by country and includes the residential address and phone number of each person. Address and phone number of the embassy and the national holiday are listed. This list begins with an "order of precedence" in which ambassadors are listed in the order of the date they assumed the post, along with that date. Retention of the current year's list is adequate. Recommended for libraries with a need for information about Washington's foreign diplomats.

Item 870
S1.38: DEPARTMENT OF STATE. East Asian and Pacific series.
Some of these materials may appear in other State Department series, but libraries supporting interests in area studies will find the consolidation useful. One or two titles on current issues and foreign policy in East Asia and the Pacific are issued annually. Written in a style to appeal to a broad audience, they are important to interests in current events and international relations. Recent titles include:

> People's Republic of China: Issues in United States foreign policy, no. 206
> The prisoners of war in Southeast Asia, no. 197
> The United States and Japan, no. 210
> U.S. trade prospects with the P.R.C.: A realistic assessment, no. 207.

Formats vary; most are under 50 pages. Recommended for academic and public libraries.

Item 872
S1.1:, S1.1/2:, S1.1/3:  DEPARTMENT OF STATE. Foreign relations of the United States. Diplomatic papers. 1861-  LC 10-3793

This series is essentially an annual survey of U.S. foreign relations including texts of some major diplomatic papers. Multivolume sets exist for war years. The annuals are published about twenty-five years after the issuance of the documents, and when the 1960s are published, annual editions will undoubtedly grow into more volumes because of the increasing role of the United States in world affairs. The 1948 papers fill nine volumes, one each for the United Nations, Germany and Austria, Western Europe, Eastern Europe, Western Hemisphere, and four volumes for the Far East. An older but notable title is Peace and war: United States foreign policy, 1931-41, no. S1.1/2:P31/8.

This series is an important chronicle of U.S. history and should be retained. Recommended for academic and larger public libraries.

Item 875
S1.71:  DEPARTMENT OF STATE.  General foreign policy series.

Recurring subseries are contained here. United States foreign policy: A report of the Secretary of State, the secretary's annual report to Congress, is a lengthy volume covering security and prosperity, social and scientific dimensions of the entire world, and serves as a foreign policy record of the year. Reprints from the Department of State bulletin, S1.3, item 864, are appended. The Battle Act Report is an annual report of the Mutual Defense Assistance Control Act of 1951. Youth travel abroad: What to know before you go is an annual pamphlet of useful information about one's relationship to, and benefit from, the State Department while abroad.

Other publications include reprints of articles from the State Department bulletin, and reprints of speeches or official statements by presidents and secretaries of state. The well-known American foreign policy, 1950-55: Basic documents, no. 117, is one of this series. Major publications of the Department of State, no. 200, is a useful annotated bibliography. Six to ten titles are issued annually. Recommended for academic and public libraries.

Item 876
S1.2:  DEPARTMENT OF STATE.  General publications.

Libraries selecting this series will find in it a number of titles which have limited, if any, use to their patrons. However, approximately half of them appear to serve libraries under consideration rather well. Examples of useful titles are
    Visa requirements of foreign governments, no. V82/2
    You and your passport, no. P26/29
    University centers of foreign affairs research: A directory, no. Un3
    Government resources available for foreign affairs research, no. F76a/4.
Occasional career guidance materials are available:
    Communications and records assistants and communications technicians, assignment: Worldwide, no. C73/6
    Assignment worldwide: Foreign service secretaries, no. Se2/2.
Publications varying from leaflets to volumes of a few hundred pages accumulate at a rate of six to twelve a year. Recommended for libraries serving patrons with general interest in U.S. affairs abroad or persons with plans for traveling, working, or studying abroad.

Item 877
S1.26:  DEPARTMENT OF STATE.  Inter-American series.

This series is a bit more active than the other regional foreign policy series issued by the State Department, perhaps reflecting greater emphasis on relations with nations to the south and north of the United States. Four or five titles are issued annually on subjects of foreign policy, current events, historical study, and cul-

tural interest.  Recent titles:
Latin America and the Trade
Act of 1974, no. 108
The Inter-American relationship, no. 107
The Andean integration movement, no. 102
U.S. policy toward Panama,
no. 106.
They vary from leaflets to 100-page
reports and are written in popular
style.  Much of this material is vital to the understanding of inter-
American relations.  Recommended for
academic and public libraries.

Item 883-A
S1.86/2:  DEPARTMENT OF STATE.  Near
East and South Asian series.
The unsettled political situa-
tion in the Persian Gulf and Arabian
Peninsula as well as the continuing
economic and resource control which
the area maintains on the rest of
the world mean that these titles are
essential to a library's information
resources.  Four or five titles are
issued annually in varying formats.
These are representative:
India, Pakistan, and Bangladesh:
Issues in United States for-
eign policy, no. 1
U.S. policy in the Middle East,
December 1973-November 1974,
no. 84
Current policy:  Persian Gulf/
Arabian Peninsula, no. 85.
Recommended for academic and public
libraries.

Item 899
S9.10:  DEPARTMENT OF STATE.  Treaties and other international
act series (TIAS).  1501-
1946-
The first published form of a
treaty, agreement, or convention between the United States and one or
more international bodies is issued
in a paper copy corresponding in
format to the Supreme Court slip
opinions, Ju6.8/b, item 740-A.  The
treaties are cumulated annually and
published in the bound volume
United States treaties and other international agreements, S9.12, item
899-A.  These paper copies may be

discarded when the bound volume is
received.  Recommended for libraries
with strong interests in international affairs.

Item 899-A
DEPARTMENT OF STATE
S9.12:  United States treaties and
other international agreements.
v.1-  1950-  LC 53-60242
S9.12/2:  Treaties and other international agreements of the
United States of America, 1776-
1949.  LC 70-600742
United States treaties and
other international agreements,
S9.12, is a continuing publication.
It is an annual cumulation which includes the texts of all treaties and
agreements entered into since January 1, 1950.  Item 899 is the pamphlet form of these treaties and
agreements and the series from which
the compilation is made.  Prior to
the annual volumes, treaties and
other international agreements were
printed in Statutes at large, a list
of which is found in 64 Statute,
part 3.
United States treaties and
other international agreements, 1776-
1949, S9.12/2, is approaching completion.  The entire set contains
the text of all treaties and agreements of the United States prior
to the initial volume of United
States treaties and other international agreements.  It therefore
supersedes the cumulations by Mal-
loy, Redmond, Trenwith, and Miller.
The set begins with several volumes
of multilateral treaties and is followed by volumes of bilateral treaties and agreements, all organized
by the name of the country with
which they were concluded.  A brief
index is included in each volume.
This set is essential for libraries
desiring a complete collection of
treaties.
The item is recommended for academic and larger public libraries.

Item 900-A
S9.14:  DEPARTMENT OF STATE.  OFFICE
OF THE LEGAL ADVISOR.  Treaties
in force; a list of treaties

and other international agreements of the United States.
LC 56-61604

The publication is an annual
which lists treaties and other international agreements in force on January 1 of the year of the volume.
Part 1 of two parts is a list of bilateral treaties and agreements by
country with subject divisions.
Part 2 lists multilateral treaties
and agreements by subject and includes names of all states which are
parties. This is a useful compilation which quickly brings treaty information up to date; several years
of the series is a good historical
record. Recommended for academic
libraries and larger public libraries.

Item 900-B
S1.111:  DEPARTMENT OF STATE.  BUR-
EAU OF INTELLIGENCE RESEARCH.
World strength of Communist
Party organizations.  LC 56-
60986

This annual publication is a
world survey of communism, present-
ing data on party membership, and
voting and parliamentary strength
where it is important. Parties are
treated by continent and by country
and are analyzed briefly in their
domestic environment. The tables
and organization are useful, and the
book provides comprehensive coverage. The annual is an important
reference source; retention for two
or three years is adequate. Recommended for academic and public libraries.

Item 900-C-2
S18.2:  AGENCY FOR INTERNATIONAL DE-
VELOPMENT. General publica-
tions.

Titles to inform the public
about the work of AID constitute
this series. Career possibilities,
conference proceedings, statistical
reports, and reports of projects are
major subject areas. Three notable
subseries are
Gross national product:  Growth
rates and trend data by region and country, no. G91

U.S. overseas loans and grants
and assistance from international organizations, no. Ov2
Selected economic data for the
less developed countries, no.
Ec7/2
The American role in disaster
relief, no. D65
Application of modern techniques to international development, no. T22.
Recommended for academic and public
libraries.

Item 900-C-6
S18.33:  Development digest.  v.1-
July 1962-   LC 66-8972

The quarterly, published by the
Agency for International Development,
is described as a journal of "ex-
cerpts, summaries, and reprints of
current materials on economic and
social development." Typical subjects of articles are fertilizer,
village technology, interest rate
reform, migration, and tourism in
developing nations. Issues are
usually focused upon a few topics
of concern to the agency, with two
or three articles falling under each
topic. Articles are scholarly and
are frequently adapted from unpub-
lished papers. Issues are about 125
pages in length. The material is
most useful to fields in the social
sciences. Recommended for academic
and for some public libraries.

Item 900-C-8
S18.34:  AGENCY FOR INTERNATIONAL
DEVELOPMENT. War on hunger.

This monthly publication is
about 20 pages in length. It contains news items, original manuscripts, speeches, and photographs
on aspects of international development. Recent issues include articles on housing in the developing
world, dental treatment, development
cooperation, and Guatemala rebuild-
ing for safety. Recommended for academic and public libraries.

Item 992
Y4.P93/1:1  CONGRESS. Congressional
directory.  LC 6-35330
The biographical directory of

senators and representatives includes in addition: lists of committees and members, congressional
office personnel, statistical data
on sessions of Congress, information about personnel in the executive departments and agencies, data
on members of the Supreme Court,
foreign diplomatic representatives
and consular offices in the United
States, U.S. diplomatic and consular
offices, members of the press admitted to the House and Senate galler-
ies and the newspapers they represent, other media representatives
admitted, and the members of the
government of the District of Columbia.

As well as being a guide to
data on members of Congress, it is
also a comprehensive source of information on all top government personnel. It is issued annually and
is indexed. Recommended as a reference title for academic and public
libraries.

Item 993
X:  CONGRESS.  Congressional record;
    proceedings and debates of the
    Congress.  43d-  v.1-
    LC 12-36438  Bound edition.
The permanent edition of the
Congressional record has sometimes
differed from the daily edition (X/a,
item 994), but at the present time,
the two issuances differ primarily
only in organization. The bound
edition, which takes up several
shelves for each session, is organized chronologically with an index
volume and a cumulative daily digest
volume. The index, as in the daily
publication, is an index to the Congressional record and contains a
cumulative history of bills and resolutions. Once all the parts of the
permanent edition have been received,
the paper daily edition can be discarded. Recommended for academic
and larger public libraries.

Item 994
X/a:  CONGRESS.  Congressional rec-
    ord; proceedings and debates of
    the Congress.  43d-  v.1-
    LC 12-36438  Daily edition.

The Congressional record is
published daily when Congress is in
session. A bound, cumulative edition is published for the entire
session (X, item 993). The daily
record contains debates and proceedings of the House of Representatives
and Senate, extensions of remarks,
and the daily digest. Lists of members with their state, party, and
office number; lists of standing
committees and the names of members;
and names of court officials are
reference features of some issues.
Members may revise remarks made in
debate and expunge material if so
desired, thus the record is not
necessarily a verbatim account of
the proceedings. The daily record
is indexed every two weeks, providing an index to proceedings, debates,
and extensions of remarks, and a
history of bills and resolutions.
Recommended for academic and larger
public libraries.

Item 1030
XJH:  CONGRESS.  HOUSE.  Journal of
    the United States House of Rep-
    resentatives.
The journals of the Congress
are the only publications which are
required by the Constitution of the
United States. The Journal is a
record of the proceedings of the
House of Representatives, and it is
the official record. Because it
omits debate, it provides easier access to procedure and chronology
than does the Congressional record,
and it is essential for this purpose.
Published at the end of each session,
and therefore annually, the House
Journal includes in addition to the
record, the House bills, joint resolutions, concurrent resolutions,
House resolutions, Senate bills, and
an index. Recommended for academic
and public libraries.

Item 1047
XJS:  CONGRESS.  SENATE.  Journal of
    the executive proceedings of
    the Senate of the United States.
    LC 9-23902
The journals of the Congress
are the only publications which are

required by the Constitution of the United States. The Journal is a record of the proceedings of the Senate, and it is the official record. Published at the end of each session, the Senate Journal has an appendix which includes "History of bills and resolutions," joint resolutions and concurrent resolutions, Senate resolutions, and an index. Because it omits debate, it provides easier access to procedure than does the Congressional record and it is essential for this purpose. Recommended for academic and public libraries.

Item 1049-D
Y3.Ad9/8:   ADVISORY COMMISSION ON INTERGOVERNMENTAL RELATIONS. Reports and publications.

Members advise the operation of the federal system, providing continual review and making recommendations for changes. In carrying out this responsibility, the commission conducts studies and investigations of government operations. The national body takes its members from the executive and legislative branches of federal, state, and local governments. Their reports are issued in this series; the following are examples:

> Toward more balanced transportation: New intergovernmental proposals, no. 2T68/2
> Property tax circuit breakers: Current status and policy issues, no. 2T19/18
> General revenue sharing, no. 2R32/5.

A series of recommendations for state action was revised in 1975. A multivolume set, ACIR state legislative program, no. L59/975, makes recommendations for state action. These topics include fiscal and personnel management, environment and land use, housing, health, and others. According to the commission, part of its responsibility to strengthen the federal system will be met by putting emphasis upon state and local governments. The series issues an average of six to eight publications a year. The

titles are strong supplements for social science programs and for civic-minded individuals.

The series is recommended for academic and public libraries.

Item 1089
Y3.   CONGRESS. COMMISSIONS, COMMITTEES, BOARDS. Reports and publications.

Commissions, committees, and boards created by Congress to investigate a specific problem or situation or to carry out a special task fall into this general publication and report series. Usually the organization is terminated upon submission of a final report or completion of a task. Examples of these commissions functioning in recent years, and in some cases, continuing, are

> The American Revolution Bicentennial Administration, Y3.Am3/6, which issued lists of activities and events and of local organizations
> National Advisory Council on Adult Education, Y3.Ed8/4, which issues annual reports to the president and Congress
> National Advisory Council on the Education of Disadvantaged Children, Y3.Ed8/2, which issues annual reports to the president and Congress
> National Commission on the Financing of Postsecondary Education, Y3.Ed8/5, which issues analyses and recommendations
> Commission on the Review of the National Policy toward Gambling, Y3.G14
> Federal Election Commission, Y3.El2/3
> Office of Technology Assessment, Y3.T22/2, which issues periodic reports and statements
> The Commission on Obscenity and Pornography, Y3.Ob7, one of the more publicized commissions of recent years.

These task forces have varying degrees of pertinence to the general public and to academic life. Scrutiny of their activities and publications is important. Recommended for academic and public libraries.

HEARINGS

Hearings are held by congressional committees for the purpose of investigating issues or pursuant to proposed legislation. When a proposed bill or resolution is referred to a committee, the committee holds public hearings to gather information in regard to the desirability of the legislation. On other occasions, hearings are held to study areas needing new or modified legislation. When a hearing has concluded, the committee writes a report of its recommendations to the House or Senate. House and Senate Reports are discussed elsewhere in this guide. House and Senate Reports do not generally include testimony or other information submitted at a hearing.

Copies of the transcripts of these hearings are printed and made available to depository libraries except in cases where the hearings are classified information or available only in limited quantities. Hearings are usually available to nondepository libraries by request to the committee or by purchase from the Superintendent of Documents.

In the following section, transcriptions of House and Senate committee hearings available in the depository list are discussed. Committee prints are sometimes issued under the item number. They are prepared for the use of a committee as background information on particular issues and proposed legislation. The distribution of committee prints is inconsistent: some are available upon request from the committee, some from a member of Congress, and some through purchase from the Superintendent of Documents.

Both hearings and committee prints are indexed in the Monthly catalog (GP3.8, item 557) and in the CIS/Index (Washington D.C.: Congressional Information Service, 1970-   ). They are indexed by subject, title, and committee in the Monthly catalog. In the CIS/Index, hearings are in-

dexed by subject, witnesses and/or organizations, committees, subcommittees, and bill and report numbers. CIS/Index, a commercial index, also abstracts contents of hearings and gives a page reference to individual testimony. Committee prints are indexed in CIS/Index by subject, committee, subcommittee, and names of some individuals named in the publication.

Because the mandate of investigation and the study of pursuant legislation are time-consuming activities involving many people and occurring daily, the hearings issued are frequent and may be voluminous. Some exceptions are noted under individual item numbers, but, for the most part, the hearings and committee prints of each committee consume from one to three feet of shelving per year. Statements of recommendation are not made for individual committee hearings. Rather, those committees listed and annotated here are included because of their applicability to undergraduate curricula in the social and natural sciences. Likewise, they are relevant material for the use of public library patron as concerned citizens, research-minded individuals, and professional people. The areas of jurisdiction of each committee are listed in detail as are, in most cases, a few examples of the subjects of recent hearings. Committee prints and hearings are commanding information resources because the testimony, research reports, and other study materials produced are prepared by people with experience and authority.

Item 1000
Y4.Ec7:  CONGRESS.  JOINT ECONOMIC
        COMMITTEE.  Hearings.
The joint committee is authorized to hold hearings which deal with legislation relating to issues covered in the Economic report, Pr39.9, item 848. The Report is transmitted to the Congress by the president and sets forth levels of employment and production desirable for recommended growth; trends in

level of employment, production, and purchasing power; a general economic review; and a program for economic growth. Federal subsidy programs, allocation of resources in the Soviet Union and China, and the public utility industry are issues recently heard in this committee.

Item 1002
Y4.T19/4:  CONGRESS.  JOINT COMMITTEE ON TAXATION.  Hearings.
The joint committee is authorized to investigate all aspects of internal revenue taxation, including the method of taxation, and the operation of the system.  They are also charged with studying the simplification of the taxation system. To these ends, hearings are held. Although publications appear infrequently, they usually report hearings on estimates of federal receipts for the fiscal year.

Item 1009
Y4.  CONGRESS.  SELECT AND SPECIAL COMMITTEES.  Hearings.
Select and special committees are established within both houses of Congress to investigate specific issues and to make recommendations to the House or Senate.  These committees do not report on legislation; however, their reports frequently constitute probes of major national problems.  When the committee's final report is made, the committee is dissolved, but it may be revived by either house and assigned a new issue.  The following select committees have existed in recent sessions of Congress:
Y4.Ag4:  Senate Committee on Aging
Y4.Ag4/2:  House Committee on Aging
Y4.B85/3:  House Committee on the Budget
Y4.In8/17:  Committee to Study Government Operations with Respect to Intelligence Activities
Y4.In8/18:  House Committee on Intelligence
Y4.Eq2:  Committee on Equal Education Opportunity

Y4.M69/3:  Committee on Missing Persons in Southeast Asia
Y4.N21/9:  Senate Committee on National Emergencies and Delegated Emergency Powers.

Item 1010
Y4.Ag8/1:  CONGRESS.  COMMITTEE ON AGRICULTURE.  Hearings.
This committee has jurisdiction over proposed legislation which affects the general areas of agriculture and forestry.  Specific examples include the protection of wildlife in forest preserves, agriculture colleges and experiment stations, the Department of Agriculture, animal and dairy industry, agriculture economics and research, production and marketing, price stabilization, rural development, crop insurance, nutrition and home economics, and commodities exchanges. Testimony about the watershed projects, review of the national wilderness preservation system, and discussion of tung nut price supports have been heard recently in committee.

Item 1011
Y4.Ap6/1:  CONGRESS.  HOUSE.  COMMITTEE ON APPROPRIATIONS. Hearings.
Jurisdiction over proposed legislation relating to the appropriation of revenue to support the federal government and over the federal budget in general is maintained by this committee.  It is also authorized to investigate rescission bills and impoundment resolutions.  In recent annual budgets, supplemental funds were needed for federal unemployment benefits and allowances, and for the Veterans' Administration. Transcripts of hearings on those subjects were issued by this committee.

Item 1012
CONGRESS.  HOUSE.  COMMITTEE ON ARMED SERVICES.
Y4.Ar5/2:  Hearings.
Y4.Ar5/2a:  Papers.
The committee has jurisdiction over bills relating to the Depart-

ment of Defense, benefits for armed services members, the selective service, research and development, materials necessary for common defense, and the size and composition of the armed services. Hearings have recently been held to review the military airlift, a national petroleum reserve, and military compensation.

Item 1013
Y4.B22/1: CONGRESS. HOUSE. COMMITTEE ON BANKING, FINANCE, AND URBAN AFFAIRS. Hearings.
Proposed legislation relating to the broad areas of banking, finance, and urban affairs are in the jurisdiction of the committee. Specific examples of topics published include banks and banking, money and credit, urban development, public and private housing, price controls, and international finance. The future of urban life and East-West trade are subjects of hearings issued recently.

Item 1015
Y4.Ed8/1: CONGRESS. HOUSE. COMMITTEE ON EDUCATION AND LABOR. Hearings.
Jurisdiction of the broad areas of educational programs and labor regulation is the concern of this committee. Specific subjects referred to this committee are labor standards, labor statistics, child labor, mediation and arbitration of labor disputes, regulation of foreign laborers, food programs in schools, wages and hours, work incentive programs, and vocational training. Hearings have been recently held on the Youth Conservation Corps program, the White House Conference on Library and Information Services, and vocational education.

Item 1016
Y4.G74/7: CONGRESS. HOUSE. COMMITTEE ON GOVERNMENT OPERATIONS. Hearings.
Authority to investigate the overall economy and efficiency of the government, reorganization in the executive branch, general rev-

enue sharing, and proposed legislation which affects these conditions rests with this committee. Members have heard testimony of telephone monitoring practices in federal agencies and on the National Women's Conference in recent hearings.

Item 1017
Y4.In8/16: CONGRESS. HOUSE. COMMITTEE ON INTERNATIONAL RELATIONS. Hearings.
Jurisdiction over proposed legislation which affects the United States and its relations with foreign nations is the general charge of this committee. Bills and resolutions referred to it may deal with these subjects: the property of embassies and legations in foreign countries, boundary lines with the United States, foreign loans, international conferences, declarations of war, interventions abroad, diplomatic service, neutrality, protection of Americans abroad, American Red Cross, commodity agreements, trading with enemy, and international education. Recent topics of hearings published include: controlling opium importation, war powers compliance, and the Vladivostok accord.

Item 1019
Y4.In8/4: CONGRESS. HOUSE. COMMITTEE ON INTERSTATE AND FOREIGN COMMERCE. Hearings.
Proposed legislation relating to the following subjects is referred to the Committee on Interstate and Foreign Commerce for investigation: inland waterways, interstate fuel agreements, railroad activities, regulation of interstate and foreign communication, securities and exchanges, consumer affairs and consumer protection, travel and tourism, public health, and biomedical research. Current topics of investigation are the Toxic Substances Control Act, health maintenance organization amendments, and railroad revitalization.

Item 1020
Y4.J89/1: CONGRESS. HOUSE. COM-

MITTEE ON THE JUDICIARY. Hearings.

The authority to investigate
proposed legislation relating to
general civil and criminal judicial
proceedings rests with this committee. These specific charges include
the apportionment of representatives,
civil liberties, constitutional
amendments, federal courts and
judges, immigration and naturalization, the Patent Office, presidential succession, claims against the
United States, copyrights, patents,
trademarks, bankruptcy, mutiny, espionage, counterfeiting, and Communist and other subversive activities
affecting the nation's internal security. Issues recently before the
committee have been surveillance,
illegal aliens, and review of administrative rule making.

Item 1022
Y4.P84/10: CONGRESS. HOUSE. COM-
    MITTEE ON POST OFFICE AND CIVIL
    SERVICE. Hearings.

The authority to investigate
proposed legislation relating to the
census, the federal civil service,
the Postal Service, the Hatch Act,
holidays, and population and demog-
raphy rests with this committee.
Recent subjects of hearings are
criteria for closing small post offices, retirement annuities of federal employees, and the date for the
census of agriculture.

Item 1023
Y4.In8/14: CONGRESS. HOUSE. COM-
    MITTEE ON INTERIOR AND INSULAR
    AFFAIRS. Hearings.

Jurisdiction over proposed legislation which corresponds in part
to the activities of the Interior
Department rests in this committee.
Specific subjects of proposed bills
and resolutions include forest preserves and national parks, the Geological Survey, Indian affairs, insular possessions, mineral rights
and mining interests, mining schools
and experiment stations, and entry
and grazing on public lands. Public timber export control, Alaska
Native Claims Settlement Act amendments, and Indian health care are
areas of recent investigation.

Item 1024
Y4.P96/11: CONGRESS. HOUSE. COM-
    MITTEE ON PUBLIC WORKS. Hear-
    ings.

Proposed legislation relating
to the following subjects is referred to this committee: maintenance
of public buildings administered by
the government including those in
the District of Columbia, the purchase of property for buildings,
pollution of navigable waters, water
power, roads and their safety,
transportation regulatory agencies,
and interstate water transportation.
Hearings have been held recently on
sound and light performances on the
east front of the Capitol, proposals
for a fourth House office building,
and emergency rail passenger service.

Item 1025
Y4.R86/1: CONGRESS. HOUSE. COMMIT-
    TEE ON RULES. Hearings.

The jurisdiction over proposed
bills and resolutions relating to
the rules and joint rules of the
House, emergency waivers authorizing
new budget authority, and recess and
the final adjournment of Congress
rests with this committee. Recently
published hearings have focused on
television and radio coverage of the
House, and on impoundment reporting
and review. Because of the nature
of the assignments of this committee,
hearings are issued infrequently.

Item 1025-A
Y4.Sci2: CONGRESS. HOUSE. COMMIT-
    TEE ON SCIENCE AND ASTRONAUTICS.
    Hearings.

The following science agencies
and activities are under the jurisdiction of the committee when legislation is proposed in their regard:
aerospace research and development,
Bureau of Standards, National
Weather Service, National Science
Foundation, National Aeronautics and
Space Administration, science schol-
arship, environmental research and
development, and nonnuclear energy
research. Some recent testimony fo-

cused on future space programs, loan guaranties for energy-conserving technology, and National Science Foundation peer review.

Item 1025-B
Y4.St2/3: CONGRESS. HOUSE. COMMITTEE ON STANDARDS OF OFFICIAL CONDUCT. Hearings.

Jurisdiction over the following areas of proposed legislation rests with this committee: the Code of Official Conduct, financial disclosure by members of the House, and general voting procedures of the House. Few hearings have been published in the last five years.

Item 1027
Y4.V64/3: CONGRESS. HOUSE. COMMITTEE ON VETERANS' AFFAIRS. Hearings.

Proposed legislation relating to veterans, their benefits, and their facilities is within the authority of this committee. Hearings and investigations focus on these issues.

Item 1028
Y4.W36: CONGRESS. HOUSE. COMMITTEE ON WAYS AND MEANS. Hearings.

Proposed legislation relating to the following subjects is in the jurisdiction of the committee: customs collection and ports of entry, revenue measures, bonded debt of the United States, transportation of dutiable goods, tax-exempt foundations and trusts, and national social security. Typical hearings have dealt with alternatives to tax-exempt state and local bonds, confidentiality of tax-return information, and unemployment compensation.

Item 1031
Y4.Sm1: CONGRESS. HOUSE. SELECT COMMITTEE ON SMALL BUSINESS. Hearings.

The assistance to small businesses by the federal government and business' participation in federal procurement are the areas of jurisdiction for proposed legislation which rest with this committee.

Typical hearings have dealt with the effect of Postal Service policies on small businesses, the federal paperwork burden, and monopolistic tendencies of auto-emission warranty provisions.

Item 1032
Y4.Ag8/3: CONGRESS. SENATE. COMMITTEE ON AGRICULTURE, NUTRITION AND FORESTRY. Hearings.

Proposed legislation referred to this committee relates to livestock and the animal husbandry industry, forest preserves and their wildlife, agriculture colleges and experiment stations, agriculture economics and research, agricultural and industrial chemistry, the dairy industry, entomology, nutrition and home economics, soils, extension services, farm credit, rural electrification, production, marketing and price stabilization, crop insurance, and soil conservation. Recent hearings have been issued by this committee on tobacco price supports; the future supply-demand situation for fertilizer, fuel, and pesticides; medical facilities in rural areas; and Rural Electrification Administration loans.

Item 1033
Y4.Ap6/2: CONGRESS. SENATE. COMMITTEE ON APPROPRIATIONS. Hearings.

Legislation relating to the appropriation of revenue for the support of the federal government is referred to this committee. From time to time most federal appropriations are debated and investigated here. The reports and hearings of such study are issued under this item number.

Item 1034
Y4.Ar5/3: CONGRESS. SENATE. COMMITTEE ON ARMED SERVICES. Hearings.

Proposed legislation on the following subjects is referred to this committee: Department of Defense; benefits of members of the armed forces; selective service; size and composition of the armed forces;

forts, arsenals, and other military property; the administration of the Panama Canal and the Canal Zone; strategic and critical materials maintained for common defense; and aeronautical and space activities relating to the development of military and weapons systems. Recent hearings held and issued have been on the nominations of top-level departmental personnel, research and development, reserve call-ups, and authorization for 1976 appropriations and procurements.

Item 1035
Y4.B22/3: CONGRESS. SENATE. COMMITTEE ON BANKING, HOUSING, AND URBAN AFFAIRS. Hearings.
All proposed legislation relating to the following subjects is referred to this committee: general financial aid to commerce and industry, deposit insurance, public and private housing, Federal Reserve System, gold and silver supplies, issuance and redemption of notes, valuation and revaluation of the dollar, price controls, and urban affairs in general. Hearings have recently been issued on problems encountered under state usury laws, on urban mass transportation, on solar home heating and cooling, and on the problems of the small business.

Item 1037
Y4.G74/6: CONGRESS. SENATE. COMMITTEE ON GOVERNMENT AFFAIRS. Hearings.
Government and accounting measures as separate from appropriation activities, and reorganization of the executive branch of government are the subjects of proposed legislation referred to this committee. Hearings recently published by the committee have been on the Watergate Reorganization and Reform Act of 1975, and travel expense amendments.
The committee was reorganized in 1977 to include the responsibilities of the former Committee on Post Office and Civil Service. This action expanded the focus of the Committee on Government Affairs to include proposed legislation relating to employees of the United States and their benefits, to the Postal Service, the National Archives, and to the census and the general collection of statistics.

Item 1038
Y4.F49: CONGRESS. SENATE. COMMITTEE ON FINANCE. Hearings.
All proposed legislation relating to these subjects is referred to the Finance Committee for study: the nation's bonded debt, deposit of public money, customs and ports of entry and delivery, reciprocal trade agreements, transportation of dutiable goods, finance in insular possessions, national social security, and tariffs and import quotas. Recent hearings held and publications issued have been on the subjects of unemployment compensation, International Trade Commission appropriations, and protecting the ability of the United States to trade abroad.

Item 1039
Y4.F76/2: CONGRESS. SENATE. COMMITTEE ON FOREIGN RELATIONS. Hearings.
Proposed legislation dealing with relations of the United States with foreign nations in general is referred to this committee. Specifically, these subjects are treaties, neutrality, boundary lines with the United States, protection of Americans abroad, expatriation, international conferences and congresses, American Red Cross, intervention abroad and declarations of war, diplomatic service, the properties for embassies and legations in foreign countries, commerce with foreign countries, and foreign loans. Recent hearings have been published following their occurrence in the committee on the following: the world situation, 1949-50, and made public in 1974; weather modification; prohibition of chemical and biological weapons; and the United States in the United Nations.

Item 1040
Y4.En2: CONGRESS. SENATE. COM-

MITTEE ON ENERGY AND NATURAL RESOURCES. Hearings.

All proposed legislation relating to the following subjects and corresponding in part to the activities of the Department of Interior is referred to this committee: entry, easement, and grazing on public lands; mineral resources of the public lands; forest reserves and national parks; insular possessions, except matters relating to revenue; irrigation and reclamation; interstate agreements on water for irrigation; mining and mineral rights; Geological Survey; mining schools and experiment stations; Indian affairs; and radium and petroleum conservation. Recent publications of hearings have focused on the following: the economic impact of President Ford's energy program, transportation of Alaskan natural gas, and oil price decontrol pursuant to corresponding proposed legislation.

Item 1041
Y4.C73/2: CONGRESS. SENATE. COMMITTEE ON COMMERCE, SCIENCE AND TRANSPORTATION. Hearings.

This committee, which was reorganized in 1977, looks at a broad spectrum of national issues: regulation of civil aeronautics, merchant fleets, the Weather Service, Bureau of Standards, registering and licensing of vessels and small boats, navigation laws, the Panama Canal and other interoceanic canals, inland waterways, fisheries and wildlife, and legislation relating to aeronautics and space activities as defined by the National Aeronautics and Space Act of 1958. Recent hearings have been held and publications issued on these subjects: the Price Disclosure Act, Materials Management Act, National Gas Pipeline Safety Act, daylight saving time, metric conversion, Skylab, and technology utilization.

Item 1042
Y4.J89/2: CONGRESS. SENATE. COMMITTEE ON THE JUDICIARY. Hearings.
Referred to this committee is

all proposed legislation relating to constitutional amendments, federal courts and judges, local courts of territories and possessions, the codification of the statutes of the United States, national penitentiaries, holidays and celebrations, Patent Office, patents, copyrights, trademarks, civil liberties, protection of commerce against monopoly, espionage, state and territorial boundary lines, mutiny, bankruptcy, counterfeiting, immigration and naturalization, apportionment of representatives, and claims against the United States. Published hearings have been issued recently pursuant to proposed legislation on benefits provided to American civilian internees in Southeast Asia and on the extension of the Voting Rights Act of 1965.

Item 1043
Y4.H88: CONGRESS. SENATE. COMMITTEE ON HUMAN RESOURCES. Hearings.

All proposed legislation relating to the following subjects is referred to this committee: mediation and arbitration of labor disputes, wages and hours, convict labor and its products, regulation of importation of foreign laborers, child labor, labor standards, statistics, the school-lunch program, vocational rehabilitation, railroad employees benefits, Gallaudet College, Howard University, public health, and the welfare of minors. Recent hearings have been held and publications issued on the following: higher education oversight, health manpower, and genetic engineering. Until early 1977, this committee was known as the Committee on Labor and Public Welfare.

Item 1045
Y4.P96/10: CONGRESS. SENATE. COMMITTEE ON ENVIRONMENT AND PUBLIC WORKS. Hearings.
All proposed legislation relating to the following subjects is referred to this committee: flood control, maintenance of rivers and harbors, benefits for navigation,

water power, pollution of navigable waters, public buildings of the United States, purchase of land, construction of various government buildings, and measures relating to the construction and maintenance of roads.  Transportation planning and priorities, current interstate needs, and energy conservation in federal buildings are examples of the concerns of recently held hearings, and the subjects of publications.

Item 1046-A
Y4.V64/4: CONGRESS.  SENATE.  COMMITTEE ON VETERANS' AFFAIRS.  Hearings.
    All proposed legislation relating to the benefits of veterans and national cemeteries is referred to this committee, and the subjects of various hearings are in published form.

SERIAL SET
    The Serial Set consists of House and Senate Reports, and House and Senate Documents.  Each volume is assigned a serial number for its organization in the set.  In addition, each Document and Report is designated by Congress, session, and individual number.  The Numerical lists, GP3.7/2, item 553, is used to determine the serial number of the volume containing a particular Document or Report.  The Serial Set is a valuable reference tool, but it requires a large allotment of shelf space.  The items on the following pages are in the Serial Set and are annotated.  They should be considered separately by libraries which cannot accomodate the entire set.  In addition to being in the Numerical lists, Reports are indexed in the Congressional record index, X, item 993; in the Digest of public general bills, LC14.6, item 807; in the Monthly catalog, GP3.8, item 557; and in the CIS/Index.  Documents are most easily approached by subject in the Monthly catalog and the CIS/Index.

Item 995-B
DAUGHTERS OF THE AMERICAN REVOLU-

TION.  Report.  1st-  1890-
    LC 8-36850
    Published annually as a separate House Document of the session of Congress to which it is submitted, the report includes an account of the past year and organization of the Daughters of the American Revolution.  Public libraries serve this constituency and may want to make the volume available.

Item 995-E
CONGRESS.  HOUSE AND SENATE.  Appropriations, budget estimates, etc.
    Proposed budget amendments, requests for appropriations, and supplemental appropriations are the particular House and Senate Documents under this item.  The difference between these and Miscellaneous Documents, item 995-G, is largely academic, but one should note that all the Document items discussed in this section under Serial Set are necessary for a complete run of the Serial Set.  Usually one or two volumes of this item, for each house of Congress, are issued per session.

Item 995-G
CONGRESS.  HOUSE AND SENATE.  Miscellaneous documents.
    Except when referring to the Serial Set, the term documents has been used synonomously with publications of the United States government.  In this case, however, Documents are specific publications of the House and Senate.  Some Documents originate in the Congress, others in executive departments and independent agencies, and a few are from national organizations which make annual reports to Congress.  (For the latter category, see items 995-B, 995-I, 995-K, 995-L, 995-P, and 995-Q.)  Documents which originate in executive departments and independent agencies, such as reports on activities relating to particular legislation or annual reports, are available to depository libraries in the departmental edition only, even though they are also

published in the Serial Set edition for congressional purposes. The Numerical lists, GP3.7/2, item 553, notes these publications which are published in two editions.

Miscellaneous House and Senate Documents which are issued under this item are publications such as presidential messages, presidential vetoes, analyses of national issues, or committee recommendations in regard to a treaty or a nomination. Recent examples of publications which are ordered by Congress to be printed as a Miscellaneous Document include: Impeachment: Selected materials, Compilation of Social Security laws, and Comprehensive energy plan. Sometimes material which might otherwise be issued as a committee print will be published as a House or Senate Miscellaneous Document. Congressional documents are also issued in unbound form, item 996. While the unbound format appears first, it is not recommended for most libraries because of the unnecessary duplication.

Item 995-I
AMERICAN LEGION. Proceedings of the national convention of the American Legion. 1st- 1919- LC 25-26630
This report of the American Legion is issued annually as a separate House Document of the session of Congress to which it is submitted. It includes some transcript of the meetings, committee reports, resolutions, and the annual report of the organization. Many members of the community the public library serves belong to the organization and may be interested in its formal report.

Item 995-J
DISABLED AMERICAN VETERANS. Proceedings of the national convention. 1st- 1921- LC 21-16790
Published annually as a separate House Document of the session of Congress to which it is submitted, the report includes transcript of the meeting, actions on rules and policy, and committee reports. Rec-

ommended for public libraries serving this particular constituency.

Item 995-K
UNITED SPANISH WAR VETERANS. Proceedings of the stated convention of the national encampment.... 1st- 1904- LC 10-5225
Published annually as a separate House Document of the session of Congress to which it is submitted, this small volume includes transcript of the meeting, organizational detail, and various reports. Recommended for public libraries if there is an appropriate group of patrons.

Item 995-L
VETERANS OF FOREIGN WARS OF THE UNITED STATES. Proceedings of the national encampment. 26th- 1925- LC 27-16417
Addresses, memorial services, reports, and elections are included in this annual volume which is submitted as a separate House Document to the current session of Congress. Some public library patrons are members of this organization and may be interested in the annual meeting.

Item 995-M
CONGRESS. SENATE. Report of the secretary.
This Senate Document, which is submitted twice a year, is issued under yet another item number. It is a complete statement of receipts and expenditures of the Senate. Accounted for here are salaries of staff members in Senate offices, disbursements for committee and subcommittee investigations, and various other expenses incurred in Senate operations. The volume has a general index.

Item 995-P
BOY SCOUTS OF AMERICA. Annual report of the Boy Scouts of America. 8th- 1917- LC 23-13721
GIRL SCOUTS OF THE UNITED STATES OF AMERICA. Report. 1950- LC 51-61149

Published annually in one volume, these reports include scouting activities, organizational detail, membership statistics, regional operation, and historical highlights. They provide interesting reading and informative data for people involved in the movement. Scouting reaches a large portion of the public library community.

Item 995-Q
VETERANS OF WORLD WAR I OF THE U.S.A.
Proceedings of the national convention.  LC 64-60773
A transcript of the annual meeting of these veterans, this is issued as a separate House Document of the session of the Congress to which it is submitted.  Recommended for public libraries serving an interested clientele.

Item 1007-A
CONGRESS.  HOUSE AND SENATE.  Reports on public bills.
After a bill or resolution has been studied by the committee to which it was referred, and after hearings are concluded, the committee writes a report to the House or Senate.  Known as House Reports and Senate Reports, they contain recommendations in regard to this legislation.  The committee may recommend passage of the bill with no qualification, or it may revise or rewrite the legislation.  Reports for uncomplicated and noncontroversial bills may be only a few pages long.  Reports which make detailed analyses of the legislation sometimes include a summary of the evidence brought out in the hearings, and occasionally the opinions of the individual committee members.  Testimony from hearings is rarely included in the Report.  Reports on bills which require appropriations usually include a cost estimate.  This comprehensive analysis of legislation is a valuable resource for determining legislative intent and for locating information on the meaning of the law.
Another category, Special Reports, is issued here.  They are written by committees at the request of Congress that a special investigation or study be made on a matter of public interest.
All Special Reports are designated by Congress, session, and individual numbers.  House and Senate Reports are also issued in unbound form, item 1008-A.  While this unbound format appears first, it is not recommended for most libraries because of the unnecessary duplication.

Item 1007-B
CONGRESS.  HOUSE AND SENATE.  Reports on private bills.
Private bills are referred to committees for study and hearings as are public bills.  Their reports provide a comparable analysis of the legislation.  One volume per house is usually adequate for all private bill Reports in each session.

Item 1029
CONGRESS.  HOUSE.  Constitution of the United States, Jefferson's manual, the rules of the House of Representatives ...and a digest and manual of the rules and practices of the House of Representatives.  LC 6-17027
Because it is one of the bound volumes of the House and Senate Document set, this manual is assigned a serial number which varies with each new Congress.  New editions are compiled periodically, and a revision is issued with each Congress. The manual is the source from which the rules of the House are derived. Included in each edition is an explanation of the franking privilege, room assignments in the House office buildings, and a detailed subject index.  This volume is a part of the Serial Set and is of permanent reference value for some collections. Likewise, it has immediate reference value for the current Congress. Recommended for academic and public libraries, to be treated in accordance with the policy for the Senate manual, item 1048.

Item 1048
CONGRESS. SENATE. Senate manual....
LC 1-9223
This manual of rules, laws, and procedures of the Senate is revised and reissued for each Congress. It corresponds to the House manual, item 1029, and should be treated similarly. In addition to the materials it contains concerning the organization and operation of the Senate, it includes some historical documents and statistical data. A detailed index is included. The manual contains material of permanent reference value for the research collection and is of immediate reference value for the current Congress. It is issued in a bound Serial Set edition or sold by the Superintendent of Documents. Recommended for academic and public libraries, to be treated in accordance with the policy for the House manual, item 1029.

## HISTORY

Item 344
D114.2: DEPARTMENT OF THE ARMY. OFFICE OF MILITARY HISTORY. General publications.
Publications are issued irregularly in this series, which will be of interest to all students of military history and war buffs. Notable titles are the following:
Directory of U.S. Army museums, no. M97
The sinews of war: Army logistics, 1775-1953, no. W19
The war of the American Revolution, no. Am3
Stalingrad to Berlin: The German defeat in the East, no. St1.
The series is important to the study of the army. The books include bibliographies, indexes, and maps and plates as necessary. Recommended for college and public libraries. Items 383-B and 399-A, respectively, provide the historical series for the Marine Corps and the Navy.

Item 345
DEPARTMENT OF THE ARMY. OFFICE OF MILITARY HISTORY

D114.7: United States Army in World War II. 1947- LC 47-46404
D114.7/2: Master index.
The multivolume series consists of accounts of various military actions in World War II. A number of subseries is in progress:
The War Department
The Army ground forces
The Army service forces
The western hemisphere
The war in the Pacific
The European theater of operations
The Middle East theater
The China-Burma-India theater
The technical services
Special studies
Pictorial record.
In addition, volumes on the Army Air Force are being published by the University of Chicago Press and are not available on deposit or through GPO. Examples of these subseries are
The framework of hemisphere defense
Salerno to Cassino
The last offensive.
Volumes are lengthy, 500 pages

or more, and contain bibliography, glossary, and indexing. They are published irregularly and at present total about 75 volumes. The present item number is the basis for future series by the Historical Division in regard to World War II. A Master Index is planned for the entire series upon its completion. An interim index, Master index reader's guide, serves the purpose in the meantime. Recommended for academic and public libraries.

Item 383-B
D214.13:  MARINE CORPS.  Historical
   publications.
   This series produces scholarly studies and bibliographies on subjects of interest to a general audience and to students.  Some will also serve librarians as reference materials.  Four to six titles a year conform to  one or two different formats.  They vary in length from booklet to book.  Most titles contain bibliography and indexes. Items 344 and 399-A, respectively, are the historical series for the Army and Navy.  Recent publications of note are
   The Marines in Vietnam, 1954-
      73:  An anthology and anno-
      tated bibliography, no.
      V67/954-73
   A pictorial history of Marines
      in the Revolution, no. R32/2
   Women Marines in World War I,
      no. W84
   Marines in the Dominican Repub-
      lic, no. D71.
Recommended for academic and public libraries.

Item 399-A
   NAVAL HISTORY DIVISION
D207.10:  Dictionary of American na-
   val fighting ships.  1959-
   LC 60-60198
D207.10/2:  Historical publications.
   The Dictionary of American na-
val fighting ships is a continuing multivolume work which gives brief historical sketches of each ship by name.  Several more volumes are anticipated, and the complete set will attract the attention of many people

with an interest in fighting ships.
   The Historical Publications series provides the historical coverage for the Navy.  Typical titles include:
   The American Revolution, 1775-
      1783:  An atlas of 18th cen-
      tury maps and charts, no.
      Am3/775-83
   Sailors, scientists and rockets,
      no. C44.
   History of United States naval
      operations:  Korea, no. K84
   On the treadmill to Pearl Har-
      bor:  The memoirs of James 0.
      Richardson, no. P31/3
   At close quarters:  PT boats in
      the U.S. Navy, no. Q2.
   Items 344 and 383-B, respectively, provide the historical series for the Army and the Marine Corps.
   The Dictionary of American na-
val fighting ships and Historical Publications are essential for adequate coverage of naval history. Recommended for college and public libraries.

Item 399-D
D207.12:  NAVAL HISTORY DIVISION.
   Naval documents of the American
   Revolution.  1964-   LC 64-60087
   This multivolume series reprints original letters and documents relating to naval and maritime history of the American Revolution. The compilation is a remarkable achievement because the documents are scattered throughout this country and Europe.  The contents are organized according to various theaters of the war and to various time periods.  Summaries precede these sections.  In most cases, the source of the document or the archive of its disposition is cited.  Both the British and American papers are included.  The series contains bibliography and is indexed.  The compilation continues and is essential to historical study.  Recommended for academic and larger public libraries.

Item 569
   NATIONAL ARCHIVES AND RECORDS
   SERVICE

GS4.2: General publications.
GS4.22: General information leaflet series.

The agency is responsible for functions of preservation, use, and disposition of records of the United States government. Presidential libraries and their operation also fall under the supervision of NARS. The publications generated by these activities have potential use for a broad segment of readers. These two series have issued only a few titles but some are useful library tools:

Indians in the United States: Select audiovisual records, no. GS4.2:In2/2/974

Index to the Journals of the Continental Congress, 1774-1789, GS4.2:C76/2/774-89

Regulations for the public use of records in the National Archives and Records Service, GS4.22:2

Regional branches of the National Archives, GS4.22:22

Suggestions for citing records in the National Archives of the United States, no. GS4.22:17.

Recommended for academic and public libraries.

Item 569-A
GS4.14: NATIONAL ARCHIVES AND RECORDS SERVICE. National Historical Publications Commission publications.

This series is not as active as it once was but does not appear to have ceased. The only regular issuance at present is Annotation, the newsletter of the commission. The quarterly carries notice of microfilming projects in and out of the government, of historical records personnel around the country, of legislation affecting the commission's functions, and of historical publishing efforts. This item will probably continue to be produced slowly but it is worthwhile for support of historical study and for local history interests. Recommended for academic and public libraries.

Item 569-B
GS4.6/2: NATIONAL ARCHIVES AND RECORDS SERVICE. Handbooks, manuals, guides.

Reference bibliographies of significance have been issued here. Though they are infrequent, two recent ones are outstanding:

Guide to materials on Latin America in the National Archives of the United States, no. L34a

Guide to the National Archives of the United States, no. N21.

Both are comprehensive and essential to the exploration of the federal archives. The item is recommended for academic libraries.

Item 569-C
NATIONAL ARCHIVES AND RECORDS SERVICE
GS4.17: Publications.
GS4.17/2: List of National Archives microfilm publications.

The most important title of this item is the Catalog of National Archives microfilm publications. It is issued periodically to list and briefly describe the records available on microfilm from the National Archives. The production of this and other guides is a part of the agency's records description program. Records vary from the basic documents of the First Continental Congress to the papers of recent presidents. The Catalog provides price and ordering information. It is organized by branch and department of government and is indexed. The most comprehensive publication for use of the archives is the Guide to the National Archives of the United States, GS4.6/2, item 569-B. The General Information Leaflet series, GS4.22, item 569, contains other useful guides to the agency and its publications. Recommended for academic and public libraries.

Item 570-A
GS4.7: NATIONAL ARCHIVES AND RECORDS SERVICE. Special lists.
Archival holdings of the General

Services Administration date from the First Continental Congress and contain the basic records of our government since then. Various organizational aids are prepared by NARS archivists to facilitate the use of some of these records and to describe their contents. Publications in the Special Lists series are of this nature. A recent one, Printed hearings of the House of Representatives found among its committee records in the National Archives of the United States, 1824-1958, no. 35, is an aid in finding particular congressional hearings. The Lists are specialized and support research. With this in mind, librarians may wish to select them for academic libraries. Public libraries with a need for reference material in government archives should also consider them.

Item 571
GS4.13:  NATIONAL ARCHIVES AND RECORDS SERVICE. Territorial papers of the United States.
    The series edits the papers found in the National Archives relating to the territories of the United States. For each territory, there are two or three lengthy volumes. Editorial policies resist random and unbalanced inclusion of documents. Papers previously edited in acceptable form are usually excluded, as are papers trivial in character, routine documents introducing no pertinent information, and documents containing duplicate information. Most papers are related to the administration of the territory. Individual territories are indexed. The series now numbers nearly 30 volumes. All libraries are interested in the papers of their region; some academics will want the entire series.

Item 574-A
GS4.113:  PRESIDENT. Public papers of the presidents of the United States.... LC 58-61050
    From the Weekly compilation of presidential documents, GS1.114, item 577-A, comes this cumulated an-

nual volume of presidential messages, transcripts, and public speeches and statements. The official series resulted from a recommendation by the National Historical Publications Commission that presidential writings and utterances be systematically compiled. Some proclamations, executive orders, and similar documents are not included, but reference to their inclusion in the Federal register (GS4.107, item 573), Code of federal regulations (GS4.108, item 572), and Weekly compilation of presidential documents is made. Additional appendixes list other releases which for one reason or another may not be included in this volume. At the present time, coverage of presidents' statements extends back to the Hoover administration. Recommended for academic and public libraries.

Item 579-A
GS6.8:  PUBLIC BUILDING SERVICE. Historical study. No. 1-1964-   LC 64-61110
    Federal buildings in the District of Columbia and throughout the country are maintained and preserved through the efforts of the General Services Administration. This series has issued only a few titles but will undoubtedly continue to produce studies for the information of federal agencies and the public as both continue to be curious about the nation's history. Some studies of the past include:
    Executive Office Building, no. no. 3
    Lucky landmark: A study of a design and its survival, the Galveston Customhouse, no. 4.
They are creatively designed publications, including pictures, blueprints, and bibliography. Other official records are cited as available. An occasional revised edition is issued, and the old one can be discarded. Knowledge of the historical prominence of these buildings may also inspire a continued national preservation program. Recommended for academic and public libraries.

Item 648-D
I29.76: NATIONAL PARK SERVICE.
National register of historic
places.

The National Historic Preservation Act of 1966 provided for the
expansion of the National register
of historic places from properties
representing only national significance to include also historic properties of state and local significance. States have surveyed their
areas for properties and developed
preservation plans. With the ap-
proval of the National Park Service,
these statewide plans qualify for
some federal funding for surveying,
acquiring, or preserving these properties. Volumes in this series are
issued periodically to include new
listings. They are organized by
state and listed alphabetically by
country. Each listing includes the
name, geographic location, date, and
brief description of the property.
If the area is not accessible to the
public, this is noted. Pictures
frequently accompany listings.

The most recent volume is the
1976 edition, which is current
through December 31, 1974. New editions are issued about every two
years. These are valuable reference
aids, as they include important historical data and useful travel information. Recommended for academic
and public libraries.

Item 811-B
LC4.7: LIBRARY OF CONGRESS. MANU-
SCRIPT DIVISION. Presidents'
paper index series.

The papers of about twenty-
three presidents are in the Library
of Congress and are being micro-
filmed, arranged, and indexed according to Public Laws 85-147, 87-
263, and 88-299. Positive copies of
the microfilm as it becomes available can be obtained from the li- ·
brary for purchase or through interlibrary loan. This item is the indexes to those presidential papers
located in the Library of Congress.
Recommended for academic and public
libraries.

Item 811-B-1
LC4.2: LIBRARY OF CONGRESS. MANU-
SCRIPT DIVISION. General pub-
lications.

Issued infrequently, all of
these provide some service as reference titles. They are listings of
Library of Congress material on persons or organizations. Recent
titles include:

The National Association for
the Advancement of Colored
People: A register of its
records in the Library of
Congress, no. C71
Manuscripts on microfilm: A
checklist of the holdings in
the Manuscript Division, no.
M58
Benjamin Franklin: A register
and index of his papers, no.
F85/973
Nelson W. Aldrich: A register,
no. Aℓ2
Owen Wister: A register ...,
no. W76.

Recommended as permanent reference
titles in some research collections.
Librarians should observe new publications of local interest.

Item 1064-A
Y3.H62: ADVISORY COUNCIL ON HIS-
TORIC PRESERVATION. Reports
and publications.

The council advises the Congress and the president on historic
preservation undertaken by federal
assistance. It reports annually to
the president on its recommendations
for the year. Titles other than reports include:

United States membership in the
International Center for the
Study of the Preservation and
Restoration of Cultural Prop-
erty, no. 2In8
Federal programs for neighbor-
hood conservation, no. 2N31.

Titles are issued from the series
infrequently. The pamphlets are
creatively inspired. The item
is recommended for academic and
public libraries.

Item 831-B-1

NF3. NATIONAL ENDOWMENT FOR THE HU-
MANITIES. Reports and publications.

NF3.1 is the annual report. It
is a review of the programs of the
year and includes the financial and
operational information which one
would anticipate.

NF3.2 contains program announcements and program descriptions.
Typical titles are

Education programs, no. Ed8
Program announcement, no. P94/2
American issues forum, no. F77.

Though not as highly developed
as the publishing program of the

National Endowment for the Arts,
this one is parallel and important.
Recommended for academic and public
libraries.

Item 831-B-3

NF1. NATIONAL FOUNDATION ON THE
ARTS AND THE HUMANITIES. Reports and publications.

These titles are few and of
limited interest at the present
time; however this item may be of
importance at a later date. Librarians and others who follow grant
programs will want this. Recommended for academic and public libraries.

Item 408-A
NAVAL WAR COLLEGE
D208.207: International law stud-
ies.   LC 41-50382
D208.207/2:  Index.

Former occupants of the chair
of international law at the Naval
War College frequently are the writ-
ers of these annual volumes.  The
specific emphasis of the scholar's
work marks this publication.  The
1962 volume was called The international law of outer space, vol. 55;
that for 1963, Modern economic warfare, vol. 56; and 1966, Studies in
the law of naval warfare:  Subma-
rines in general and limited wars,
vol. 58.  Each has a different author, and each represents some of
the material presented by the author
in the classroom of the Naval War
College.

Volumes are indexed individually and also by cumulative indexes.
They purport to be decennial but are
rather slow in appearing.  Recommended for academic libraries supporting courses in law, military
history, international politics.
The series will also be useful in
larger public libraries.

Item 572
GS4.108:  Code of federal regula-
tions.... 1949-   LC 49-46198
GS4.108/2:  Supplements.

Fifty titles, similar to those
in the United States code, incorporate the provisions currently in
force and as updated by the Federal
register, GS4.107, item 573.  The
CFR is revised annually and issues
monthly the "Cumulative list of CFR

sections affected," that is, affected by the daily documents of the
Federal register.  CFR is issued by
the General Services Administration.
Recommended for libraries maintaining the Federal register.  Some libraries may consider one or the
other depending upon the immediacy
of their need for the information.

Item 573
GS4.107:  Federal register.... v.1-
March 14, 1936-   LC 36-26246
Published daily Tuesday through
Saturday, this title includes all
presidential proclamations, executive orders, administrative rules,
regulations, and similar documents
unless the president determines that
they lack general applicability or
legal effect.  It generates monthly,
quarterly, and annual indexes.  The
Federal register cumulates provisions in force into the Code of federal regulations, GS4.108, item 572,
which is currently revised annually.
The Register contains a page of
highlights and reminders, a table of
contents, and a cumulative list of
parts affected for titles of the
Code to date.

Because of the magnitude and
complexity of the Privacy Act of
1974, the Office of the Federal Register published in one volume, under
this item number, a digest of all
systems of government records and
the text of all implementing regulations published to date in the Federal register under the Privacy Act.
It provides aid to individuals in
exercising their rights under the
act by listing names of record sys-

tems maintained by the federal government, the categories of persons about whom records are maintained, and the steps an individual should take to find information in a record system covered by the Privacy Act regulations. This volume is called Protecting your right to privacy, no. GS4.107/a:P939. A 1976 compilation of similar information was issued in early 1977.

Libraries may consider Code of federal regulations as an alternative to this if both are not possible, or if compilation is of greater importance than daily information.

Item 575
GS4.110:   OFFICE OF THE FEDERAL REGISTER.   Slip laws.

The first official publication of new legislation is called a "slip law." It is a printed pamphlet and at this stage is assigned a Public Law number. The two-part number, 92-34 for example, means that the law was passed during the 92nd Congress and that it is number 34 in the sequence of legislation passed. These slip laws are bound into volumes, the Statutes at large (GS4.111, item 576), at the end of each session. Slip laws may be discarded upon receipt of the volume. Recommended for libraries needing ready access to current legislation.

Item 576
GS4.111:   LAWS, STATUTES, ETC.
United States statutes at large.... LC 7-35353

Laws passed during each session of Congress are compiled into these volumes. They are arranged chronologically by date of passage. In addition, the volume for each session contains reorganization plans, concurrent resolutions, proclamations, a guide to the legislative history of public laws, and a subject index. A "Table of laws affected" is appended to each volume and is periodically cumulated into a separate volume, GS4.111/2, also issued under this item. The statutes are preceded in form by the Slip

Laws, GS4.110, item 575, and are followed by the United States code, Y4.J89/1:Un3/3, item 1020, which cumulates and codifies laws. Recommended for academic and public libraries.

Item 738
Ju6.2:   SUPREME COURT.   General publications.

Perhaps the most notable and most frequently issued publication from this series is the pamphlet The Supreme Court of the United States, no. Su7. It is a history and description of the court that includes pictures and sketches of the justices and describes the building and its furnishings. The pamphlet is periodically revised and reissued. The series issues other titles infrequently. Recommended for public libraries.

Item 740-A
Ju6.8/b:   SUPREME COURT.   Decisions.

Individual decisions of the Supreme Court, also known as "slip opinions," are printed in booklet form for use until the reports, Ju6.8, item 741, appear. Because there is a period of about two years between the decision and the issuance of the bound volumes, this is an important interim source. The Decisions may be discarded when the reports arrive. Recommended for libraries maintaining the reports.

Item 741
Ju6.8:   SUPREME COURT.   United States reports. Cases adjudged in the Supreme Court.... v.1- Sept. 1754-   LC 1-26074

At the present time there are about three volumes of Supreme Court decisions per term. In the period between individual decisions and bound volumes, Supreme Court Decisions, Ju6.8/b, item 740-A, are available. The United States Reports are of permanent reference value but consume considerable space over a period of years. Recommended for larger academic and public libraries.

Item 864-A
S7.12/3:  DEPARTMENT OF STATE.  Di-
    gest of United States practice
    in international law.  1973-
The beginning of this series
represents a new approach by the
State Department to the publication
of materials of interest to the international legal community.  Previously multivolume surveys, the di-
gests by Francis Wharton, John
Bassett Moore, Green Hackworth, and
Marjorie Whiteman, have been issued
to include a comprehensive account
of U.S. practice in international
law.  There is a growing demand for
the continuous flow of these materials.  To meet that need the department began this annual volume
series, which is quite different
from the previous comprehensive di-
gests.  The annual digest is shaped
almost solely by the international
legal events of the year.  The 1975
volume, of nearly 1000 pages, summarizes the role of Secretary of
State Henry Kissinger as mediator in
the Middle East conflict.  It notes
the U.S.'s lifting of the arms em-
bargo against India and Pakistan,
the growing concern of the U.S. with
foreign boycotts, and many other international issues of 1975.

The series has permanent reference value.  Recommended for academic and public libraries serving a
pre-law curriculum or the legal profession.

Item 991
Y4.J89/1:Un3/3/  LAWS, STATUTES,
    ETC.  United States code, con-
    taining the general and perma-
    nent laws of the United States.
    1925-   LC 65-61024
The United States code is a
consolidation of all the permanent
laws of the country which are in
force at a given time.  It is arranged by fifty numbered titles
(Title 16, Conservation; Title 17,
Copyrights; Title 18, Crimes and
Criminal Procedure, etc.), which
serve as a subject organization.
New editions are issued every six
years.  Each edition contains about
fifteen volumes; three or four supplemental volumes are added annually.  The index is by popular
names of legislation and by subject.
It is necessary to consult the Statutes at large, GS4.111, item 576,
for the full text of a law.  Recommended for large academic and public libraries.

## LIBRARY AND INFORMATION SCIENCE

Item 460-A-15
HE19.338:  NATIONAL CENTER FOR EDU-
    CATION STATISTICS.  Library
    statistics of colleges and
    universities.
Issued about three years after
the data are gathered, this report
compares library holdings, operating
expenditures, staff, salaries, etc.,
among various types of institutions.

Charts, tables and appendixes amplify the information.  The annual
is about 70 pages in length.  Academic librarians should use this as
a professional reference with the
hope that it will not always suffer
from as much time lag as it does at
present.  Some of the data may also
be of use in public libraries.

Item 551
GP3.2:  SUPERINTENDENT OF DOCUMENTS.
    General publications.
    No titles have been published
in this series in the last few years.
However, because of the relationship
of libraries to the Superintendent
of Documents, it seems desirable to
subscribe to this series because of
the possibility of its issuing
titles of use to documents collections.  Recommended for academic
and public libraries.

Item 785
LC1.1:  LIBRARY OF CONGRESS.  Report
    of the Librarian of Congress.
    1865/66-   LC 6-6273
    Obviously of more interest to
librarians than the average annual
report, this series is essential to
libraries.  It is an important summary of activities over a year at
the library.  Most libraries, regardless of size, have a link to the Library of Congress through its cataloging and classification system.
Some librarians are increasingly
drawn into the debate about copyright, whose center of registry is
the Copyright Office of the Library
of Congress.  The appendixes include
statistics of the operation and a
list of publications issued during
the fiscal year.  An index is included.  Recommended reading for academic and public librarians.

Item 785-A
LC1.12/2:  LIBRARY OF CONGRESS.
    Bibliographies and lists of
    publications.
    A bibliography series kept con-
siderably more up-to-date than those
of some other agencies and departments, this item carries an annual
Library of Congress publications in
print, no. P96.  The annual is comprehensive and provides excellent
acquisition information.  Other aids
appear occasionally, such as Library
of Congress catalogs in book form
and related publications.  Recommended for academic and public libraries.

Item 785-B
LC1.32/2:  FEDERAL LIBRARY COMMIT-
    TEE.  General publications.
    Another series which is of more
interest for what it might publish
in the future than for what has been
published, these titles are devoted
primarily to the coordination among
government libraries.  Many librarians have found Guidelines for library handbooks, no. L61/2, useful.
Recommended for academic and public
libraries.

Item 785-C
LC1.18:  LIBRARY OF CONGRESS.  In-
    formation bulletin.  v.1-
    Jan. 23, 1942-   LC 51-3324
    The weekly is primarily an in-
house publication for employees of
the Library of Congress, but it contains much information of interest
to the library world at large.  News
of performances, consultants, significant acquisitions, and publications at the library are regular
features.  Staff news, library world
events, and coming events are also
featured.  Librarians in smaller institutions find this particularly
important because it provides news
which otherwise might be missed.
Retention for six months is adequate.
Recommended for academic and public
libraries.

Item 786
LC1.2:  LIBRARY OF CONGRESS.  Gen-
    eral publications.
    Few titles have been issued in
this series in the last few years.
The following are recent:
    Teaching creative writing, no.
    P93/3
    Information for readers, no.
    R22/5/975
    Composite MARC format, no.
    M18/18.
The series is useful for what it
might issue in the range of general
publications of interest to librarians.  Recommended for academic and
public libraries.

Item 788
LC1.17:  LIBRARY OF CONGRESS.  Quar-

terly journal.  v.1- July/
Sept. 1943-  LC 44-40782
A scholarly journal of articles
by persons involved in rare book and
manuscript work or by persons whose
professional interests are naturally
combined with rare books and manuscripts. Issues sometimes bear a
contemporary theme, such as capital
punishment, women's rights, and explore the past using materials from
the Geography and Map, Manuscript,
and Rare Book divisions to illustrate and provide historical data.
There was recently a fine issue
which focused on women in history
that was prepared as a means of re-
vealing the rich resources which the
Library of Congress offers for the
study of women.  Issues are 75 to
100 pages in length.  Recommended
for librarians and scholars.

Item 819
LC26.9: LIBRARY OF CONGRESS. SUB-
JECT CATALOGING DIVISION.
Classification.
The Library of Congress classification schedules, used in many
other libraries as well, are issued
in book form.  The tables of numbers
and letters are broken down into
classes (K, law; L, education; and
P, general philology and linguistics)
and subclasses (KF, law of the
United States; PG, Russian literature) for separate publications.  At
present, the entire classification
schedule is in about 35 volumes.
The tables are useful as reference tools even in libraries using
the Dewey Decimal classification.

Item 820
LC26.2: LIBRARY OF CONGRESS. SUB-
JECT CATALOGING DIVISION. General publications.
As they provide amplification
for the cataloger and reference librarian, these titles have usefulness for the library staff.  Publications generally focus on the discussion of a specific grouping of
subject headings and their shades of
difference, the use of decimal classification, and guides to period
subdivisions.  LC classification

guides and other guides to common
subject-cataloging problems are typical titles.  Recommended for academic and public libraries.

Item 821
LC26.9/2: LIBRARY OF CONGRESS.
SUBJECT CATALOGING DIVISION.
L.C. classification--additions
and changes.  List 1- Mar./
May 1928-  LC 40-31400
This quarterly supplements the
LC classification, LC26.9, item 819,
and should be subscribed to if li-
brary uses the LC classification.
If not, add according to cataloger's
wishes, but it is useful for ref-
erence even if Dewey Decimal classi-
fication is used.

Item 823
LC26.7: LIBRARY OF CONGRESS. SUB-
JECT CATALOGING DIVISION. Subject headings.
Subject headings used by the
Library of Congress occur in this
series in a cumulative edition.
Currently the eighth edition (1975)
is in use and kept up to date by
monthly supplements.  The eighth
edition is a large, two volume set.
Of obvious necessity in all libraries, it is useful to have a second copy for use by patrons at the
card catalog.

Item 823-A-1
LIBRARY OF CONGRESS. SUBJECT
CATALOGING DIVISION.
LC26.7: Subject headings. Microfiche edition.
LC26.7/2: Quarterly cumulation.
Some librarians find the microfiche (reduction ratio 24x) to be of
use in the reference area and/or the
cataloging area.  This edition is an
alternative to a second copy of the
hard bound edition for some.  Recommended where facilities can accommo-
date and need warrants.

Item 1061-F
Y3.L61: NATIONAL COMMISSION ON LI-
BRARIES AND INFORMATION SCIENCE.
Reports and publications.
This body is concerned with
making recommendations for library

and information resources to meet the needs of all the people of the United States. It is an essential series for librarians to be aware of and to respond to. Some of their activities have been the study of a national library system, library education, and library funding. Publication in this regard includes:

> Library and information service needs of the nation, no. 2N28
> Resources and bibliographic

support for a nationwide library program, no. 2R31
Alternatives for financing the public library, no. 2F49
Continuing library and information science education, no. 2Ed8/2.

Recently titles have been issued at a rate of six to eight a year. The series is recommended for academic and public libraries.

# MATHEMATICS

Item 246-B
C13.22/sec.B  NATIONAL BUREAU OF STANDARDS.  Journal of research. B.  Mathematics and mathematic physics. v.63B-  July-Sept. 1959-  LC 62-4414

Research conducted by the bureau as it provides the national basis for measurement, scientific and technical service to the private sector, and various other technical services is reflected in this periodical.  Issued quarterly, it includes articles on mathematical statistics, experimental design, numerical analysis, logical design, and the programming of computers and computer systems.  Each issue contains five to eight articles.  Papers are submitted by bureau scientists and on invitation by persons working outside the federal government.  The research is technical but of interest to students doing advanced work.

Item 444-F
HE1.42: DEPARTMENT OF HEALTH, EDU-
CATION, AND WELFARE. Syncrisis:
The dynamics of health.

Health problems and programs in
selected developing countries are
analyzed in these studies. They
seek to identify areas in health and
socioeconomic development which may
be influenced by the cooperation of
the government in question and international assistance agencies.
The studies do not develop a plan of
action but they may serve as a point
of departure for developing activities which benefit the country.
Syncrisis is written for persons
working in international health programs in these various countries;
however, the series is found to be
useful to others because of the resources it provides for the general
study of developing nations. Individual studies typically include
data on population, climatic conditions and geography, the political
situation, education and communication, economics, and nutrition and
agriculture as they interact to produce the conditions that affect the
health of the population. This information frequently does not exist
elsewhere; consequently these studies are unique reference sources.
Revisions are issued as they become
desirable. Nations under consideration are covered by individual issues. Three or four are made available annually. Length is under 200
pages. Recommended for academic and
public libraries.

Item 467-A-5
HE20.8214: NATIONAL INSTITUTE ON
DRUG ABUSE. Research issues.

Topics for study and inclusion
here are chosen because they present
a challenging issue to the research
community. Most topics have received little previous attention
from the research world, according
to the project officer. The following are recent additions to the series and seem to support this con-
tention:

Drugs and addict lifestyles,
no. 7
Drug themes in science fiction,
no. 9
Predicting adolescent drug
abuse: A review of issues,
methods, and correlates,
no. 11.

Six or eight titles are issued annually, and they vary in length from a
few pages to a few hundred. They
include indexes and bibliographies
as necessary. The unique subject
matter is a welcome addition to the
literature. Recommended for academic and public libraries.

Item 475
HE20.4002: FOOD AND DRUG ADMINIS-
TRATION. General publications.

Many consumer questions are answered by the material in this series. Eight or ten titles are issued annually, but many of them are
in leaflet form. There is a "We
want you to know about ..." series
of leaflets which are periodically
revised that provide consumer infor-

mation about such subjects as salmonella and food poisoning, diagnostic x-rays, nutrition labels on food, impact resistant eyeglass lenses, microwave oven radiation, cosmetics, drugs for food-producing animals, etc. These are excellent sources of information for the general public. Other titles are occasionally specialized reports, but the majority are easily comprehended. Recommended for public libraries.

Item 475-H
HE20.4010:  FOOD AND DRUG ADMINIS-
     TRATION.  FDA consumer.  1967-
     Published ten times a year, the Consumer is an attractively designed and aesthetically appealing periodical.  It reports research and results of the FDA's business of consumer protection.  Typical articles are about the action of the agency with regard to polyvinyl chloride, the cost of prescription drugs, the consumer's relationship to metric measures, animals used in research, and appropriate labeling of products. Regular features include a consumer forum, news highlights, regional reports, and actions by states.  Violations of the Federal Food, Drug, and Cosmetic Act and ensuing seizures are reported monthly.  Two or three years of back files are desirable.  Recommended for academic and public libraries.

Item 475-Q
HE20.4003/3:  FOOD AND DRUG ADMINIS-
     TRATION.  FDA drug bulletin.
     Issued irregularly, but about four times a year, this 4-page leaflet reports information of interest to health professionals.  The information is technical, but portions of it are comprehensible to the general reader.  The bulletin is included here because patrons are also patients and should have the opportunity to review research which affects them directly.  Each issue contains four or five health or drug notes. Recent briefs include discussion of risks to users of oral contraceptives, insulin dosage errors, mammography, health hazards of aerosol propellants, the dangers in the use

of saccharin, and risks in the use of tranquilizers.  Recommended for academic and public libraries.  Five years of back files are desirable.

Item 481-A
HE20.11:  PUBLIC HEALTH SERVICE.
     Bibliography series.
     The main feature of this item is the Bibliography on smoking and health, which is published annually. Other bibliographies reflecting the interests of the Public Health Service are issued irregularly.  Recommended for academic and public libraries.

Item 483-F-1
HE20.8210:  NATIONAL INSTITUTE ON
     DRUG ABUSE.  Marijuana and
     health, annual report to the
     Congress from the Secretary of
     Health, Education and Welfare.
     1st-  1971-  LC 74-610590
     The study of the use of marijuana and its implications for the American people has been a high priority program of the department since the late 1960s.  This annual report is designed to describe the program's progress over the year. It is a source of information about the extent and nature of cannabis use in the United States, preclinical research, behavior, various effects, and therapeutic aspects. Written in a scientific style, the report includes references which provide useful bibliography.  The sixth report is brief and represents a change in focus from previous reports.  It is addressed to a general audience.  Previously, the publication has aimed to reach persons involved in public policy deliberations and the technically trained.
     Two or three years of back files may be desirable.  The report is indexed and contains less than 100 pages.  Recommended for academic and public libraries.

Item 483-I
HE20.13:  PUBLIC HEALTH SERVICE.
     CCPM pamphlets.
     The professionals employed by the Public Health Service are members of either the Civil Service

or the Commissioned Corps of the PHS. These pamphlets are written for the latter group, and they describe career opportunities, benefits, and rewards of the system. One or two are issued annually. The titles are important components of the career literature maintained by libraries.

Item 486
HE20.10:   PUBLIC HEALTH SERVICE.
      Health information series.
      This series of pamphlets and leaflets is about individual health problems. Articles describe the symptoms, cause, and prognosis in simple language, and also give the progress of research in curing or eradicating the ailment. Typical titles include:
      Research explores pyorrhea and
         other gum diseases, no. 133
      Learning disabilities due to
         minimal brain dysfunction,
         no. 140
      Typhoid fever, no. 72.
They serve to educate people to precautions and public health services. Recommended for public libraries.

Item 486-E-1
HE20.5002:   HEALTH SERVICES ADMINIS-
      TRATION. General publications.
      The delivery of health services in community health programs is the focus of the Health Services Administration. The series issues annually one or two titles of varying lengths and with various purposes. Most are directed at the general public. Recent titles include:
      Books that help children deal
         with a hospital experience,
         no. C43
      The National Health Service
         Corps, no. N21h.
Other subjects which may be covered are health maintenance organizations, Indian health care, and professional standards review. The series is recommended for libraries supporting persons involved with health services professions.

Item 486-I-2
HE20.5302:   INDIAN HEALTH SERVICE.
      General publications.

The average library patron would have little personal interest in these titles, but they are notable for their social and educational impact. Most citizens are probably unaware that there is an Indian Health Service. It administers over 50 hospitals, 83 health centers, and 300 health stations, serving 500,000 native Americans and Alaskan natives. These publications serve to describe the program, recruit personnel, and provide literature for the native Americans on health care. Two or three are issued annually. Most are pamphlets. Recommended for academic and public libraries.

Item 491-B-10
HE20.6509:   NATIONAL CENTER FOR
      HEALTH SERVICES RESEARCH.
      Bibliographies and lists of
      publications.
      Useful bibliography is published here, covering such topics as the ethical issues of abortion, euthanasia, genetic engineering, malpractice, and the right to health care. Recent titles include:
      The utilization of health ser-
         vices, no. H34/3
      Health services research, no.
         H34.
Bibliographies, generally annotated, provide useful reference for persons studying or practicing in health fields. About one title is issued annually. Recommended for academic and public libraries.

Item 494-D-4
HE20.7110:   NATIONAL INSTITUTE FOR
      OCCUPATIONAL SAFETY AND HEALTH.
      Standard occupational exposure
      to....
      Workers are exposed to increasing health and safety hazards at their places of work. Since the Occupational Safety and Health Act of 1970, standards in this area have been sought and established to protect workers. The agency has created a formal research program and is actively producing data from which standards can be derived. This series focuses on the perni-

cious effects of exposure to dangerous substances. Three or four studies, 100 to 200 pages in length, are
issued annually. The papers are
technical and are of primary interest to the industrial community.
However, they may also appeal to the
nonspecialist worker under exposure.
Recent subjects of exposure include
zinc oxide, sulfur dioxide, inor-
ganic arsenic, and organic fluorides.
Typically the report contains recommendations for a standard, discussion of the biologic effects of exposure, environmental data, work
practices, and various analyses.
References are included. Recommended for libraries serving patrons
who have interest in the field or
who work under possibly harmful conditions.

Item 497
HE20.6011:  Public health reports.
    Subtitled the official journal
of the Public Health Service, Public
health reports publishes scientific,
technical, administrative, and analytical articles of interest to the
public health profession. The journal is published six times a year.
Issues are usually built around
themes, recently including health of
the elderly, health manpower training, and suicide statistics and so-
ciological variables. Ten to fifteen articles and comment on programs, practices, and people compose the 100-page issue. The layout
is attractive and the journal has
broad appeal. Recommended for academic and public libraries.

Item 497-C-1
HE20.3452:  NATIONAL INSTITUTE OF
    GENERAL MEDICAL SCIENCES. Gen-
    eral publications.
    Reports of progress and find-
ings in medical treatment and services are issued here. Two or three
are published annually in varying
forms. Typical titles include:
    The study of injured patients:
        A trauma conference report,
        no. In5
    What are the facts about ge-
        netic disease?, no. G28/3

Perspectives on engineering in
    biology and medicine, no. En3.
The publications are specialized and
written for the student or professional in the health sciences. Recommended for academic and public libraries.

Item 497-D-1
HE20.8002:  ALCOHOL, DRUG ABUSE, AND
    MENTAL HEALTH ADMINISTRATION.
    General publications.
    These titles are not essential
to any collection, but they are of
value to patrons with concerns similar to those of the agency. Helping states and communities to meet
the needs of Americans suffering
from alcoholism, drug abuse, and
mental illness is the goal of the
agency. The publications reflect
this concern in reports of research
to find means of preventing these
human problems. Most of the titles
are brief. Three or four are produced annually. Recommended for
public libraries.

Item 498-C-1
HE20.8302:  NATIONAL INSTITUTE ON
    ALCOHOL ABUSE AND ALCOHOLISM.
    General publications.
    Educational, outreach, and pub-
lic relations materials compose this
series of titles. Four or five are
issued annually in varying sizes and
formats. Recent titles include:
    Directory of occupational pro-
        gram consultants, no. Oc1/2
    Diagnosis and assessment of al-
        cohol abuse and alcoholism,
        no. Al1/5
    Someone close drinks too much,
        no. D83
    Alcohol: A family affair, no.
        Al1/2.
Individual publications are designed
to reach a broad audience. Recommended for academic and public libraries.

Item 498-C-6
HE20.8313:  NATIONAL INSTITUTE ON
    ALCOHOL ABUSE AND ALCOHOLISM.
    Special report to the U.S. Con-
    gress on alcohol and health.
    1st-  1971-

The existence of this report recognizes the concern of the country about the misuse of alcohol and the control of alcoholism. It is issued infrequently and serves as a comprehensive review of research in the field. Existing areas of knowledge about alcohol and advances in certain aspects of alcohol and health are reported. The second Special report, issued in 1974, includes such topics as economic costs of alcohol-related problems; health consequences and specifically heart disease, cancer, liver disorders, and the central nervous system; health insurance; and heredity and congenital effects. Contributors are from both public and private agencies. The text is written as a research report, but most of the material does not require specialized knowledge of the user. The first Special report was reissued by a commercial publisher. Recommended for academic and public libraries.

Item 499-F-5
HE20.7108/2:  NATIONAL INSTITUTE OF OCCUPATIONAL SAFETY AND HEALTH. NIOSH health and safety guides for various businesses.

These booklets are of a specialized nature, yet many public library patrons either operate or work in one of the types of business under consideration. Each booklet is devoted to one particular business and is about 50 pages in length. It contains information about health and safety guidelines, frequently violated regulations, and emergency procedure. A "fire extinguisher chart" and a "how to lift safely chart" are included in most. Fire protection, good housekeeping, hazardous materials, first aid, etc., are standard topics. The series is new and titles have been issued at a rapid rate. When most businesses have been covered, publication will probably slow up until revisions are needed. Thus far, grain mills, paints manufacturers, paperboard industries, millwork shops, dry cleaners, printers, hotels and motels,

and retail bakeries are some of the operations covered. Recommended for public libraries.

Item 504
HE20.7002:  CENTER FOR DISEASE CONTROL. General publications.

The symptoms and treatments for individual diseases are discussed here in booklets or leaflets and in a popular style. Venereal disease as an individual problem and as a community problem, smoking, ringworm, family planning, and insects are examples of subjects considered in relation to disease-control. An occasional title is a research report, but most have broad appeal. Three or four are issued annually. Recommended for academic and public libraries.

Item 505-A-1
HE20.3252:  NATIONAL INSTITUTE OF ALLERGY AND INFECTIOUS DISEASES. General publications.

A few specialized reports and proceedings are issued here but most are addressed to the general patron. The breadth of the series is best described by recent titles:
  Viruses: On the border of life, no. V81
  Poison ivy allergy, no. P75
  Miscellaneous microbes, no. M58/2
  Bacteria: The littlest cells, no. B13
  The primate malarias, no. M29.
In addition, brief reports are available on rabies, influenza, hepatitis, dust allergy, common cold, strep infections, tuberculosis, mononucleosis, malaria, and numerous other diseases. Most titles are under 20 pages in length; six or eight are issued annually. Recommended for academic and public libraries.

Item 506-A
NATIONAL INSTITUTES OF HEALTH
HE20.3009:  NIH publications list.
HE20.3012:  Bibliographies and lists of publications.

The NIH publications list is issued annually and cites all materials currently available from the

National Institutes of Health. It contains ordering information, and a title and subject index. The list is essential to identifying the available printed materials of this group of institutes.

Bibliographies are issued periodically on subjects related to the research of the institutes. Titles are both general and specialized.

The two series are important acquisitions for the library supporting programs in health science fields.

Item 506-C
HE20.8123: NATIONAL INSTITUTE OF MENTAL HEALTH. Mental health directory. 1964-   LC 65-60647

The directory, published biennially in recent years, provides current details for persons seeking the location and nature of mental health services available throughout the country. It includes listings of state mental health authorities and facilities, organized by state. For each facility, the address, telephone, geographic areas served, auspices, and services provided are listed. The appendix includes other mental health organization listings and a bibliography of similar directories. A useful reference title, this publication is recommended for academic and public libraries.

Item 506-D-2
HE20.3352: NATIONAL INSTITUTE OF CHILD HEALTH AND HUMAN DEVELOPMENT. General publications.

The physical and mental development of children as administered and nurtured by the agency is the basic concern of these publications. Population research, family planning, nutrient requirements, social behavior, disease, and educational progress are typical of the subjects covered by the materials. Some are written for the specialist, but most are easily comprehended by parents and teachers of children and adolescents. Three or four titles are issued annually. Recommended for public libraries and for academic libraries supporting human development in their curricula.

Item 506-D-3
HE20.3361: NATIONAL INSTITUTE OF CHILD HEALTH AND HUMAN DEVELOPMENT. Bibliographies and lists of publications.

This institute conducts research on child health, maternal health, mental retardation, family structure, population dynamics, and human reproduction. Recent and useful bibliographies include:
  Selected bibliography on death and dying, no. D34
  Sudden infant death syndrome: Selected annotated bibliography, no. In3/960-71.
The titles are infrequent. Recommended for academic and public libraries.

Item 507
HE20.3002: NATIONAL INSTITUTES OF HEALTH. General publications.

Six or eight titles are issued annually in this series which reveals and communicates something of the work of the institutes. The publications are written in nontechnical language and in a style which appeals to the average patron. Some serve as reference sources, and some report on surveys. Recent titles include:
  Associate training programs in the medical and biological sciences, no. T68/6
  Volunteer to fight high blood pressure, no. V88/2
  How medical students finance their education, no. M46
  Students: Consider a career in podiatry, no. P75.
The National Institutes of Health are a group of about fifteen research institutes and support services. Their mission is to improve the health of the American people. For more specific research and activity of the individual institutes (the National Cancer Institute, the National Institute of Environmental Sciences, the National Institute of Child Health and Human Development, etc.) one should see the General Publications series of those institutes.

The item is recommended for academic and public libraries.

Item 507-A-25
HE20.3302:  NATIONAL INSTITUTE OF
    ARTHRITIS, METABOLIC AND DI-
    GESTIVE DISEASES.  General pub-
    lications.

A few of these publications are
written for the specialist, but most
have general appeal and serve to
publicize the progress of research.
Other series issued by this agency
are suitable only for professionals
in health research.  Typical subjects include human growth hormones,
nutrition, organ transplants, and
artificial devices.  Recommended for
libraries serving the health professions.

Item 507-B-2
HE20.8117:  NATIONAL INSTITUTE OF
    MENTAL HEALTH.  Mental health
    program reports.

The concern of the National Institute of Mental Health with problems of social importance and the
breadth of its approach are evidenced in these reports.  The reports are made by investigators
working on institute-supported projects.  The papers span some of the
major scientific and clinical themes
in the contemporary study of human
behavior.  A volume of ten or twelve
such reports is issued irregularly,
usually at a rate of one a year.
Recently the investigations have
taken the following topics:  communication through nonverbal behavior,
instrumental training of visceral
functions, death and bereavement,
Chinatowns, biological bases of mem-
ory, reeducation of criminals, and
clinical studies in alcoholism.
This series is a reasonable alternative to similar material being published commercially.  The papers
have broad appeal to students of the
social sciences and to public library patrons as well.

Item 507-B-5
HE20.8102:  NATIONAL INSTITUTE OF
    MENTAL HEALTH.  General publi-
    cations.

Mental health service administered through the agency and throughout society is the focus of these

titles.  Six or eight publications
are issued annually in varying formats and lengths.  Typical titles
include:

> A report:  National Conference
>   on Child Abuse, no. C43/3
> Resource materials for commun-
>   ity mental health program
>   evaluation, no. C73/3
> Directory:  Federally funded
>   community mental health cen-
>   ters, no. C73.

Consultation, continuing education,
finance, and facilities are also
treated in the context of mental
health.  Some titles are obvious
reference materials while others
contribute substantive literature to
the field.  Recommended for academic
and public libraries.

Item 507-B-9
HE20.8113:  NATIONAL INSTITUTE OF
    MENTAL HEALTH.  Bibliographies
    and lists of publications.

These bibliographies focus on
subjects of general concern to the
institute's research.  They cite materials produced by federal agencies
as well as by commercial publishers.
Most are annotated.  They cover current topics often sought after by
patrons.  One or two may be issued
annually.  Recent titles include:

> Family health indicators, no.
>   F21
>
> Selected references on the
>   abused ...child, no. C43/2
> Latino mental health:  Bibliog-
>   raphy and abstracts, no. L34
> Women and mental health, no.
>   W84.

Recommended for academic and public
libraries.

Item 507-B-10
HE20.8108:  NATIONAL INSTITUTE OF
    MENTAL HEALTH.  Handbooks, man-
    uals, guides.

Three or four publications are
issued annually in this series intended for persons working in the
field of mental health.  In effect,
however, these titles have appeal to
a broader population:  to persons
and families served by mental health
agencies, to the person contemplat-

ing a career in mental health, and to the community at large.  Typical titles include:

> A guide for nursing home per-
> sonnel:  Making each person
> count, no. N93
> A consumer's guide to mental
> health services, no. M52
> Film discussion manual, no. F48.

In addition, long-term care facili-ties, communication, educational ma-terials, foundation support, and so-cial work are treated in the context of mental health by various publica-tions.  Recommended for academic and public libraries.

Item 507-B-12
HE20.8116:  NATIONAL INSTITUTE OF
     MENTAL HEALTH.  Statistical
     notes.

Mental health subjects which generate statistics are presented in these 10- to 20-page booklets.  Some subjects are a bit esoteric, but most are relevant to the needs of students and employees of mental health facilities.  Recent studies have analyzed the cost of mental illness annually, alcoholic admis-sions in state and county mental hospitals, staffing of mental hospi-tals, and admission rates by highest level of education attained.  Many of these studies are issued annually. A total of six to eight reports ap-pear in a year.  Recommended for li-braries supporting mental health in-terests.

Item 507-B-19
HE20.8309:  Alcohol health and re-
     search world.  v.1-   Spring
     1973-   LC 73-642496

A quarterly publication pro-duced by the National Institute on Alcohol Abuse and Alcoholism, it is intended for persons working in re-search, treatment, and prevention of alcohol abuse.  Each issue is about 30 pages in length and contains five or six articles about such subjects as young people, residential treat-ment programs, detoxification, and highway accidents.  Accounts of ex-periences are given by alcohol abusers and persons who have worked

with them.  Regular features include book reviews and subject bibliogra-phies.  The quarterly provides im-portant information to the groups mentioned and to families and educa-tors as well.  Recommended for aca-demic and public libraries.

Item 507-C-3
HE20.3710:  JOHN E. FOGARTY INTERNA-
     TIONAL CENTER FOR ADVANCE STUD-
     IES IN THE HEALTH SCIENCES.
     Fogarty International Center
     proceedings.

Conference proceedings on prob-lems in medical care and medical science are published in this series. Recent topics include human genetic defects and early diagnosis; social, demographic, and economic forces which are reshaping the family; poly (ADP-ribose); and reform of medical education.  Proceedings are usually published in bound volumes at a rate of one a year.  Each volume includes the names and affiliations of parti-cipants, the papers presented, and occasionally summary of the discus-sion.  A bibliography is also in-cluded in some papers.  Because many of the symposia deal with broad questions in the field of medicine, public library patrons may find this of interest as well as comprehen-sible.  Libraries supporting health service fields should consider the series.

Item 507-G-2
     NATIONAL CANCER INSTITUTE
HE20.3152:  General publications.
HE20.3168/2:  National Cancer Pro-
     gram strategy plan.
HE20.3168/3:  National Cancer Pro-
     gram publications.
HE20.3169:  National Cancer Program
     progress against....

General Publications provide an overview of the research and pro-gram of the institute.  They are usually nontechnical publications which have broad appeal.  Recent titles include:

> The leukemic child, no. L57/3
> Employment opportunities in the
> National Cancer Institute,
> no. Em7

Treatment and survival patterns
for black and white cancer
patients, 1955-64, no. C16/7/
955-964
The cancer story, no. C16.
Six or eight titles are issued annually.

Progress against (cancer of the
uterus, cancer of the lung, the
mouth, the prostate, the bone, the
bladder, etc.) is reported in a
group of about twelve leaflets that
are revised periodically.

National Cancer Program strategy plan and publications are of
little use to the lay population.
Several are issued annually, but
they should not cause a serious
space problem.

The item is recommended for academic and public libraries.

Item 507-H
HE20.3008: NATIONAL INSTITUTES OF
HEALTH. Handbooks, manuals,
guides.

Three or four guides are issued
annually and are intended for use by
NIH staff. Many guides have application to work outside the institutes and are, therefore, possible
library acquisitions. Recent titles
include:
Guide for the care and use of
laboratory animals, no. An5
The institutional guide to DHEW
policy on protection of human
subjects, no. H88
The National Institutes of
Health radiation safety guide,
no. R11
A guide to the NIH research con-
tracting process, no. R31.

Publications on these and other
subjects covered by the series are
needed by libraries and so the series may be a good alternative to
titles published commercially. The
series is somewhat specialized but
not highly technical. Recommended
for libraries supporting health science programs.

Item 507-H-3
HE20.6015: Commitment.

A quarterly magazine for health
professionals, Commitment contains

material relating to the practice of
health care in underserved areas.
Issues are about 30 pages in length
and are attractively designed. Recent articles have focused on facing
the challenge of health care in a
large city, pharmacists in the Indian Health Service, and a nurse
practitioner clinic. The periodical
is issued by the Health Resources
Administration and has broad appeal.
Recommended for academic and public
libraries.

Item 507-P-1
HE20.3552: NATIONAL INSTITUTE OF
ENVIRONMENTAL HEALTH SCIENCES.
General publications.

This agency is charged with ad-
vancing fundamental knowledge of the
effects of environmental agents on
human health and, ultimately, with
preventing any harmful effects,
which may be chemical, physical, or
biologic. Publications from this
agency have been few to date and focus primarily on the research program. Recent titles include:
National Institute on Environmental Health Sciences Research Programs, no. En8
Man's health and the environment: Some research needs,
no. M31.
In addition, other work of the
agency is covered in the series.
Recommended for libraries serving
interests in environmental health.

Item 507-Y-1
HE20.3752: NATIONAL EYE INSTITUTE.
General publications.

The results and progress on eye
research are reported here. The
most useful materials are the occasionally produced leaflets on eye
disorders--glaucoma, diabetic reti-
nopathy, and cataracts. The publications are useful educational materials for the general audience. A
group of eight or ten are maintained
by occasional revisions. Other research reports and program proceedings are sometimes issued in the series. Recommended for public libraries.

Item 508-E
    NATIONAL LIBRARY OF MEDICINE
HE20.3612:  Index medicus.
HE20.3612/3:  Cumulated Index medi-
    cus.
HE20.3612/3-2:  Cumulated list of
    new medical subject headings.
HE20.3612/4:  List of journals in-
    dexed in Index medicus.

    Index medicus is an index to
biomedical periodical literature,
including original articles, letters,
editorials, biographies, and obitu-
aries of substantive content.  It is
issued monthly; Cumulated Index medicus is an annual.  Both may be ap-
proached by the author or subject
indexes.  The Cumulated list of new
medical subject headings is issued
annually, as is the List of journals
indexed in Index medicus.  Each annual cumulation totals eight lengthy
volumes at present.  Approximately
2,250 journals are indexed.

    The Index medicus is useful to
undergraduates only if they are engaged in rigorous biomedical research.  Public libraries must jus-
tify the need.


Item 508-H-2
HE20.3616:  NATIONAL LIBRARY OF MED-
    ICINE.  Selected references on
    environmental quality as it re-
    lates to health.

    This monthly bibliography cites
selected articles from biomedical
journals which are also cited in the
corresponding monthly issue of Index
medicus, HE20.3612, item 508-E.  Arrangement is by subject headings,
and an author section is included.
The citation includes basic bibliographic information.  Each issue is
about 50 pages in length.  The bibliography cites scientific and technical articles for the most part.
Because these same articles are included in Index medicus, it seems
unnecessary for libraries to receive
both.  This bibliography is recommended for libraries supporting
health professions and similar interests, and in the absence of Index medicus.


Item 509-A-1
HE20.6102:  BUREAU OF HEALTH PLAN-
    NING AND RESOURCES DEVELOPMENT.
    General publications.

    Medical practitioners, support
personnel, and their training are
the themes of several of these publications.  One title which is a
useful reference in some libraries
is Health occupation training programs administered by hospitals:  A
directory, no. Oc1.  Other recent
titles include:
    Foreign medical students in the
        Americas, no. F76/97
    Preparing registered nurses for
        expanded roles, no. N93/3
    Special project grants and con-
        tracts awarded for improve-
        ment in nurse training, no.
        N93/12.
All are profession related and are
useful guidance materials.  Three or
four titles are issued annually.
Recommended for libraries supporting health-related interests.


Item 509-A-2
HE20.6108:  BUREAU OF HEALTH PLAN-
    NING AND RESOURCES DEVELOPMENT.
    Handbooks, manuals, guides.
    The training of health care
professionals is the subject of most
of these guides.  They are important
to guidance, placement, and general
collections of career literature.
Recent titles include:
    Entering an agreement to prac-
        tice in a shortage area, no.
        P56
    Handbook for loan cancellation
        benefit, no. L78
    What can you do?, no. W55.
One or two titles are issued annually.  Recommended for academic and
public libraries.


Item 509-B
HE20.6212:  NATIONAL CENTER FOR
    HEALTH STATISTICS.  Health re-
    sources statistics.  1965-
    LC 66-62580
    Published annually, the volume
provides current and comprehensive
statistics on a wide range of health

fields. It is divided into three categories: employment, inpatient health facilities, outpatient and nonpatient health services. An appropriate amount of textual material accompanies the data. The 600-page volume contains a wealth of reference information and is indexed. Holding the current year only is usually adequate. Recommended for academic and public libraries.

Item 512-C
HE22.102: MEDICAL SERVICES ADMINIS-
TRATION. General publications.
Medicare and medicaid are administered by this office, and these publications reflect that responsibility. Titles are intended to acquaint people with the services. Typical titles include:

Health treatment and screening
for children, no. C43
Medicare, medicaid: Which is
which?, no. M46/4
When you go to the doctor, no.
D65.
One or two publications are issued annually. Recommended for public libraries.

Item 515-A
HE3.51/5: SOCIAL SECURITY ADMINIS-
TRATION. Directory of medi-
care/medicaid providers and
suppliers of services....
The Directory may not have high potential for use as it is intended, but it has possibilities for use as a general directory of medical ser-

vices, including names and addresses. It is a compilation of all medical services which participate as providers or suppliers of medicare services, including hospitals, skilled nurse facilities, home health agencies, outpatient physical therapy, independent laboratories, portable x-ray units, and renal disease treatment centers. The participation of these services in the program set up by the Health Insurance for the Aged Act means that they meet its requirements and are approved by the Department of Health, Education, and Welfare. The directory is organized alphabetically by state and city and is revised as necessary. Recommended as a reference for general medical facilities.

Item 831-C-1
HE20.8215: NATIONAL INSTITUTE ON
DRUG ABUSE. Report series.
One of the functions of this agency is to disseminate information to the public. In this series, significant research is gathered and published on drug-related subjects in an effort to give the general public an overview. The publications are issued about once a month and are 10 to 50 pages in length. Recent subjects include detecting drugs of abuse in body fluids, narcotic antagonists, and treatment of drug abuse. Reports are aimed at a general audience, and they contain references. Recommended for academic and public libraries.

Item 125-A-8
AC1.16: ARMS CONTROL AND DISARMA-
    MENT AGENCY. World military
    expenditures and arms trade.

This report was previously an
annual report of data for the current year, but it has become, since
the 1963-73 edition, an annual of
data for a ten year period. Part of
the data presented here can probably
be found in other publications; however, there is no comparable world
survey. Statistics are presented
textually, in graphs, charts, and
tables; historical data for compilation are included. Appended matter
includes definitions of terms and
notes on the data collection activity. Annuals are about 100 pages in
length. A back file of a few years
is useful. Recommended for academic
and public libraries.

Item 304-G
D1.41: DEPARTMENT OF DEFENSE.
    Profile.

This publication appears
monthly, October through April, to
inform high school students of the
opportunities available to them in
the armed services. It also serves
to keep the public informed of activities of the military. Issues
are about 14 pages in length except
for Basic facts about military service, which appears once a year and
is longer. Regular issues have
three or four short articles. Retention of the current year is adequate. Recommended for public libraries.

Item 306
D1.2: DEPARTMENT OF DEFENSE. Gen-
    eral publications.

There are a number of titles in
this series which are useful to public and academic libraries. Career
materials such as Time for decision:
The Armed Services vocational apti-
tude battery, no. T48, and An auditing career, no. C18/3, recur. The
challenge of change, no. C36, 100
companies receiving the largest dollar volume of prime contract awards,
no. C764/4, and Selected manpower
statistics, no. M31/7, are among
those providing information of reference value to the public. A significant portion of the publications
are related to internal military operations. The series accumulates at
a rate of six to ten titles a year.
Recommended for public and academic
libraries with a need for certain
military information.

Item 315-C
D5.12: JOINT CHIEFS OF STAFF. JCS
    publications.

The most prominent title in
this series is the Dictionary of
military and associated terms, no. 1.
It is revised and updated periodically and should be discarded as the
new edition appears. Terms with
broad significance to defense and to
the military are included. The Dictionary is produced in an effort to
standardize terminology and to improve communication within the department, among agencies of the government, and with the civilian com-

munity.  This is a valuable reference tool in some collections.  Recommended for libraries serving patrons interested in the military.

Item 322
D101.12:  Soldiers.  v.1-    1948-
    The official magazine of the United States Army has a place in some libraries.  This monthly serves the civilian public as a source of information on policies of, and changes in, this branch of the service.  Each issue contains feature articles on army assignments, benefits, obligations, and personnel. Articles feature historical subjects such as the participation of black Americans in the war for independence, the Battle of the Alamo, and other military expeditions.  Consumer advice, tax tips, legal aid, and recreation are other typical subjects.  One or two years' back files are adequate.  Recommended for academic and public libraries, but it should be given the same treatment as Airman, D301.60, item 422-D, and All hands, D207.17, item 401.

Item 325
D101.2:  DEPARTMENT OF THE ARMY.
    General publications.
    Of use in career guidance, these materials also show up at army recruitment offices.  The entire series has a broader scope than recruitment, however, for it informs the public of army programs.  Career publications, many of which describe programs, scholarship, benefits, and obligations, include:
    Army ROTC, no. R31/21, frequently updated, a comprehensive look at the program
    Add flying to your college career in Army ROTC, no. R31/15
    Assignment ...AG, no. Ad4
    Let yourself grow:  The women's Army corps, no. Y8/3.
Of more popular interest are
    Spirit of America, no. Am3, commemorating the two hundredth anniversary of the army
    Willamette  National Cemetery,

no. W66
Your Army, 200 years. no. Ar5/17.
    Some are updated; superseded titles should be discarded.  Recommended for academic and public libraries, or in accord with policy for items 370, 424, and 383.

Item 356
D12.2:  NATIONAL GUARD BUREAU.  General publications.
    This series produces only two or three titles a year and is primarily concerned with publicity for the National Guard.  The brochure format predominates:
    Spend a weekend with the boys, no. Ar5/5
    What every veteran should know about the Army National Guard, no. Ar5/4
    A great field for a woman, no. Ai7/4.
Recommended to support career materials in libraries maintaining them.

Item 370
D201.2:  NAVY DEPARTMENT.  General publications.
    Unlike the corresponding series for the other branches of the military, this navy series does not emphasize recruitment and career materials.  It is a combination of glossy public relations and technical publications.  They provide important information, and, even without recruitment materials, have a use in libraries.  Recent titles include:
    Hydroballistics modeling, no. H99
    The Navy in Vietnam, no. V67
    Navy birthday:  A family tradition, October 13, 1973, no. N22/5.
As with other general publications of military services, these vary in length and format.  Usually there are three or four published a year. Recommended for academic and public libraries, or in accord with the policy regarding items 424, 383, and 325.

Item 383
D214.2:  MARINE CORPS.  General pub-
     lications.
     This series was more active in
the 1960s when the Marine Corps was
more active.  It is probably the
chief group of titles to convey Marine Corps activities to the general
population.  Subject matter varies
from public relations and career
aids to books of internal interest
only.  Recent examples include:
     Sing and be joyful:  The chapel
         songbook, no. Si6
     Challenges in leadership:  A
         text for U.S. Marine Corps
         ROTC, no. L46/2
     Occupational opportunities, no.
         Oc1
     The Marine officer candidate
         handbook, no. Of2/3
     Telling the Marine Corps story,
         no. St7.
Recommended for academic and public
libraries, or in accord with policy
for items 370, 424, and 325.

Item 390-A
D208.109:  NAVAL ACADEMY, ANNAPOLIS,
     MARYLAND.  Catalog.
     The annual catalog of courses,
activities, and staff, should be ac-
quired by all libraries maintaining
a college catalog collection.  Previous editions may be discarded.

Item 401
D207.17:  All hands:  The Bureau of
     Naval Personnel information
     bulletin.  LC 43-37008
     The magazine of the United
States Navy lacks the appeal of the
comparable army publication, Soldiers, D101.12, item 322.  The
monthly includes consumer advice and
articles of popular interest, but it
is heavy on in-house material:  naval strategy, submarine adventures,
and other technical features.  Nevertheless, because of the prevalence
of the military in American life,
many libraries will want to give it
the same treatment as Soldiers, Airman, D301.60, item 422-D.  One or
two years of back files are adequate.

Item 421-F
D301.79:  DEPARTMENT OF THE AIR
     FORCE.  Soviet military thought
     series.  No. 1-  1970-
     Significant books in recent So-
viet military writing are translated
into English and published in this
series.  Persons interested in contemporary Soviet affairs will find
it important.  The volumes are published at a rate of about one a year.
The philosophical heritage of V. I.
Lenin and problems of contemporary
war, no. 5, was published in the Soviet Union in 1972, and the U.S. ed-
itor conjectures that the book is
for use in the Soviet military.  It
applies Lenin's philosophy and methodology to modern warfare and Soviet
military organization.  Basic principles of operational art and tac-
tics, no. 4, was published in 1972
and was recommended reading for the
armed forces.  All of these titles
are heavy reading regardless of language and it would be surprising to
find them widely read anywhere.
Nevertheless, they are representative Soviet military writing and
recommended for academic libraries.

Item 422-D
D301.60:  Airman.  v.1-  Aug. 1957-
     LC 59-43590
     This monthly carries features
of a similar scope of content as
does All hands, D207.17, item 401.
As the official magazine of the
United States Air Force, it is of
greater value to persons involved
in the service than it is to civil-
ians.  Recent articles of broad appeal include such subjects as the
Soviet armed forces, Americans living in Turkey, and the adoption of
foreign children.  Airman communicates to the nonmilitary person
something of the air force's activity and should be treated as All
hands and Soldiers, D101.12, item
322, by libraries.

Item 424
D301.2:  AIR FORCE.  General publi-
     cations.

This series contains the expected materials on career guidance, recruitment and public relations, along with a few technical documents of interest only to air force personnel. The formats vary from leaflets to books of several hundred pages. Publications are issued at a rate of three to ten a year. Examples include:

Dynamic response of materials to intense impulsive loading, no. M41/2

Find yourself as a physician, no. P56/4

Get off the ground with Air Force ROTC, no. R31/8

Welcome to Britain: Base guide to RAF Lakenheath, no. B72.

Patrons with an interest in the air force will be attracted to, and served by, this item. It also informs the general public of the service's activities. Recommended for academic and public libraries, or in accord with the policy regarding items 325, 370, and 383.

Item 425-A

D305.8: AIR FORCE ACADEMY, UNITED STATES AIR FORCE ACADEMY, COLORADO. Catalog.

The annual catalog of courses, facilities, and requirements for this service academy should be included in any library maintaining a college catalog collection. Previous editions may be discarded.

Item 865-B

AC1.11/2: ARMS CONTROL AND DISARMAMENT AGENCY. Documents on disarmament. 1945-59- LC 60-64408

A compilation of the basic documents of arms control and disarmament developments in a given year, this volume also includes the annual report of the agency. Listed topically and chronologically, documents are typically: statements made by members of principal disarmament organizations and conferences, resolutions, working papers, and agreements coming out of various groups working toward arms control and disarmament. The series chronicles the

work of the agency since its establishment in 1961. Each volume is indexed, contains bibliographies of other federal and United Nations publications pertinent to the subject, and is several hundred pages in length. Recommended for academic and public libraries.

Item 930-B

TD5.16/2: COAST GUARD ACADEMY, NEW LONDON, CONNECTICUT. Bulletin of information.

The bulletin follows the standard college catalog format. It includes information about staff, facilities, and requirements, and it lists courses. Recommended for college catalog collections of academic and public libraries.

Item 934

TD5.2: COAST GUARD. General publications.

Interspersed with a few technical reports on Coast Guard discoveries are printed materials of interest to travelers, placement and guidance personnel, and boaters. Formats and lengths are varying. Titles of interest to library patrons are

Historically famous lighthouses, no. L62/2

Coast Guard reserve, no. Of2

A civilian career in the Coast Guard, no. C49

Marine communications for the boating public, no. C73.

Other subjects include Coast Guard history, navigation, and research reports. Six or eight titles are issued a year. Revisions are issued frequently and older editions should be discarded. Recommended for academic and public libraries.

Item 982-F-1

TD5.15: COAST GUARD ACADEMY. Cadet profile.

This annual leaflet provides information on curriculum, selection of candidates, qualifications for admission, and data on typical cadets: class standing, test performance, age and extracurricular activities. These facts are useful to persons making choices toward careers.  Recommended to accompany college materials in public libraries.

Item 1075
     SELECTIVE SERVICE SYSTEM
Y3.Se4:2  General publications.
Y3.Se4:10-2/  Handbooks, manuals, guides.
     In times of an active conscription, these publications would probably be issued more frequently. They are useful pamphlets for persons affected by the system and for persons working with registrants. Recent titles include:
     Conscientious objectors, no. Y3.Se4:2/C76/2
     Perspective on the standby Selective Service System, no. Y3.Se4:2/P43
     Why Selective Service?, no. Y3.Se4:10-2/W62
     Reconciliation service, no. Y3.Se4:10-2/R24.
Selective Service materials are important for public perusal.  Recommended for all libraries.

Item 1076
Y3.Se4:1  SELECTIVE SERVICE SYSTEM. Report of the director.  1950/51-  LC 52-60414
     This country has only in the last few years ended a period of over a quarter of a century in which armed forces personnel have been procured by conscription.  The reports of the years of conscription are of quite a different nature than those of today.  General subjects of registration, classification, medical specialists, alternative service programs, amnesty, training, and re-

serve officers are reported on.  Appendixes support these topics.  The present status of the Selective Service program determines the report. Recommended for academic and public libraries.

Item 1077-C
Y3.Se4:25  SELECTIVE SERVICE SYSTEM. Draft information series.
     This series has no reason to be active at this particular time.  A decade ago, families and men of draft age could not get enough information about their responsibilities and alternatives.  This series remains important for that reason. It once produced these titles:
     The doctors' draft, no. D65
     Hardship benefits, no. H22
     Draft:  Past, present, and future, no. D78/2
     Lottery and class 1-H, no. L91.
If this country abolishes the Selective Service System, libraries can abandon the series.  Meanwhile, recommended for all libraries.

Item 1079-B
Y3.Se4:24  SELECTIVE SERVICE SYSTEM. List of local boards of the Selective Service System.  LC 74-644841
     The List is organized by state, giving each local board with its code number, jurisdiction, mailing address, and telephone number.  The Selective Service System and its boards have retreated from the public eye, but they should not be forgotten.  Revised periodically, this directory has been an important reference item in academic and public libraries.

Item 909
SI1.1: SMITHSONIAN INSTITUTION.
    Smithsonian year. 1964/65-
    LC 67-7980
    Annual reports of many agencies
are not essential to the interests
of the bulk of the libraries under
consideration, but this publication
is an exception in several respects.
It supersedes the Smithsonian Institution's former Report of the secretary, the Annual report of the Board
of regents, and the U.S. National
Museum's Annual report. In addition,
because the activities of the Smithsonian Institution have broad appeal
to the population, both scholar and
citizen, the annual reports of the
various agencies are also likely to
be enjoyed by library patrons. The
Smithsonian year, along with other
publications of the institution,
partially fulfills the behest of
James Smithson, "to found at Washington, under the name of the
Smithsonian Institution, an establishment for the increase and dif-
fusion of knowledge among men."
    The volumes are long, now ap-
proaching 500 pages, and are written
with expression and enthusiasm which
characterizes the institution. They
are attractively designed and include illustrations. Each volume is
organized by its bureaus and carries

reports of the year's activity in
the sciences, history and art and in
its museums and public services.
Appended material includes a list of
publications of the Smithsonian Institution Press for the year, a useful section for librarians. Recommended for libraries serving patrons
with keen interest in arts and sciences, whether academic or popular.

Item 910
SI1.2: SMITHSONIAN INSTITUTION.
    General publications.
    Titles typically describe the
program and bureaus of the Smithsonian Institution, or are accounts
of historical or natural subjects
available for observation in the
collections of the institute. (In
the heat of Bicentennial activity,
this series perhaps generated more
publications than in other years.)
Recent issuances include:
    We the people: The American
        people and their government,
        no. Am1/2
    And the band played on, 1776-
        1976, no. B22/776-976
    The First Ladies Hall, no. F51
    The Hirshhorn Museum and Sculp-
        ture Garden, no. H61/7.
Three or four titles are issued a
year in varying lengths. Recommended for all libraries.

## PHYSICS AND CHEMISTRY

Item 246-A

C13.22/sec.A NATIONAL BUREAU OF
STANDARDS. Journal of research.
A. Physics and chemistry.
v.63A- July-Aug. 1959-
LC 62-37059

Four to six articles are included in each issue of this journal published six times a year. The papers are of primary interest to persons in the fields of physics and chemistry. Articles are written by scientists employed by the bureau and on invitation, by persons outside the federal government. Properties of water, fundamental constants, and a wide range of physical and chemical research are reported here. Advanced undergraduates should have access to this.

## RECREATION AND TRAVEL

Item 85

A13.13: FOREST SERVICE. Information pamphlets relating to national forests.

These pamphlets and brochures are items which are frequently available at visitors' centers in national forests but are useful to people in making plans before they arrive. They include the maps available for all forests and descriptive materials about some areas. Points of interest, scenic tours, trails, winter sports, etc., are all features of the publications. Recommended for libraries serving interests in outdoor recreation.

Item 271-A-1

C47.2: TRAVEL SERVICE. General publications.

The agency serves primarily to attract tourism to the United States from abroad, and to acquaint visitors with this country. Some of the brochures are also of use to Americans traveling in this country. Other materials include studies of travel habits of various nationalities and statistical summaries of international travel to the United States. Recommended for public libraries.

Item 314
D2.8:  DEPARTMENT OF DEFENSE.
     Pocket guides.
     Prepared for the use of U.S.
military personnel stationed in
other countries, these guides provide useful information for all
Americans traveling abroad. The
guides are pocket size and vary from
75 to 125 pages. They include pictures of military uniforms, flags,
background and history, language
guides, currency aids, and other information typically found in travel
books. The guides are available for
major countries or areas of the
world and provide an alternative for
libraries that cannot afford comprehensive travel collections. Guides
are revised about every ten years,
and old ones should be discarded.
Recommended for libraries as need
dictates.

Item 431-A-1
TD4.17:  FEDERAL AVIATION ADMINIS-
     TRATION. FAA publications.
     What has been an annual bibli-
ography is becoming less frequent
but, presumably, has not been discontinued. It is a list of publications of the agency which may be of
interest to the public, pilots, and
the aviation industry. Basic bibliographic information, annotations,
and ordering information are included. As a reference tool, it
provides increased control of the
agency's publications. Recommended
for academic and public libraries.

Item 431-A-11
TD4.9:  FEDERAL AVIATION ADMINISTRA-
     TION. FAA aviation news.  v.1-
     May 1962-   LC 67-3244
     Published monthly by the agency,
the periodical serves to acquaint
the public with its policies and
programs. Issues are brief as are
the articles. Much of the emphasis
is on safety, and articles deal with
emergency responses, proper maintenance, runway hazards, and weather.
Other topics include famous flights,
visual illusions, lighting systems,
and passenger screening. Most writing is directed to private pilots

and small aircraft. Patrons are attracted to this periodical written
in nontechnical language. Recommended for public libraries.

Item 431-C-8
TD4.2:  FEDERAL AVIATION ADMINISTRA-
     TION. General publications.
     Some titles here are adminis-
trative and intended for the aviation industry. Several, however,
are guides for the individual or
groups using aircraft privately.
Typical of those titles are
     Look before you lease ..., no.
     L48
     A flight to grandmother's, no.
     F64/2
     Advisory circulars: Mainte-
     nance records ..., no. M28/5
     FAA film catalog, no. F48, an
     annual.
Other subjects covered are conference reports, noise, individual airport studies, aviation statistics,
education. They vary in format and
length. Six or eight titles are issued a year. Local private pilots
and aviation clubs will be interested in this series. Recommended
for public libraries.

Item 431-C-14
TD4.20:  FEDERAL AVIATION AGENCY.
     FAA statistical handbook of
     aviation. 1944-   LC 46-26093
     Published annually, the primary
purpose of the handbook is to serve
as a source of data to persons interested in civil aviation. The
functions of the FAA, all features
of air traffic, airport facilities,
etc., are represented by tabular
data in this statistical report. It
is over 100 pages in length and contains quite a bit of data which are
more detailed than the needs of most
patrons. It is, nevertheless, an
important reference tool for large
collections.

Item 612-C
I49.44:  FISH AND WILDLIFE SERVICE.
     Refuge leaflets.
     The Wildlife Refuge System is a
collection of lands and waters selected for their value to the na-

tion's wildlife populations, particularly migratory birds and endangered species of mammals.  Leaflets
in this series describe the system
as a federal agency and the individual refuges, mammals, and birds to
be found in them.  They include maps,
visitors' guides, and regulations.
Some list species of wildlife protected and bibliography for further
study.  Examples include:

> Wheeler (Alabama) National
>   Wildlife Refuge, no. 7R
> Mammals of Santa Ana (Texas)
>   National Wildlife Refuge, no.
>   312
> The National Wildlife Refuge
>   System, no. 1A/4.

These titles have broad popular appeal.  Recommended for academic and
public libraries.

Item 612-E
I49.6/2:  FISH AND WILDLIFE SERVICE.
     Handbooks, manuals, guides.
     Visitor information booklets,
tour guides, master plans, etc.,
compose this item.  Titles are not
issued frequently, but they are useful.  All are brief and of interest
to patrons who frequent wildlife
refuges.  Recommended for academic
and public libraries.

Item 613
     BUREAU OF SPORT FISHERIES AND
     WILDLIFE.
I49.24:  Hunting regulations.
I49.24/2:  through I49.24/6:  Summary
     of federal hunting regulations
     governing the hunting, posses-
     sion, transportation, and im-
     portation of [various birds in
     various flyways].
     Issued annually, these guides
contain federal regulations governing the hunting, possession, transportation, and importation of migratory birds in the United States.
Laws for individual states, which
are sometimes more restrictive than
federal law, are not included in
this announcement.  Addresses of
sources of more complete information
are included.  The announcements are
reprinted from the Code of federal
regulations, GS4.108, item 572,

title 50, chapter 1, subchapter B,
part 20.  Smaller libraries that do
not receive CFR will want to keep
these guides current.

Item 631
I53.2:  BUREAU OF LAND MANAGEMENT.
     General publications.
     Yet another group of materials
which serve as guides to tourists
and people using federal lands for
recreational purposes, these titles
also include environmental impact
statements and other publications
which describe BLM responsibilities.
Representative titles include:

> Public land facts, no. P96/8
> BLM recreation guide for Ore-
>   gon, no. R24/2
> Lewis and Clark:  A brief ac-
>   count of their expedition,
>   no. L58
> Fact sheet:  Wild horses, no.
>   H78.

Varying formats.  Three or four
titles are issued annually.  Recommended for public libraries.

Item 632
I53.9:  BUREAU OF LAND MANAGEMENT.
     Information bulletins.
     Five subjects are dealt with in
leaflets revised periodically:

> What are the "public lands"?,
>   no. 1
> What about land in Alaska, no.
>   2
> Camping on the public lands,
>   no. 3
> How to buy public lands, no. 4
> The Taylor Grazing Act, no. 5.

Patrons will find these interesting.
Some of the subjects are typical of
the kinds of questions that the public has about federal land.  Maintaining current editions of these
bulletins is performing an important
public service.  Recommended for
public libraries.

Item 633
I53.7/2:  BUREAU OF LAND MANAGEMENT.
     Handbooks, manuals, guides.
     Some of these titles are admin-
istrative, but even so they have potential usefulness to users of public lands, such as ecology or

recreation. Some may be useful in
the classroom. They vary in format
and size. Representative titles include:

> Lower Salmon River guide, no.
> Sa3
> All around you: An environmen-
> tal study guide, no. En8
> Learning all about the environ-
> ment, no. En8/2.

Two or three titles are issued annually. Recommended for academic and
public libraries.

Item 633-A
I53.12: Our public lands. v.1-
    Apr. 1951-  LC 60-33660
    Published by the Bureau of Land
Management, this quarterly periodical reflects the responsibility of
the department for nationally owned
public lands and natural resources.
Articles are brief, as are the quarterly issues, and cover the subjects
of water, fish, wildlife, minerals,
park and recreational resources, and
Indian and territorial affairs. The
conservationist citizen and student
will enjoy this title. A few years
are adequate for back file. Recommended for academic and public libraries.

Item 646-B
I29.66: NATIONAL PARK SERVICE.
    Areas administered by the Na-
    tional Park Service. LC 49-
    45754
    This list issued periodically
includes basic statistics on the
properties: name and location,
acreage, outstanding characteristics
and pertinent data, and postal address. It is organized by category
of area. This is a useful reference.
Recommended for academic and public
libraries.

Item 646-C
I29.71: NATIONAL PARK SERVICE.
    Camping in the National Park
    System.
    A guide, revised periodically
to update camping information on all
the facilities of the system, the
publication charts all park and
campground areas. It gives for each

a map reference, the camping season,
limit of stay, campground type, number of sites and spaces, group camps,
fee, and other comfort and recreational facilities available. Brief
textual remarks outline some rules
and regulations. A useful reference
recommended for academic and public
libraries.

Item 646-G
I29.80: NATIONAL PARK SERVICE.
    Scientific monograph series.
    Research conducted by and/or
financed by the National Park Service is published here. The new series has issued impressive works so
far. Two examples:

> The bison of Yellowstone Na-
> tional Park, no. 1
> Invasion and recovery of vege-
> tation after a volcanic erup-
> tion in Hawaii, no. 5.

While scientific, the reports have
potential appeal to a broad group of
patrons. They are interesting reading and seem to be the beginning of
a promising series. Recommended for
academic and public libraries.

Item 648
I29.2: NATIONAL PARK SERVICE. Gen-
    eral publications.
    In this series there is a broad
range of travel materials: for individual geographical areas, for facilities maintained by the agency,
for seasonal activities, types of
recreation, buildings. Careers with
the Park Service, its educational
programs, authority, and responsibilities are subjects of some titles.
Four or five titles a year are issued. Formats and lengths vary.
Representative titles include:

> Welcome to Washington, no.
> W27/5
> Seasonal employment, no. Em7
> Environmental education, no.
> En8/2
> Delaware, an inventory of his-
> toric engineering and indus-
> trial sites, no. D37.

Revised editions of earlier titles
are issued periodically. Materials
from this and other National Park
Service series are a boon to public

library travel collections and to those maintained at academic libraries.

Item 648-A
I29.9/2:  NATIONAL PARK SERVICE.
   Handbooks, manuals, guides.
   Some titles are administrative guides, but most are of interest to the park system user.  They are booklets issued infrequently about some feature of the park program. Representative titles include:
   Campfire programs, no. C15
   Mountaineering, Mount McKinley National Park, Alaska, no. M86
   National Park Service guide to historic places of the American Revolution, no. Am3
   National Park guide for the handicapped, no. H19.
Recommended for academic and public libraries.

Item 649
   NATIONAL PARK SERVICE
I29.58:  Historical handbook series.
I29.58/2:  National Park Service history series.
   The history and development of individual National Park Service facilities are written into visitors' handbooks less than 100 pages in length and issued irregularly.  Pictures, maps, and artist's conceptions usually accompany the text of the Historical Handbook series.  The series is an important contribution to the historical literature of the country.  Titles include:
   Whitman Mission, National Historic Site, no. 37
   Antietam, National Battlefield Site, no. 31.
   Events, persons, and historical situations, rather than places, are the subjects of the National Park Service History series.  They have a format similar to the Historical Handbook series and are written in a popular style.  Representative titles include:
   John Brown's raid, no. B81
   Booker T. Washington, no. W27
   Campaign for Petersburg, no. P44.

The two series are recommended for academic and public libraries.

Item 650
I29.21:  NATIONAL PARK SERVICE.
   Information circulars on National Monuments and Military Parks.
   Publications similar to those found in Information Circulars, I29.6, item 651, are issued here for national monuments and military parks.  The guides contain maps and explanatory material about the sites. Examples include:
   Wilson's Creek National Battlefield, Missouri, no. W69
   White Sands National Monument, New Mexico, no. W58
   Wright Brothers National Memorial, North Carolina, no. W93.
Revisions are issued periodically. Recommended for academic and public libraries.

Item 651
   NATIONAL PARK SERVICE.
   Information circulars.
I29.6:  National Parks.
I29.6/2:  National Seashores.
I29.6/3:  National Lakeshores.
I29.6/4:  National Rivers.
I29.6/5:  National Scenic Trails.
   These circulars are the sort of publication available at a National Park Service Visitor Center.  However, many persons enjoy seeing them in advance and appreciate finding the printed material available. Some include regulations of the area, warnings about plants and animals, and pictures.  Revisions are issued periodically.  Some of the more popular installations and those in multilingual locations issue circulars in other languages.  Representative guides include:
   Mount McKinley, no. I29.6:M86
   Haleakala, no. I29.6:H13
   Fire Island National Seashore, no. I29.6/2:F51
   Sleeping Bear Dunes National Lakeshore, no. I29.6/3:Sℓ26
   Ozark National Scenic Riverways, Missouri, no. I29.6/4:Oz1
   Appalachian Natural Scenic Trail, no. I29.6/5:Ap4.
Recommended for all libraries.

Item 651-A

I29.8:  NATIONAL PARK SERVICE.
   Maps.
   The maps for individual national parks show physical relief,
political units, roads, bike routes,
trails, camp grounds, picnic areas,
and other useful park features.  In
addition, textual description is included for the area.  Recommended
for academic and public libraries.


Item 654

I29.39:  NATIONAL PARK SERVICE.
   National Recreational Areas,
   information circulars.
   Identical in format and coverage to items 650 and 651, these circulars are distinguishable only by
the facility they describe.  Examples:
   Delaware Water Gap National
      Recreation Area, no. D37
   Bighorn Canyon National Recrea-
      tion Area, no. B48.
Recommended for academic and public
libraries.


Item 654-A

I29.62:  NATIONAL PARK SERVICE.
   Natural history handbooks.
   These are beautifully written
stories of particular National Park
Service facilities.  Recent ones in-
clude:
   Saguaro National Monument,
      Arizona, no. Sa1
   The nature of Shenandoah, no.
      Sh4
   Everglades wildguide, no. Ev2.
They are about 100 pages in length,
replete with color photography of
wildlife.  Most are written by naturalists who know and love the area.
Included are discussions of the
flora and fauna, the geology of the
area, native Americans of the area,
the impact of white man, and maps.
Appendixes include supplementary detail.  The appeal is to all ages.
Recommended for academic and public
libraries.


Item 657-B-1

I66.2:  BUREAU OF OUTDOOR RECREATION.
   General publications.
   Typical of general publications,

these provide materials and studies
of various features of outdoor recreation.  Representative titles include:
   Islands of America, no. Is4
   Outdoor recreation:  A legacy
      for America, no. Ou8/2
   Nationwide outdoor recreation
      plan:  Final environmental
      statement, no. En8
   Off-road vehicle use on federal
      lands, no. V53
   Working for the Bureau of Out-
      door Recreation, no. W89.
There are also ecological studies of
facilities.  Format and length vary;
many are beautifully designed travel
guides.  Three or four titles are
issued a year.  Recommended for academic and public libraries.


Item 657-B-5

I66.17:  BUREAU OF OUTDOOR RECREA-
   TION.  Outdoor recreation action.  Aug. 1966-   LC 67-60945
   Published quarterly, the periodical reports actions, both governmental and private, which support
recreation.  Typical articles are
about protecting land, seasonal recreation activities, local recreation
groups, legislation, conference reports, and regional cooperation.
Book reviews, publications lists,
and research reports are regular
features.  Articles vary in length
and issues are about 50 pages each.
With a larger budget, the bureau
could undoubtedly produce a more
attractive periodical complete with
color illustrations.  The publication is still an important addition
to academic libraries supporting
recreation and athletics in the
curriculum, and for public libraries.
An extensive back file is not necessary.


Item 657-B-7

I66.8:  BUREAU OF OUTDOOR RECREATION.
   Handbooks, manuals, guides.
   Publications reflecting outdoor
needs and activities are found here.
Representative materials include:
   Miniature environments:  An en-
      vironmental guidebook, no. En8
   Recreational community garden-

ing, no. G16
A catalog of guides to outdoor
recreation areas and facilities, no. G94.
Titles are issued irregularly, and
they are good reference sources for
both public and academic libraries.

Item 950
T17.2:  CUSTOMS SERVICE. General
publications.
TD5.12/2:  COAST GUARD.  Merchant
vessels of the United States.
LC 6-35358
Titles in the General Publications series are primarily guides to
the importation of goods by United
States citizens.  They reflect the
functions of the Customs Service as
it is engaged in handling goods to
and from abroad.  Most publications
are in pamphlet format and are designed to inform the public.
Customs hints for returning
residents:  What to know before you go, no. C96/13

Trademark information, no. T67
Importing a car, no. C17
Customs highlights for government personnel, no. G74
The customs concept for merchandise and revenue pro-
cessing, no. M54.
Most titles are revised annually.
Older ones can be discarded.  The
series is an important component of
a library's travel collection.  Recommended for academic and public libraries.

The major drawback of this item
is the inclusion of Merchant vessels
of the United States.  It is an annual, listing the names of American
merchant vessels and yachts having
current marine documents during the
given year.  Changes of names are
noted and there is an index to managing owners.  The volume is large
and takes up space needed by less
esoteric titles.  The most practical
decision for all libraries is to
purchase T17.2.

## SOCIOLOGY AND SOCIAL SERVICE

Item 30-A-2
AA1.11:  ACTION. Pamphlets.
Youth, the retired, and persons
midstream in their careers are attracted to this series for the ideas
it offers.  Pamphlets are frequently
devoted to one traditional profession and suggest the transferability
of one's training and skills to volunteer service.  The publication describes the need for the service,
project examples, and the procedure
for joining one of the volunteer
services.  Examples:
Nurses in Peace Corps and Vista,
no. 4000-1
Lawyers in ACTION, no. 4300-2/2

Your next move as an engineer,
no. 4200.5.
Some pamphlets are descriptions of
service programs:
Service corps of retired exec-
utives, no. 4600-1
Foster grandparent program,
no. 4400-2.
At least one subseries appears to be
emerging:
Directory of college student
volunteer programs, no.
4000.10.
Other material describes general opportunities and gives accounts of service performed.  The
series can alert both those who have

skills and time to volunteer and
those in need of the service or the
opportunities available to them.
Ten to fifteen titles are issued annually. They are brief and do not
conform in size and format. Recommended for academic and public libraries.

Item 74-C-2
AA1.13:  Interaction.  1972-
  LC 74-646318
    A publication for persons in
volunteer service, this monthly tab-
loid is of interest to many people
outside the service area. News stories by and about persons in both
domestic and foreign volunteer programs, regular columns on educational resources materials, and communication from the ACTION administration are standard features. In
addition there is a column of educational opportunities, particularly
graduate or intern programs, which
may be of interest to persons currently doing volunteer service. A
recent issue contained a notice of
free books available to help volunteers in their work from a women's
group and also information on the
availability of single copies of a
"how to fix" series of books. This
sort of information is in every issue and adds to the general appeal
of the periodical. Because ACTION,
the agency which issues the periodical, has enfranchised older Americans into its volunteer group and
therefore gives them coverage in
this publication, Interaction has
another reason for being important
reading material in a public library.
Academic libraries should also consider it as a part of their career
literature.

Item 74-C-4
AA1.1:  ACTION. Annual report.
  1st-  1972-
    Most ACTION publications serve
as an introduction to the programs
of the volunteer agency, and they
are an important acquisition if a
wide range of ideas is desired.
However, for a comprehensive account
of the year and of programs contin-

uing in various regions, this Annual
report is most useful. About 50
pages in length, it contains pictures and other graphics to further
describe the projects. Recommended
for academic and public libraries.

Item 74-D-1
AA3.9:  Synergist.  v.1-  Fall
  1971-
    This periodical, published
three times a year by the National
Student Volunteer Program of ACTION,
differs from Interaction, AA1.13,
item 74-C-2, in that Synergist follows closely the activities of the
student volunteers. A typical issue
is 50 to 70 pages in length and includes a variety of articles about
student volunteer programs around
the country and abroad. Practical
advice on such things as organizational techniques, project budget-
ing, and faculty roles in off-
campus volunteer service appear as
articles in most issues. Regular
features include announcements of
various information resources available from the government and commercial outlets, legal advice on how
state and federal laws may be useful
to the programs of various volunteers, and a report from London on
volunteer activities in Great Britain. The publication is of greatest
interest to the student volunteer,
but it will also be attractive to
the high school or college student
contemplating a service program.
Synergist is good browsing material.
Recommended for academic and public
libraries.

Item 208-A-1
J23.2:  COMMUNITY RELATIONS SERVICE.
  General publications.
    This agency was created by the
Civil Rights Act of 1964 to help
groups of individuals solve dis-
agreements relating to perceived
problems of discrimination. The
agency seeks to settle these disputes which may grow out of racial
encounters and to promote justice.
Publications reflect the conflicts,
conciliation, and mediation which
are the work of the agency. Some

titles merely explain the services offered. Some are attempts at solutions, such as New minority enterprises, no. M66, which is a list of data. There is also a group of pamphlets describing various disputes and the appropriate action to take. One or two titles are issued annually. Recommended for public libraries.

Item 208-A-2
J23.8:  COMMUNITY RELATIONS SERVICE.
    Handbooks, manuals, guides.
    The only title issued here recently is Guidelines for effective human relations commissions, no. H88/2. It is a pamphlet, revised periodically, and useful for ideas about organization, membership, budget, staff, etc. Recommended for public libraries.

Item 288-A
    COMMISSION ON CIVIL RIGHTS
CR1.2:  General publications.
CR1.8:  Hearings.
CR1.10:  Clearinghouse publications.
CR1.12:  Civil rights digest.
    At present all depository series of the Civil Rights Commission are included in this item number. The commission was established in 1957 as a temporary, independent, and bipartisan office to monitor the constitutional rights of all persons, to serve as a clearinghouse for information about the commission's service and actions, and to prepare reports about their work.
    In the General Publications series one finds reports of civil rights problems in, for instance, minority or ethnic populations, made by state advisory committees to the commission, and reports of the commission about current civil rights issues. Note particularly:
    Route 128: Boston's road to
        segregation, no. B6
    Twenty years after Brown:
        Equality of economic oppor-
        tunity, no. B81
    Federal civil rights enforce-
        ment effort, various numbers
    Freedom to the free, century of
        emancipation, 1863-1963, no.
        F87.

    The transcripts of hearings held at various places around the country are issued by this item. The commission is empowered by law to hold hearings and issue subpoenas as necessary to investigate allegations that individual civil rights are being denied. Examples are hearings held at Window Rock, Arizona, in 1973, concerning Navajo Indian rights, and at Cairo, Illinois, in 1972, concerning racial discrimination in that community.
    Titles in the Clearinghouse Publications series support the commission's function of serving as a clearinghouse for information. The publications are varied and roughly fall into the categories of handbooks, guides, directories, and case studies. Note these examples:
    A guide to federal laws pro-
        hibiting sex discrimination,
        no. 46
    School segregation in ten com-
        munities, no. 43
    Civil rights directory, 1975,
        no. 15/3
    American Indian civil rights
        handbook, no. 33.
Other publications are reports of the commission about a situation in which civil rights have been denied, similar to some of the reports in the General Publications series.
    Also serving the clearinghouse function, the Civil rights digest contains articles on civil rights concerns. Some issues carry reviews of books, films, and pamphlets, as well as annotated lists of reports published by the commission and by state advisory committees to the commission. Articles deal with such subjects as sex discrimination, prison reform, bussing, fair housing, ethnic minorities, and voting rights. The Civil rights digest is issued quarterly.
    This item is relatively prolific and is recommended for all libraries.

Item 444-A
HE1.210:  Aging. No. 1-   June 18,
    1951-   LC 67-115021
    A monthly publication of the Administration on Aging, this peri-

odical lacks the glossiness and design of some federal magazines. It is, however, the chief source of information about programs to the elderly and for persons working with them. Issues run about 30 pages in length and contain eight to ten brief articles. These articles report on activities and programs, spotlighting individuals and areas of concern. Typical articles feature foster grandparents and children, transportation, senior Peace Corps volunteers, education, fitness, and consumer advice. Standard columns are devoted to a conference calendar, news of state, area, and federal agencies, aging around the world, and publications. One or two years of back file are desirable. Recommended for public libraries.

Item 444-B
    DEPARTMENT OF HEALTH, EDUCATION
    AND WELFARE
HE1.18:  Catalog.
HE1.18/3:  Bibliographies and lists
    of publications.
    The bibliographies are issued irregularly on subjects of broad concern to the work of the Department of Health, Education, and Welfare. The Catalog lists by title all available publications printed by the department during the current fiscal year. It is issued in July. Several agencies within the department issue their own lists of publications, but they will be covered in this catalog as well. The Catalog is organized by agency and subagency and gives basic bibliographic information for each title. A subject and title index is included. The Catalog is an essential tool for the bibliographic control of the department's publications. Recommended for academic and public libraries.

Item 445
HE1.2:  DEPARTMENT OF HEALTH, EDUCA-
    TION AND WELFARE.  General pub-
    lications.
    Because of the breadth of the responsibility of the Department of Health, Education, and Welfare, this series offers a greater variety of materials than exists with most other agencies. The item issues six or eight titles a year in a variety of formats. Some are subseries and are updated annually. Medicine, foods, schools, handicapped individuals, old age assistance, community services, civil rights, and research are all subjects likely to be treated in this broad series. Recent titles include:
    A summary of selected legisla-
        tion relating to the handi-
        capped, no. H19
    Historical women in health, ed-
        ucation, and welfare, no. W84
    Responsibility and responsive-
        ness, no. R31/3
    Records, computers, and the
        rights of citizens, no. R24/3.
This department touches the lives of every citizen, many of whom will be attracted to its literature. Recommended for academic and public libraries.

Item 445-A
    DEPARTMENT OF HEALTH, EDUCATION
    AND WELFARE
HE1.6:  Regulations, rules, and in-
    structions.
HE1.6/3:  Handbooks, manuals, guides.
HE1.6/6:  Catalog of HEW assistance
    providing financial support and
    service to states, communities,
    organizations, individuals.
HE1.6/7:  Grants administration man-
    ual.
HE1.6/7-2:  Grants administration
    manual circulars.
HE1.6/7-3:  PHS grants policy memo-
    randum.
    Of obvious administrative intent, these individual publications have application in the educational and health communities at large. At a glance one would expect the entire item to be quite prolific, but in fact, only four or five titles are issued annually. The most useful group are the handbooks and manuals, HE1.6/3, which have produced the following:
    Higher education guideline,
        Executive order 11246, no.
        H53

A common thread of service:  An
historical guide to HEW, no.
Se6
A guide for colleges and universities:  Cost principles
and procedures for ..., no.
C68.

Throughout this item, the un-
derlying theme is grant administration.  Guidelines, regulations, and
compliance in the use of federal
money make up the bulk of the subjects covered.  The series is an important reference for local institutions involved in grants and contracts with the Department of Health,
Education, and Welfare.  Recommended
for libraries serving these users.

Item 447-A-1
    ADMINISTRATION ON AGING
HE1.202:  General publications.
HE1.213:  Fact sheets.

Titles in the General Publications series are intended to serve
both the elderly and persons who
plan assistance for them.  The publications communicate to older Americans opportunities and services
open to them in, for example, health
care, nutrition, and housing.  Persons involved in providing such services find useful materials here.
The following are good examples of
both:
    Protective services for the
      aged, no. P94
    Homes for the aged:  Super-
      vision and standards, no. H75
    Dissertation research grant
      program, no. G76
    Older Americans are a national
      resource, no. Ol1.
Four or five titles are issued annually.  Some are revised periodically,
and some are written in Spanish.

The Fact Sheet series is a miscellaneous series of pamphlets covering topics pertinent to the program on aging.  Recent subjects of
the series are employment and volunteer opportunities, model projects
for the aging, and transportation
serving the elderly.  Four or five
are issued annually.  Most are brief.

The series is recommended for
public libraries.

Item 447-A-6
HE1.212:  ADMINISTRATION ON AGING.
    Bibliographies and lists of
    publications.

This is a comparatively new series and has not issued many titles.
It is, however, notable because of
the increasing national attention
which is being placed on older Americans and gerontology in general.
Of special interest is the bibliography, Words on aging, no. HE17.311:
Ag4 (HE1.212 is the new classification).  It contains selected annotated references from a variety of
fields dealing with aging.  A valuable reference tool in an area where
limited material is available, the
bibliography is organized by subject and indexed by author.  Publications of the Administration on
Aging, no. P96, is also issued periodically.  The bibliography series
is recommended for academic and public libraries.

Item 452-C
HE1.458:  CHILDREN'S BUREAU.  Hand-
    books, manuals, guides.

These publications offer guidance and suggestions to persons who
work with children.  They are general and they appeal to a broad audience.  Examples include:
    Becoming a child development
      associate, no. C43/2
    Pocket guide to babysitting,
      no. B11
    Comprehensive emergency ser-
      vices, no. Em3.
Titles are issued infrequently.
Recommended for public libraries.

Item 454-C-1
HE1.402:  OFFICE OF CHILD DEVELOP-
    MENT.  General publications.

This agency is responsible for
serving children with special needs,
such as:  children from low income
families, abused and neglected children, children in institutions and
in foster families, and migrant and
native American children.  Programs
which serve these children are described, and reports of various
projects may also be issued here.
    Typical titles include:

Child abuse and neglect, no.
    C43
Project Head Start:  Directory
    of full year and summer pro-
    grams, no. P94.
Three or four titles are issued annually.  All are of interest to parents, educators, and program plan-
ners.  Recommended for academic and
public libraries.

Item 467-A-1
HE20.8202:  NATIONAL INSTITUTE ON
    DRUG ABUSE.  General publica-
    tions.
    These titles have a tendency to
serve those dealing with drug
abusers rather than the abusers
themselves.  Many publications deal
with training programs for teachers
or are resources for use in the community.  Recent titles include:
    National Institute on Drug
        Abuse training grants direc-
        tory, no. T68/3
    The rap kit, no. R18
    A catalogue of alternatives for
        young Americans, no. A27.
Four or five titles are issued annually in various formats.  Recommended for academic and public libraries.

Item 507-B-13
    NATIONAL INSTITUTE OF MENTAL
    HEALTH
HE20.8114:  Crime and delinquency
    issues, monograph series.
HE20.8114/3:  Crime and delinquency
    topics, monograph series.
    Two or three papers are issued
annually on current issues and di-
rections in the area of crime and
delinquency.  In sponsoring these
series, the agency encourages the
expressions of opinions on issues of
mental health and law, their analyses, and recommendations for the future.  Recent monographs include:
    Mental health and law:  A sys-
        tem in transition, no. HE20.
        8114/3:L41
    Observing the law:  Applica-
        tions of field methods to
        the study of the criminal
        justice system, no. HE20.
        8114/3:L41/2.

The studies are 200 to 300 pages in
length, contain references, and are
indexed.  Recommended for libraries
supporting interests in mental
health and criminology.

Item 507-B-20
HE20.8114/2:  NATIONAL INSTITUTE OF
    MENTAL HEALTH.  Center for
    Studies of Crime and Delin-
    quency:  Research reports.
    The reports are individually
numbered pamphlets of about 8
pages in length, and are written to
make available information gained
from the research programs.  Researchers, program administrators,
persons involved in the fields of
crime and juvenile delinquency, and
parents will appreciate these brief
descriptions of projects of the center.  Recent reports include:
    The Juniper Gardens project:
        A study in community crime
        control, no. 4
    Teenage delinquency in small
        town America, no. 5
    Predictive sentencing:  How to
        best rehabilitate teenage
        traffic offenders, no. 6.
Recommended for public libraries and
academic libraries supporting social
service programs.

Item 512-A-1
HE22.2:  HEALTH CARE FINANCING AD-
    MINISTRATION.  General publi-
    cations.
    The Health Care Financing Ad-
ministration is a new agency.  It is
responsible for medicare and medicaid, the Medical Services Administration and other medical assistance
programs.  These publications reflect those responsibilities.  Two
or three are issued annually.  The
item is recommended for academic and
public libraries.

Item 516
HE3.2:  SOCIAL SECURITY ADMINISTRA-
    TION.  General publications.
    Historical, administrative, and
instructive materials are issued
here.  Titles appear at a rate of
six or eight a year, although frequently in pamphlet format.  Recent

substantive titles include:
> History of the provisions of
> Old-Age, Survivors, ...and
> Health Insurance, no. H62
> National health systems in
> eight countries, no. H34/10
> Personal health care expendi-
> tures by state, no. H34/8.

There is an endless list of
leaflets which serve to inform citizens of their rights and responsibilities to the system. This information includes instructions to
farmers on how to report their income for social security, disability
benefits, retirement and survivor
benefits, supplemental security income payments, and social security
income advice for young families.
Academic and public libraries have
patrons with needs for this varying
group of publications.

Item 516-B
HE3.38:  SOCIAL SECURITY ADMINISTRA-
         TION.  Bibliographies and lists
         of publications.

Occasional subject bibliographies and catalogs of Social Security publications are issued here.
They are useful reference guides to
the literature. Of interest to librarians and patrons is the bibliography, The impact of medicare, no.
M46/2.  It is an annotated list of
selected sources, organized by subject, and indexed by author. Recommended for academic and public libraries.

Item 516-C
     SOCIAL SECURITY ADMINISTRATION
HE3.6/3:  Handbooks, manuals, guides.
HE3.6/4:  Health insurance for the
          aged.

The handbooks and guides are
similar to some of the instructive
titles found in the General Publications series, HE3.2, item 516. Examples include:
> A guide to supplemental secur-
> ity income, no. In2
> A woman's guide to social se-
> curity, no. W84
> Social Security handbook, no.
> Sol/3.

The latter is a standard source, re-

vised periodically, of the provisions of the Social Security Act.
It is intended for the use of persons who need details in regard to
federal retirement insurance, survivors' insurance, disability insurance, health insurance, black lung
benefits, and supplemental security
income. One or two titles are issued annually. These handbooks and
guides have obvious value to some
public libraries.

The Health Insurance for the
Aged series is new to the item
and cannot be evaluated at this
writing.

Item 522-A
HE3.49:  SOCIAL SECURITY ADMINISTRA-
         TION.  Research reports.
         No. 1-  1963-  LC HEW 63-129

A numbered report series which
goes back several years, these monographs make detailed analyses of the
history and performance of the features of social security in this
country and around the world. Recent examples include:
> The benefit structure of pri-
> vate health insurance, no. 32
> Public attitudes toward social
> security, 1935-65, no. 33
> Community hospitals:  Inflation
> in the pre-medicare period,
> no. 41
> Women and social security:  Law
> and policy in five countries,
> no. 42
> International social security
> agreements, no. 43.

These reports provide the most
comprehensive review of the system,
which, since 1935, has undergone
scrutiny by politicians, actuaries,
and social scientists of all varie-
ties. The reports are issued infrequently. Recommended for libraries
serving both participants in and
students of the system.

Item 523
     SOCIAL SECURITY ADMINISTRATION
HE3.3:  Social Security bulletin.
        Mar. 1938-
HE3.3/3:  Statistical supplement.
          1955-  LC 40-29327
          The official monthly publica-

tion of the agency, the Social Security bulletin focuses on one or
two broad areas of social maintenance in each issue.  Private health
insurance, the coming decade,
women's work lives, and social welfare expenditures over 25 years are
recent examples.  In addition, each
issue includes a review of social
security program operations, notes
and brief reports, and current operating statistics.  Quarterly statistics are available in the March,
June, September, and December issues.
The Statistical supplement is issued annually and includes statistical tables for social security and
the economy; poverty data; inter-
program social security data; old-
age, survivors, disability, and
health insurance; black lung benefits; and public assistance.  Many
statistical tables contain historical data.  A back file should be
considered in light of increased
concern in the general population
over the future of social security.
The Social Security bulletin is 70
to 80 pages in length.  The Statistical supplement is about 150 pages.
The two publications are of reference value to both academic and pub-
libraries.

Item 532-A-13
HE22.3:  HEALTH CARE FINANCING AD-
    MINISTRATION.  Record.  v.1-
    Apr. 1977-
    Until recently this agency was
known as the Social and Rehabilitation Service and the publication as
the Social and Rehabilitation record.  Now titled Record, the monthly
serves as a management tool to aid
personnel in state and local agencies to administer human assistance
programs.  It also serves to communicate information about services to
those in need and to the general
public.  Assistance payments, individual and family social services,
and medical services are the responsibility of the agency and, therefore, general subjects of the articles.  Recent issues have contained articles about resettling
Vietnamese refugees, revenue sharing

as a source of program funds, and
child neglect.  Regular features include notes about current research,
state news, and publications.  Issues are creatively designed and are
about 35 pages in length.  They are
of interest to persons in any aspect
of social service.  Two or three
years of back files are desirable.
Recommended for academic and public
libraries.

Item 532-B-1
HE1.902:  PUBLIC SERVICES ADMINIS-
    TRATION.  General publications.
    This agency was established in
1969 and renamed in 1976 but many
of its programs existed prior to
1969 in other agencies.  It now has
responsibilities in the areas of job
training, child care, education, and
other support services for Americans
with low income.  These publications
are indicative of some of the activities:
    A right to a decent home, no.
        H75
    Protective services project for
        older Americans, no. Oℓ1
    Door to opportunity, no. Op5.
No more than one title is issued a
year.  Recommended for public libraries.

Item 532-C-2
HE1.302:  OFFICE OF YOUTH DEVELOP-
    MENT.  General publications.
    The Youth Development Office
funds many programs and living quarters around the country for youth
who, for various reasons, can no longer live at home.  State, local, and
private agencies usually pick up
some or all of the support of this
project, which seeks to assist
troubled youth in their search for
maturity.  In this series are found
descriptions of some of these projects:
    Focus Runaway Hostel, Las Vegas,
        Nevada, no. Im1/2
    Better tomorrows:  Girls' Ad-
        venture Trails, Dallas, Texas,
        no. B46
    Catalog of federal youth pro-
        grams, no. F31.
Other publications describe various

approaches of the agency, and state
and local agencies, in dealing with
youth. One or two are issued annually. The series is an important
one for libraries serving professionals and students of the social
services.

Item 532-E-1
HE20.5102:  BUREAU OF COMMUNITY
    HEALTH SERVICES.  General pub-
    lications.
    Guides to programs, communica-
tions of services, and health needs
of the community are found among
these titles.  Some titles attempt
to recruit personnel, and these belong in career literature collections.  Others are exemplified by:
    Vision screening of the pre-
        school child, no. V82
    The hassles of becoming a teen-
        age parent, no. T22
    Sickle cell screening and edu-
        cation clinics, no. Sil/3
    Building a rural health system,
        no. R88
    Projects for intensive infant
        care, no. In3.
All are under 100 pages.  Four to
six titles are issued annually.
Recommended for public libraries and
for academic libraries serving social service or health-related programs.

Item 627
I20.2:  BUREAU OF INDIAN AFFAIRS.
    General publications.
    The federal government's admin-
istration of native American affairs
is demonstrated here in its miscellaneous series.  Federal policy, Indian history, education, culture,
and government are subjects of these
publications.  Three or four titles
are issued a year.  They vary in
length and format.  Typical titles
include:
    A history of Indian policy,
        no. H62
    Governing bodies of federally
        recognized groups, no. G74/4
    Federal Indian policy, no. F31/2
    Indian education, no. Ed8/9
    American Indian calendar, no.
        C12/2.

Recommended for academic and public
libraries.

Item 627-A
    BUREAU OF INDIAN AFFAIRS
I20.51:  Indians of various states.
I20.51/2:  Indians.
    The Indians of Various States
series, published in the 1960s, will
perhaps be revised.  Each publication briefly notes by geographic
area, tribes, history, and contemporary life of these groups of
people.  The series has some merit
but users should bear in mind that
this is the bureau's story of the
Indians rather than a personal account told by Indians.
    The Indians series is a loose-
leaf series of three or four pages
each; individual titles focus on a
tribe or a feature of native American life.  Legends and myths, no.
L52, is essentially a bibliography;
The Nez Perce, no. N49, gives introductory commentary and three pages
of selected readings.  The series
serves as a useful teaching or library aid if supplemented by non-
government sources.
    Both series are recommended for
academic and public libraries.

Item 716-C
J1.32/2:  DEPARTMENT OF JUSTICE.
    Attorney General's annual re-
    port, federal law enforcement
    and criminal justice assistance
    activities.
    While the Constitution of the
United States reserves principal authority for promulgation and enforcement of criminal law to state
and local governments, the federal
government also makes some contributions to this area.  It is responsible for the enforcement of all
federal law and assumes a role in
helping state and local governments
improve their justice systems.  Both
of these responsibilities are surveyed here.  Major federal law enforcement activities such as violations occurring on national forest
lands, in federally insured banks,
in interstate commerce, and in various other areas of federal juris-

diction are summarized here.  Federal assistance programs working to prevent crime and to educate and rehabilitate are also noted.  Organization is by agency.  The publication appears irregularly and is a few hundred pages in length.  The current edition is an adequate reference source.  Recommended for academic and public libraries.

Item 717
    DEPARTMENT OF JUSTICE
J1.2:  General publications.
J1.33:  LEAA grants and contracts.
J1.33/2:  LEAA grants and contracts dissemination documents.
J1.42/3:  National Criminal Justice Reference Service.
J1.44:  Research series.
J1.44/2:  Monograph series.
    The General Publications series includes judicial reviews, directories, career guides, standards for criminal justice, and guides to the jurisdiction of the department.  Formats and lengths vary, as does the specialization required of the readership.  Eight to ten titles are issued annually.  Recent titles include:
    The American student left, no.
        St9
    Legal aspects of impeachment:
        An overview, no. Im7/2
    High impact anti-crime program,
        no. C86/32
    Crimes and victims:  A report
        on the Dayton-San Jose pilot
        survey of victimization, no.
        C86/25.
    The people of the nation have an obligation to be knowledgeable about their criminal justice system. Reading agency publications about what they say they are doing is part of the job.
    Titles in the LEAA Grants and Contracts series and the LEAA Grants and Contracts Dissemination Documents series are issued infrequently and have not appeared for several years.  They are not particularly useful to the patrons of the libraries under consideration.
    Major surveys of state and local public facilities in the crim-

inal justice system are reported on in the National Criminal Justice Reference Service series.  Papers usually are less than 100 pages and are issued at a rate of three or four a year.  Recent titles include:
    Children in custody, no.
        SD-JD-2
    Census of state correctional
        facilities, no. SD-NPS-SR-1
    National survey of court organ-
        ization, no. SD-C-2.
    The Research series and the Monograph series report on projects funded by the National Institute of Law Enforcement and Criminal Justice. Some are specialized legal reports, but most will appeal to the general public and students interested in the broad area of criminal justice. Examples of research reports:
    Bail and its reform:  A national
        survey, no. J1.44:B15
    The law of detainers, no.
        J1.44/2:D48
    Ethnic succession in organized
        crime, no. J1.44/2:Et3
    The utilization of experience
        in parole decision-making,
        no. J1.44:Ex7.
Three or four titles a year are issued.
    The series of the item are varied.  Recommended for academic and public libraries.

Item 717-A
DEPARTMENT OF JUSTICE
J1.8:  Regulations, rules, instructions.
J1.8/2:  Handbooks, manuals, guides.
J1.8/3:  Prescriptive package.
    Primarily administrative publications, the series of rules and guides is in the interest of the general public, who have a right and obligation to know about regulations governing and procedures followed by law enforcement officials.  Training manuals for personnel at all levels, guidelines for state and local agency planning grants, crime prevention councils procedures, and manuals of juror usage are all in the range of publications issued here.  Recent titles include:
    Police guide for organized

crime, no. J1.8/2:P75
Handbook on the law of search
   and seizure, no. J1.8/2:Se1
Basic elements of intelligence,
   no. J1.8/2:In8/2
Guidelines and standards for
   halfway houses and community
   treatment centers, no.
   J1.8/2:H13
Job training and placement for
   offenders and ex-offenders,
   no. J1.8/3:J57.

Some titles are revised periodically. Three or four are issued
annually; length and format vary.
The more crucial regulations and
procedures of the department will
not be issued for public consumption,
but this series goes a long way in
keeping the public informed, as well
as providing materials and programs
for local citizen groups. Recommended for public libraries and for
academic libraries supporting criminal justice or law enforcement programs.

Item 717-B-1
J1.33/3: DEPARTMENT OF JUSTICE.
   LEAA newsletter.
   Essentially a publication of
the law enforcement community, this
monthly is published by the Law Enforcement Administration. News and
notes are included about justice
programs in the academic environment,
personnel activities in the agency,
studies of inmates, patterns of
crime, and the experience of officers. Because the agency is also a
project funder, news of grants and
research is prevalent. The Newsletter is 14 to 20 pages in length.
Retention of the current year is
adequate. It provides a welcome
forum for both specialists in criminology and officers in the field.
Recommended for public libraries and
for academic libraries supporting
parallel programs.

Item 717-D
J1.36: DEPARTMENT OF JUSTICE. PR
   series.
   Titles here tend to report research funded by the National Institute of Law Enforcement and Criminal

Justice by grant or contract. The
topics are related to human needs,
patterns of crime, the administration of justice, and the training of
law enforcement officials. Recent
titles include:
   Higher education programs in
      law enforcement and crim-
      inal justice, no. 71-2
   An inventory of surveys of the
      public on crime, justice, and
      related topics, no. 72-16
   Criminal justice--The consumer's
      perspective, no. 72-9.
They vary in length from a few pages
to a few hundred. While they are
comprehensive and sometimes exercise
the methodology of social science,
they have broad appeal. They are
issued irregularly. Recommended for
academic and public libraries.

Item 717-E
DEPARTMENT OF JUSTICE
J1.37:   National Criminal Justice
         Information and Statistics Ser-
         vice, SC-EE series.
J1.37/2:   Statistics center reports.
J1.37/3:   Criminal justice mono-
         graphs.
J1.37/4:   Criminal justice research.
   Various data in statistical and
textual form on all aspects of criminal justice are issued in these
publications. The costs of prosecu-
tion, maintenance, and rehabilita-
tion of criminal offenders, reports
on correctional institutions, studies of types of crime, and papers on
law enforcement systems are typical
subjects. Recent titles include:
   Historical statistics on expen-
      diture and employment for the
      criminal justice system, 1971
      to 1973, no. J1.37:6
   Local jails, no. J1.37/2:1a
   Determinants of police behavior,
      no. J1.37/3:P75
   Prevention and control of col-
      lective violence, no. J1.37/4:
      V81.
   Both the public and student audience should be attracted to these
issues because of concern for the
relationships between police and
citizens and the increase in vio-
lence in recent years. Four or five

titles are issued a year. Various formats and lengths prevail. Recommended for academic and public libraries.

Item 717-G
DEPARTMENT OF JUSTICE
J1.20/2: Bibliographies and lists of publications.
J1.20/3: Library book catalog.

A variety of bibliographies are issued here with appeal for a range of users. Some of the topics are administrative, some vocational. Others are appropriate for use by sociology students approaching the problems of criminal justice and urban studies. Two or three are issued a year. Typical titles include:

> Selected literature on evaluation, no. Ev1
> Abstracts: Police-community relations, no. P75.

Others are lists of publications issued by agencies of the Justice Department, similar to those appearing in other publication groups.

The Library book catalog has lapsed in publication and is less interesting.

The item is recommended for increased bibliographic control in academic and public libraries.

Item 721
J1.14/2: FEDERAL BUREAU OF INVESTIGATION. General publications.

Informing the public of the work of the bureau is the primary function of this group of printed materials. Few titles are issued and most are pamphlets, annually or periodically revised. Typical titles include:

> 99 facts about the FBI: Questions and answers, no. F31/3
> The FBI laboratory, no. L11
> The science of fingerprints, no. F49/12.

Other titles are about patterns of crime, officer fatalities, and bureau adventures. An introduction to the agency is provided. Recommended for public libraries.

Item 721-A
J1.14/1: FEDERAL BUREAU OF INVESTI-

GATION. Annual report. 1920-
LC 20-26159

This chronicle of the FBI's year is not an essential title until one considers the increasing charges made against the agency for what the public considers to be inappropriate activity. Unlawful wiretapping and the collection of dossiers on thousands of citizens by the FBI will probably not be reported in the series. However, domestic intelligence activities are summarized, and even the summaries may serve to alert concerned citizens of the extent to which the agency surveys citizen activity. The 1972 report includes the following headings under its domestic intelligence section: revolutionary activities, Weathermen, foreign intelligence activities, sabotage, bombing matters, black extremism, white extremism, and antiwar movement. The Annual report is about 50 pages in length. Recommended for academic and public libraries.

Item 722
FEDERAL BUREAU OF INVESTIGATION
J1.14/7: Uniform crime reports for the United States. Aug. 1930-
LC 30-27005
J1.14/16: Handbooks, manuals, guides.

Issued annually since 1930, Uniform crime reports was initiated to better identify the crime problem. Certain standards and procedures have been maintained and only those crimes which come to the attention of enforcement agencies are included. Seven criminal acts have been selected for measuring crime in the United States. Known as the Crime Index offenses, they are murder, forcible rape, robbery, aggravated assault, burglary, larceny-theft, and motor-vehicle theft. Most of each volume consists of statistical tables, but there is a reasonable amount of text which amplifies the data. Crime factors, nature of crimes committed, victimization, prosecution, and the Uniform Crime Reporting Program are discussed.

Each annual approaches 300 pages in length. Few historical data series are included, and, therefore, a back file of annuals is necessary if the library needs historical data for comparison. Most libraries will suffice with the current report and those for a few random years. Recommended for academic and public libraries.

Titles in the Handbooks, Manuals, and Guides series are infrequent and tend to be related to the administration of the reports.

Item 831-C-3
HE20.8215/2: NATIONAL INSTITUTE ON DRUG ABUSE. Selected reference series.

Bibliographies of drug abuse information are issued infrequently from this series. They are under 100 pages and recommended for use in academic and public libraries.

Item 831-C-8
HE20.8216: NATIONAL INSTITUTE ON DRUG ABUSE. Research monograph series.

This series began in the mid-1970s. It issues research monographs on subjects of both the social and medical complications of drug abuse. The monographs are research reports, surveys, and conference papers. They are written in technical style but have appeal throughout the library audience. Recent publications have included the subjects of socio-behavioral drug abuse research and alternatives to methadone. They are 50 to 300 pages in length. Two or three titles are issued annually. Recommended for academic and larger public libraries.

Item 853-A-1
PrEx2.20: OFFICE OF MANAGEMENT AND BUDGET. Catalog of federal domestic assistance. 1971-

A comprehensive list of domestic assistance programs administered by federal agencies, this catalog is issued annually and updated semi-annually. New editions indicate the addition of new programs and the deletion of old programs, and note substantive changes in continuing programs. The Catalog is an important reference item because it identifies assistance for the potential user. It also intends to improve coordination among federal, state, and local agencies. The 1975 edition contained 1,030 programs administered by 55 different federal departments. The information provided for each program is detail about the assistance provided, the purpose for which it is available, who may apply, and how one should apply. Federal offices associated with the program are also identified. Recommended for academic and public libraries.

Item 857-B-3
PrEx20.9: SPECIAL ACTION OFFICE FOR DRUG ABUSE. Special Action Office monograph series.

Federal drug abuse prevention and treatment are the functions of this office. The series offers studies and ideas regarding these services. Examples include:

Drug incidence analysis, no. A/3

Estimating the prevalence of heroin use in a community, no. A/4

Outpatient methadone treatment manual, no. C/2

Looking ahead: The youth health center, no. E/1.

Three or four titles are issued annually. Publications are not highly technical and have a range of possibilities for use by individuals and groups in the community. Recommended for academic and public libraries.

Item 967
J24.2: DRUG ENFORCEMENT ADMINISTRATION. General publications.

Titles here are primarily pamphlet materials embracing the work of the agency, and one or two are issued annually. They are addressed to the subjects of enforcement and prevention, to persons who use narcotics, to those who encounter users, and to the legal trade of narcotics and dangerous drugs. Typical titles

include:
> Katy's coloring book about
> drugs and health, no. K15
> Workshop for college deans and
> campus security officials,
> no. W89
> You think you have problems,
> no. P94.

Recommended for academic and public
libraries.

Item 968-A
J24.8:   DRUG ENFORCEMENT ADMINISTRA-
TION.   Handbooks, manuals,
guides.

Titles for laymen, law enforcement officers, physicians, and parents are present here.  They alert
persons dealing with drug offenders
and with the concerned community to
pharmacology, physiology, and the
sociology of narcotics use.  Some
titles support the special training
for control of narcotics and dangerous drugs provided by the federal
agency to local and state adminis-
trations.  Titles may reflect the
legal trade in narcotic and dangerous drugs regulated by the bureau.
Some handbooks deal with prevention
and others with legislation.  Two
or three are issued annually.  Most
are in booklet form.  Recommended
for academic and public libraries.

Item 1088
Y3.W58:  WHITE HOUSE CONFERENCES.
Reports and publications.

White House conferences are
called rather infrequently, primarily to look at a problem in society
or at a group of people in need of
attention.  In the last decade the
two major conferences have been
those of aging and youth.  The White
House Conference on Youth, no.
3-3:1/971, was held in 1971, in an
effort to provide interaction between youth and adults.  Ten issues
were chosen for the two groups to
find common ground on:  the draft,
drugs, employment and economy, education, environment, foreign relations, legal rights and justice,
poverty, ethics, race and minority
groups.

The Conference on Aging, no.
4:971, also held in 1971, was the
second such conference.  It dealt
with the problems of aging and generated fifteen to twenty publications, including summaries of the
conference and recommendations for
action.

This series is recommended for
academic and public libraries because of the importance of the conferences and the publications which
ensue.

## STATISTICS AND DEMOGRAPHY

Item 138
> BUREAU OF THE CENSUS.  Catalog
> of United States census publi-
> cations.  1946-   LC 47-46253
C3.163/2:  Monthly supplements.
C3.163/3:  Quarterly catalogs.
C3.163/4:  Bibliographies and lists
> of publications.
C56.222/2-2:  Historical compila-
> tions.

Monthly Supplements, issued
several weeks after the fact, list
census reports as they become available for purchase by the public.
All bibliographic information available at the time is included, as is
ordering information.  Monthly Supplements are 4- to 8-page briefs.

Quarterly Catalogs are cumulated annually.  They are divided

into two parts: publications, a classified and annotated guide to all titles issued during the time period; and data files and special tabulations, primarily a list of computer tape and punch cards available to customers on a cost basis. Used together, the annual catalogs serve as a basic bibliographic guide to census publications.

Titles in the Bibliographies and Lists of Publications series are issued infrequently with the exception of Census Bureau methodological research, no. M56, an annual annotated list of papers and reports on the status of research currently underway. It seeks to provide an interchange of information and to encourage dissemination of other reports. It contains about 100 citations and is useful to persons practicing or studying survey methodology.

The most recent historical compilation is the Catalog issued in 1974 which includes publications from 1790 to 1972. It combines two catalogs: one issued in 1950 for 1790-1945, and the second, 1946-1972, in one binding. It is indexed by subject.

The group of series is recommended for academic and public libraries.

Item 146
C3.2: BUREAU OF THE CENSUS.
     General publications.
     Descriptions and methods of data collecting and data analysis are standard features in these titles. Social, economic, and political statistics are issued from time to time. Typical titles include:
     World population: 1973, no. P81/2
     Census data for community action, no. C73
     A student's introduction to assessing the 1970 census, no. St9
     Centers of population for states and counties, no. P81/3.

Two or three titles are issued annually, of which many are useful references. Lengths and formats vary, but most are under 100 pages. Recommended for academic and public libraries.

Item 146-A
C3.6/2: BUREAU OF THE CENSUS.
     Handbooks, manuals, guides.
     Guides and directories for census takers and census users are published here. They are issued infrequently but serve as aids to new census materials. Recent issuances include:
     Guide to programs and publications: Subjects and areas, no. P94
     Mini-guide to the 1972 economic censuses, no. Ec7
     1970 census users' guide, no. C33/2.
Recommended for academic and public libraries.

Item 146-H
C56.234: BUREAU OF THE CENSUS. We the Americans series.
     These numbered booklets are designed as educational materials and discuss various categories of Americans and their social and cultural life as reported in the 1970 census. Text, pictures, graphs, and tables combine to present the income levels, occupations, ages, education, and political importance in the electorate of the groups of persons. Each booklet is devoted to one group such as women, the elderly, the foreign born, youth, and native Americans. A few summarize social and economic characteristics associated with American living patterns or institutions, including incomes, education, and cities and suburbs. According to the Department of Commerce, this series is now complete. In some libraries it is useful in retrospect. For others, it would be advisable to watch for a similar series to emerge from the 1980 census. Recommended for academic and public libraries.

Item 146-K
   BUREAU OF THE CENSUS
C3.62/4:  United States maps, GE-50.
C3.62/8:  United States maps, GE-70.
   The older series is GE-50, and
it now includes more than 70 maps.
The appearance of GE-70, with its
first map based on an older one previously issued by GE-50, suggests
the possibility that GE-70 will replace the older series.  At any rate,
librarians making use of maps in
both public and academic libraries
should note these materials.  They
are statistical maps (scale of
1:5,000,000 for GE-50 and
1:7,500,000 for GE-70) which present
relationships of data generated by
the census.  Typical subjects cover
the percentage of total population
that are of Spanish origin, median
gross rent, number of owner-occupied
housing units, number of Chinese,
and urban and rural distribution of
population, with most distributions
made by county units.  GE-50 maps
are 42 x 30 inches; GE-70,  30 x 20
inches.  Recommended for academic
and public libraries.

Item 150
C3.134:  BUREAU OF THE CENSUS.  Statistical abstract of the United
   States.  1st-   1878-
   LC 4-18089
   A one-volume annual, this standard reference source combines a selection of statistics from the publications and records of various
governmental and private agencies.
It is also a guide to these other
sources, and it includes bibliographic information for them below
each table and in an appendix.  The
major social, political, and economic variables are treated in the
more than 1400 tables and charts of
the 34 subject categories.  Emphasis
is given primarily to national data,
although regions and cities are
sometimes represented.  Some tables
have historical series, but for comprehensive historical coverage, see
Historical statistics of the United
States, colonial times to 1970,
C3.134/2:H62/789-970, item 151.
This two-volume work is linked to

the Statistical abstract by an appendix in the latter which notes
tables appearing in both.  The annual is indexed.  Long backfiles are
not essential to most libraries.
Recommended for academic and public
libraries.

Item 150-A
C3.134/3:  BUREAU OF THE CENSUS.
   Pocket data book.  1967-
   LC A66-7638
   Issued biennially, the Pocket
data book combines narrative, charts,
and graphs in an introductory summary section to include population,
economic and social welfare, government, elections, industry and business, agriculture, finance, and foreign commerce.  The book totals
about 300 pages, and its parts provide a selection of data on major
facets of the social, economic, and
political organization of the country.  Sections of statistics include
population, vital statistics, immigration, land and environment, government, elections, national defense,
law enforcement, labor, health, education, science, welfare, income,
prices, parks and recreation, agriculture, forests and fisheries,
business enterprise, manufactures,
transportation, etc.  Appended is an
explanation of terms, the index, and
a list of charts.  A useful ready-
reference, this is recommended for
academic and public libraries.

Item 151
C3.134/2:  BUREAU OF THE CENSUS.
   Statistical abstract of the
   United States.  Supplements.
   The following are issued as
statistical supplements:
   The Congressional district data
book, no. C76, is issued for each
Congress.  It compiles various census data and recent election statistics by the districts of each Congress into a meaningful statistical
picture.  Organized by state, it includes for each maps and several
pages of statistics.  The volume is
several hundred pages in length and
an important reference title.
   County and city data book, no.

C83, is issued about every five years, or after a group of major censuses have been taken. A comprehensive compilation of local area data, standard metropolitan statistical areas, cities, counties, urbanized areas, and unincorporated places are treated. Social and economic data typical to the census, such as family income, housing, and agriculture are presented. Maps, numerous explanatory notes, source citations and appendixes are included. The volume is lengthy and is a companion to the Congressional district data book.

USA statistics in brief, no. St2, is a folded, pocket size reference of summary statistical data. It may be useful for personal reference or for the classroom. It is issued annually.

Historical statistics of the United States, no. H62, is issued as a compilation of thousands of statistical series from as early as 1610. The first volume issued was Historical statistics, 1789-1945, followed by Colonial times to 1957, and revisions. Most recent is Historical statistics of the United States, colonial times to 1970, known as the Bicentennial edition. It is a two volume work which has drawn heavily on the previous editions both in form and content. The Statistical abstract, no. C3.134, item 150, contains a table in the appendix which links its tables to those of the Historical statistics. The compilation is an indispensible reference.

These supplements are recommended for academic and public libraries.

Item 159
   BUREAU OF THE CENSUS
C3.223/10:  Census of population. Final volumes, other than by states and areas.
C3.223/11:  Census of population. Census tract reports.

A major portion of the data from the census of population appears in the Characteristics of the population (no. C3.223/9, item

159-A-1 to A-54) and is designated as volume 1. The volumes in this series, known as subject reports, are the accompanying volume 2. They focus on national and regional data for a particular subject and include the characteristics of national origin, race, education, fertility, marital status, occupation, industry, etc. About forty subject reports were issued for the 1970 census, including School enrollment, no. 5A; Americans living abroad, no. 10A; Government workers, no. 7D; Journey to work, no. 6D; and State of birth, no. 2A.

Census tracts are individual statistical reports for a standard metropolitan area. The comparability of 1970 tracts to 1960 areas tracted is recorded in tables in each report, and the population and housing subjects included are those generally used throughout the census. In the 1970 census, 241 tracts were issued. Each tract is about 60 pages in length.

These two series are not essential to reference collections of census data, but libraries with some research needs should acquire them--at least those which pertain to the local area.

Item 159-A-1 to A-54
   BUREAU OF THE CENSUS.  Census of population.  State and area series.
C3.223/2:  Preliminary reports.
C3.223/4:  Advance reports.
C3.223/5:  Number of inhabitants.
C3.223/6:  General population characteristics.
C3.223/7:  General social and economic characteristics.
C3.223/8:  Detailed characteristics.
C3.223/9:  Characteristics of the population (bound).
C3.223/13:  General demographic trends.
C3.223/17:  Employment profiles of selected low income areas.

A census of population is conducted at the end of every decade. Observations here are based on the 1970 census publications which were similar in framework to the 1960

census publications. An official of
the Bureau of the Census has indicated that the guidelines for 1980
census publishing will attempt to
maintain comparability, but some
changes will undoubtedly occur because of the demands of new data and
the necessity for the increased use
of microform. Librarians should
watch for changes in classification
numbers and for explanatory publications in advance of the 1980 census.

Population data gathering and
reporting result in numerous preliminary reports, advance reports, and
other nonpermanent materials which
should be discarded, in most libraries, upon the receipt of final
volumes for the particular reporting period. The series Preliminary
Reports, Advance Reports, Number of
Inhabitants, General Population
Characteristics, General Social and
Economic Characteristics, and Detailed Characteristics are issued
in separate advance copies but are
later combined in part into Characteristics of the population, the
permanent edition. The latter bound
set of volumes is issued in parts
with one numbered part devoted to
each state and outlying area. The
set is preceded by a summary part.
These reports present a major portion of the information compiled for
the state in the previous census of
population. Each part is several
hundred pages in length and largely
tabular. The appendixes include explanatory text on data collection.

General demographic trends for
metropolitan areas is a series con-
sisting of 52 reports, one of which
is a United States summary and the
others for each of the states and
the District of Columbia. These
statistics are drawn from the Advance Reports of the population census and the housing census. The reports are tabular with some explanatory text and average about 50
pages in length. The principal focus is the presentation of data on
population, by age and race, by standard metropolitan statistical area,
and on housing detail, such as race
of owner, plumbing facilities, and

persons per room.

Employment profiles of selected
low income areas totaled 76 reports
of about 300 pages each for the 1970
census. Each compiled data on the
social and economic characteristics
of residents of a particular low-
income area, such as Toledo, Ohio,
no. 57; Selected rural counties in
Alabama, no. 69; and Zuni Reserva-
tion, New Mexico, no. 76. Low income neighborhoods in 51 cities and
7 rural poverty areas are reported
on by statistics on employment, education, availability for work, job
history and income, and other economic and housing variables.

The entire item consumes several shelves of space, but it is
only issued once a decade. Libraries with room and need for the
detail should subscribe to all of
it. Libraries which serve a smaller
population or have limited space
should subscribe to the item number for their own state and, perhaps,
surrounding states. All libraries
will be interested in item 159-A-1,
the national summary. It is possible to select only the volumes
wanted because of the structure of
the item: it is actually 54 item
numbers.

Item 508-A
HE20.7009:  CENTER FOR DISEASE CON-
    TROL. Morbidity and mortality
    weekly report. v.1-  Jan. 11,
    1952-

Provisional data issued by
state health departments are published here weekly. Weekly and cumulative totals are available for
cases of specified diseased in the
United States, (such as measles,
malaria, tetanus) and diseases of
low frequency, such as anthrax and
plague. These data are broken
down by state. Deaths are charted
for 121 U.S. cities by age group.
In addition, textual material accompanies the tables to account for interesting cases, outbreaks, environmental hazards, or other public
health problems. Influenza trends
are usually reported throughout the
critical months. An annual issue

is compiled as the last issue in
each volume. An annual supplement,
Health information for international
travel, includes recommended and required immunizations for the traveler. All of these combine to serve
reference functions. Retention of
the annual summary, which includes
some historical series, is an adequate permanent record. Recommended
for academic and public libraries.

Item 508-B
HE20.6217: Monthly vital statistics
        report. v.1-  Apr. 4, 1952-
        Births, marriages, divorces,
and deaths for each month are reported by the National Center for
Health Statistics. These statistics
are compiled annually and issued in
separate publications by this series.
The final, permanent edition of the
tabulation is published annually as
Vital statistics of the U.S., HE20.
6210, item 510. Textual material
accompanies the tables and amplifies the monthly data with discussions of causes of death, life ex-
pectancy, autopsy reports, the fertility rate, etc. The statistics
are usually broken down by states
and by year for the current year and
two or three preceding years. Issues of annual statistics are the
only records which librarians need
to retain in most cases, and then
only until the Vital statistics
volume is issued. Issues are 10
to 30 pages in length. A useful
reference item this is recommended
for academic and public libraries.

Item 510
HE20.6210: NATIONAL CENTER FOR
        HEALTH STATISTICS. Vital sta-
        tistics of the United States.
        1937-  LC 40-26272
        Statistics on natality, mortal-
ity, and marriage and divorce are
published annually. Detailed demographic and geographic backgrounds
and other characteristics pertinent
to these subjects are included, such
as interval since last birth, legit-
imacy status, prenatal care, and
seasonal variations for births; maternal mortality and accident mor-

tality for deaths; and median age of
bride and groom, previous marriage
status, and race or color for the
marriage and divorce category. Over
100 pages are produced annually.
These data are published monthly as
provisional vital statistics in the
Monthly vital statistics report,
no. HE20.6217, item 508-B. A comprehensive source of statistical
reference data, the title is recommended for libraries holding other
sources of vital statistics.

Item 633-C
I53.1/2:  BUREAU OF LAND MANAGEMENT.
        Public land statistics. 1962-
        Data on all land owned by fed-
eral agencies, and therefore public land, are compiled here. Tables
list various categories of allocation and acquisition. Basic facts
such as grants to states, area of
national forests, federally owned
land by agency and states, grants to
railroads, and area of states are
listed in early tables. Further divisions define the area of the Bureau of Land Management programs
(such as homestead entries, forests,
outdoor recreation sites, range
management, mineral leases) and the
administration and finance of land.
A subject index is included. The
publication is annual; a brief back
file may be desirable. This is a
relatively specialized reference,
but yet it contains much general
data in a small volume. Recommended
for academic and public libraries.

Item 853-A
PrEx2.10:  OFFICE OF MANAGEMENT AND
        BUDGET. Federal statistical
        directory.
        The Federal statistical direc-
tory is worth knowing about, and for
larger libraries, worth having in
the collection. Persons responsible
for statistical programs in all departments and agencies of the federal government are listed, along
with their office address and telephone number. The massive prolif-
eration and complex organization of
federal statistics necessitates the
availability of this source to some

persons. The current year is adequate. The directory is issued every two or three years.

Item 855-C
PrEx2.11: Statistical reporter,
   current developments in federal
   statistics.
      This monthly periodical carries
regular features reporting developments in federal statistics. It is
issued by the Management and Budget
Office, Executive Office of the
President. Typical features include
the announcement of new publications
or of the release of new editions,
changes in categories of data
classes, tips on locating selected
statistical reports, and new reporting plans and forms. Recent examples of these features:
   "Racial/Ethnic categories for
      educational statistics," dis-
      cussion and definitions of

five categories which may be
implemented by all federal
agencies
"Dial 443-NCHS," announcement
of automatic service for
placement of orders with the
National Center for Health
Statistics
"1975 Pennsylvania statistical
abstract" report of the release of a publication.
One lead article in each issue frequently has useful information for
librarians. One such recent article,
"Some current thoughts on the 1980
census," is useful for learning of
the data dissemination to anticipate
for the 1980 product. The periodical is a valuable tool for librarians. It is also useful to the social and natural scientist. Recommended in libraries where there is
a moderate use of statistical
sources.

## URBAN LIFE AND STUDIES

Item 156-A-1 to A-54
   BUREAU OF THE CENSUS. Census
   of housing.
C3.224/3: Reports by states and
   areas.
C3.224/4: Metropolitan housing.
C3.224/5: City blocks.
      A census of housing is con-
ducted at the end of each decade.
Classification numbers and formats
may vary and some series change from
one census to the next, but the focus and functions remain the same.
Observations here are based on the
1970 census. Librarians should
watch for explanations in the reporting of the 1980 census. There
will undoubtedly be needs for different kinds of data and increased

use of microforms.
      With this type of item, deposi-
tory libraries have the option of
choosing only those materials about
their state or region if they so desire. States and small areas con-
stitutes volume 1 of the housing
census in 58 parts. Each part is devoted to a state or outlying area,
and one is a summary for the United
States. The two chapters, "General
housing characteristics" and "Detailed housing characteristics," are
bound together in the final volume
but are also issued as individual
paperbound reports initially. Within
each state, statistics on plumbing
facilities, number of rooms, fuels,
air conditioning, sewage, gross

rent, etc., are presented. Parts
average about 200 pages in length.

Volume 2 of the housing census
is Metropolitan housing characteristics. The housing subjects are covered in detail, with one report for
each standard metropolitan statistical area, as well as a national summary report. For the 1970 census,
248 reports were issued.

City block statistics are issued for each urbanized area, show-
ing data for individual blocks. Selected population and housing subjects are covered in reports number-
ing about 20 pages. Some selected
areas outside urbanized areas are
also included. For the 1970 census,
278 block statistics reports were
issued.

Other items and series are issued to report the census of housing,
but the series noted here are most
appropriate for the needs under consideration. These items are recommended in total or in part for academic and public libraries.

Item 265-B
TD2.23: FEDERAL HIGHWAY ADMINISTRA-
TION. Highway statistics.
1945-  LC 47-32330
An annual volume of highway
data, this publication presents statistical data and analytical tables
on motor fuel, motor vehicles,
driver licensing, highway-user taxation, state highway finance, highway mileage, and federal aid for
highways. Data are also included
for municipalities, counties, town-
ships, and other local government
units. There are no historical series in the annual volume; thus it
is necessary to keep each annual if
one needs comparative data. Summary editions have been published
in the past, and will probably occur in the future. A recommended
reference item for academic and public libraries.

Item 581-D
HH1.23: DEPARTMENT OF HOUSING AND
URBAN DEVELOPMENT. Bibliographies and lists of publications.

This is one of the most impressive and active bibliography series
of the entire federal publishing
arena. Leaflets appear such as Bibliography on mortgage finance, no.
M84. Some works are lengthy bibliographies:
The North American Indian:  A
bibliography of community development, no. In2
Equal opportunity in housing:
A bibliography of research,
no. Eq2.
Most are compiled by the library of
the department. When old titles are
revised, the superseded edition
should be discarded. Recommended
for academic and public libraries.

Item 581-E-5
HH1.46: DEPARTMENT OF HOUSING AND
URBAN DEVELOPMENT. Community
development evaluation series.
These technical assistance reports are prepared by consultants
under contract with the Department
of Housing and Urban Development.
They are potentially interesting to
persons involved in community development activities or to students of
urban problems. Recent studies have
covered annual planning procedures,
local authority, federal grants, and
federal assistance. Some are case
studies and all are based on respec-
table methods of research. Publications are issued irregularly.
Length is about 75 pages. Recommended for college and public libraries.

Item 582
HH1.2: DEPARTMENT OF HOUSING AND
URBAN DEVELOPMENT. General
publications.
Covering the spectrum of hous-
ing and development publications, a
few subseries fall into the sequence:
Financing condominium housing,
no. C75/2
The home buying serviceman, no.
Se6
Buying and financing a mobile
home, no. M71/2
Buying lots from developers, no.
L91.
These are brief pamphlets and are

made obsolete by the publication of a new edition.

Many single publications are statistical. The following are exemplary:

> Housing in the seventies, no. H81/47, a review of federal housing programs
> Historic preservations in San Francisco's Inner Mission, no. Sa1974
> Older Americans:  Facts about incomes and housing, no. Oℓ1.

An older reference title distributed in this series is Chronology of major federal actions affecting housing and community development, July 1892 through 1963, no. H81/34.

Other subjects include housing project reports of the Department of Housing and Urban Development, housing investments, property tax studies, urban research, and rent costs. Formats and lengths vary. About one linear foot of shelf space is published annually. The series is useful to both public and academic libraries because it contains items of both popular and scholarly nature.

Item 582-K
HH1.36:  DEPARTMENT OF HOUSING AND URBAN DEVELOPMENT.  HUD challenge.  v.1-  1969-
The official magazine of the department serves as a forum for persons in the department and is also of interest to outsiders.  It describes policy, programs, and projects while it seeks to encourage nationwide involvement in solving problems.  Regular features include a review of publications, statistics, and HUD-related news items.  Articles are typically about day care, neighborhood renovation, public housing abroad, housing for the elderly, minority problems, and environmental quality.  The magazine is published monthly and contains 30 to 40 pages.  It has a pleasing format and is attractively designed.  Recommended for college and public libraries.

Item 582-L
HH1.15/4:  DEPARTMENT OF HOUSING AND URBAN DEVELOPMENT.  HUD newsletter.  LC 74-645737
The 4-page leaflet is published weekly and contains news of legislation, mortgage money, HUD services, publications issued, reports of HUD-financed contracts, statistics, and conferences.  The Newsletter is a good reference for librarians, and it has particular usefulness to persons involved in community action. It is dated and need not be held longer than one year.  Recommended for public libraries, and academic libraries supporting interests in urban studies.

Item 582-M
HH1.38:  DEPARTMENT OF HOUSING AND URBAN DEVELOPMENT.  Statistical yearbook.  1966-
LC 68-62733
The source of the data in this yearbook is the program and financial activity of the Department of Housing and Urban Development. Community planning, insurance, disaster assistance, mortgages, and other federal responsibilities of the department provide comprehensive statistical information for most of the sections.  However, a section of census data concludes the volume.  Other HUD publications contain statistics, but this title is the most comprehensive.  Recommended for academic and public library reference collections.

Item 831-A
NC2.  NATIONAL CAPITAL PLANNING COMMISSION.  Reports and publications.
The commission was established as the planning agency for the preservation of historical and natural features in the District of Columbia.  As a result of the activity of the commission, many publications have been issued which describe landmarks, proposed physical development, and landscape plans, all of which have potential appeal to the

citizenry of this country. As well as having patriotic appeal, the publications have broad application to land-use planning and to natural and historic preservation throughout the country. The materials, usually pamphlets, maps, or booklets, are attractively designed and accumulate at a rate of three or four a year. Titles are not usually distinctive. Recommended for public libraries and some academic libraries.

Item 982-C
TD1.1:   DEPARTMENT OF TRANSPORTA-
TION. Annual report. 1st-
1967-  LC 72-600917
    The oil embargo, rail passenger service, bicycling, attempted hijackings, car pools, and seatbelts have touched the lives of many Americans. The department is directly involved in planning, developing, or controlling these and many other activities of individuals. The Annual report is an interesting summary of the year in transportation programs. The establishment of the Department of Transportation in 1966 provided for the consolidation of numerous agencies, and now it includes the United States Coast Guard, the Federal Aviation Administration, Federal Highway Administration, Federal Railroad Administration, National Highway Traffic Safety Administration, Urban Mass Transportation Administration, and the St. Lawrence Seaway Development Project. Progress reports, photographs, tables, and charts serve to tell the year's story for all of these programs and agencies. Recommended for academic and public libraries.

Item 982-C-1
TD1.2:   DEPARTMENT OF TRANSPORTATION.
General publications.
    Four or five miscellaneous titles are issued per year. Most have popular appeal, but some are administrative materials. Among them we find the standard career-oriented pamphlets, public relations materials of the department, reports, conference proceedings, etc. Energy, safety, mass transit, funding, and

noise control are some topics of consideration. Typical titles include:
    National transportation statis-
        tics, summary report, no. St2
    Better transportation for our
        senior citizens, no. Se5
    Metropolitan transportation
        planning seminars, no. M56
    Bicycling for recreation and
        commuting, no. B47.
Titles vary in format and length. They provide material of greater interest to public library patrons than to those of academic libraries.

Item 982-C-6
TD1.26:   DEPARTMENT OF TRANSPORTA-
TION. National transportation report. 1972-
    Over the past few years Americans have become increasingly aware that transportation is closely tied to social and economic forces. Lower rates of energy consumption per unit of transportation activity are now a national goal in the minds of conserving citizens. This annual summary is an important chronicle of the federal government's response to transportation. It discusses regulation of transportation, state and local activity, development of urban transit facilities, highways and airports, and the general area of the effects of higher energy prices on transportation. The series began in 1972 and is a periodic report on the state of the nation's transportation system. In 1974, three reports were produced: a summary report, an appendix, and a final report. The reports are several hundred pages in length, containing supporting tabular material and profiles of public transportation plans and programs. Recommended for academic and public libraries.

Item 982-C-8
TD1.27:   Transportation USA. v.1-
Summer 1974-  LC 74-647158
    Published quarterly by the Office of Public Affairs, of the Department of Transportation, this periodical is intended to apprise the public of transportation pro-

grams and to stimulate interest in improving transportation.  It is the principal popular publication of the department, with five to ten short articles in each issue.  Electric cars, women road builders, pedestrian safety, and local project reports are recent topics covered. Regular features of the 30-page issue include department news, editorials, safety commentary, and lists of department publications. The periodical is beautifully designed and illustrated with color photographs. Recommended for academic and public libraries.

Item 982-G-7
TD2.18:  Highway transportation.
    LC 72-626540
    Published irregularly two or three times a year, the periodical describes programs of the Federal Highway Administration and the Urban Mass Transportation Administration. Eight to ten brief articles make up each issue, which runs about 35 page pages in length.  Typical features include the design of transportation systems in various cities, coordination of urban mass transit and other aspects of urban planning, car pool programs, land use, property values and zoning, social effects of transportation, and recent legislation. The publication is written for the nonspecialist.  Three or four years of back files are adequate.  It addresses itself to the needs of undergraduates in urban planning programs and to public library patrons with civic planning interests. Recommended for academic and public libraries.

Includes page references to titles of series and subjects. Subjects are in capital letters.
An index to item numbers follows this index.

166   Index

MLR, monthly labor review, 46
Manuals, See Handbooks, manuals, guides
MANUFACTURES, 32
MANUSCRIPTS-U.S., 103
MAPS, 10, 78, 133, 149
Maps and atlases, 78
MARIJUANA, 112
Marijuana and health, 112
Marine Corps historical publications, 100
MARINE CORPS-U.S., 124; HISTORY, 100
MATHEMATICS, 110
MEDIATION, 38
MEDICAL SCIENCE, 114, 118
MEDICARE, 121, 139
MEDICINE, 111-21
MENTAL HEALTH, 114, 116-18
Mental health directory, 116
Mental health program reports, 117
Merchant vessels of the United States, 134
METABOLIC DISEASES, 117
METEOROLOGY, 30, 66
MIDDLE EAST, 85
MILITARY, 90, 93, 122-26
MILITARY SERVICE, 122; COMPULSORY, 126
MILITARY THOUGHT-U.S.S.R., 124
Minerals yearbook, 27
MINES AND MINERAL RESOURCES, 26-27
Mines Bur. bulletin, 26
Mines Bur. research, 27
MINORITY BUSINESS ENTERPRISES, 29
MINORITY GROUP RELATIONS, 135-36
MISCELLANY, 127
MONEY-U.S., 40, 52
Monthly catalog of United States government publications, 72
Monthly checklist of state publications, 74
Monthly energy review, 22

Monthly labor review, 46
Monthly vital statistics report, 152
Morbidity and mortality weekly report, 151
MORTGAGES, 40
Mosaic, 77
Motor vehicle safety defect recall campaigns, 62
MOTOR VEHICLES-SAFETY, 19-20, 62, 63

NASA activities, 2
NASA EP series, 1
NASA facts, 1
NASA report to educators, 2
NBS consumer information series, 18
NIOSH health and safety guides for various businesses, 115
NOAA (quarterly), 21
National Archives and Records Service general information leaflet series, 101
National Archives and Records Service special lists, 101
National Cancer Program, Progress against..., 118; Publications, 118; Strategy plan, 118
National Criminal Justice Information and Statistics Service, SC-EE series, 144; Statistics center reports, 144
National Criminal Justice Reference Service, 143
National electric rate book, 38
National food situation, 7
NATIONAL FORESTS-U.S., 128
National Historical Publications and Records Commission publications, 101

National Institute on Drug Abuse report series, 121
NATIONAL LAKESHORES-U.S., 132
NATIONAL MILITARY PARKS-U.S., 132
NATIONAL MONUMENTS-U.S., 132
National Park Service historical handbook series, 132
National Park Service history series, 132
National Park Service information circulars, National Lakeshores, 132; National Military Parks, 132; National Monuments, 132; National Parks, 132; National Recreation Areas, 133; National Rivers, 132; National Scenic Trails, 132; National Seashores, 132
National Park Service maps, 133
NATIONAL PARKS-U.S., 131-33; HISTORY, 132, 133
NATIONAL RECREATION AREAS-U.S., 133
National register of historic places, 103
NATIONAL RIVERS-U.S., 132
NATIONAL SCENIC TRAILS-U.S., 132
NATIONAL SEASHORES-U.S., 132
National transportation report, 156
National Weather Service regulations, rules, and instructions, 66
National zip code directory, 48
Natural history handbooks, 133
NATURAL RESOURCES, 3-4, 23-24, 92, 95
NATURALIZATION-U.S., 60, 80
Naval Academy catalog, 124

## INDEX TO ITEM NUMBERS